Vue.js 2 Web Development Projects

Learn Vue.js by building 6 web apps

Guillaume Chau

Packt>

BIRMINGHAM - MUMBAI

Vue.js 2 Web Development Projects

Copyright © 2017 Packt Publishing

All rights reserved. No part of this book may be reproduced, stored in a retrieval system, or transmitted in any form or by any means, without the prior written permission of the publisher, except in the case of brief quotations embedded in critical articles or reviews.

Every effort has been made in the preparation of this book to ensure the accuracy of the information presented. However, the information contained in this book is sold without warranty, either express or implied. Neither the author, nor Packt Publishing, and its dealers and distributors will be held liable for any damages caused or alleged to be caused directly or indirectly by this book.

Packt Publishing has endeavored to provide trademark information about all of the companies and products mentioned in this book by the appropriate use of capitals. However, Packt Publishing cannot guarantee the accuracy of this information.

First published: November 2017

Production reference: 2081217

Published by Packt Publishing Ltd.
Livery Place
35 Livery Street
Birmingham
B3 2PB, UK.

ISBN 978-1-78712-746-3

www.packtpub.com

Credits

Author
Guillaume Chau

Reviewer
Eduardo San Martin Morote

Commissioning Editor
Ashwin Nair

Acquisition Editor
Shweta Pant

Content Development Editor
Arun Nadar

Technical Editor
Diksha Wakode

Copy Editor
Dhanya Baburaj

Project Coordinator
Sheejal Shah

Proofreader
Safis Editing

Indexer
Tejal Daruwale Soni

Graphics
Jason Monteiro

Production Coordinator
Shantanu Zagade

About the Author

Guillaume Chau is the creator of integrations with Meteor (vue-meteor) and Apollo GraphQL (vue-apollo) to help developers build highly interactive, real-time, Vue-powered apps. He also created the official vue-curated app , which helps you to discover great packages, and he contributes to the ecosystem with tools such as vue-virtual-scroller and vue-supply. He built a customer portal app for a big energy company with large datasets and performance challenges and is now working with an innovative French start-up (WebRTC and real-time data).

> *First, I would like to thank my partner. With her constant support and love, I was able to get through the huge amount of work required to write this book.*
> *I would also like to thank my parents, my family and my friends for their support as well, and also the other Vue.js Core Team, and more specifically Posva for his technical review of the book, the Packt staff members I worked with, and my very cute black and white cat.*

About the Reviewer

Eduardo San Martin Morote is a frontend developer who loves open source. He has been contributing to open source since he started crafting applications. He mostly maintains Vue.js-related projects as Vue itself, vuefire, and vue-router. When he develops applications, he likes to focus on UX, and always works in a pragmatic way. He tends to reduce waste as much as possible by applying the lean methodology wherever he can. He also trains people in web development, and is patient and adapts his teaching to different levels.

www.PacktPub.com

For support files and downloads related to your book, please visit www.PacktPub.com. Did you know that Packt offers eBook versions of every book published, with PDF and ePub files available? You can upgrade to the eBook version at www.PacktPub.com and as a print book customer, you are entitled to a discount on the eBook copy. Get in touch with us at service@packtpub.com for more details.

At www.PacktPub.com, you can also read a collection of free technical articles, sign up for a range of free newsletters and receive exclusive discounts and offers on Packt books and eBooks.

Mapt

https://www.packtpub.com/mapt

Get the most in-demand software skills with Mapt. Mapt gives you full access to all Packt books and video courses, as well as industry-leading tools to help you plan your personal development and advance your career.

Why subscribe?

- Fully searchable across every book published by Packt
- Copy and paste, print, and bookmark content
- On demand and accessible via a web browser

Customer Feedback

Thanks for purchasing this Packt book. At Packt, quality is at the heart of our editorial process. To help us improve, please leave us an honest review on this book's Amazon page at `www.amazon.in/dp/178712746X`.

If you'd like to join our team of regular reviewers, you can email us at `customerreviews@packtpub.com`. We award our regular reviewers with free eBooks and videos in exchange for their valuable feedback. Help us be relentless in improving our products!

Table of Contents

Preface — 1
Chapter 1: Getting Started with Vue — 7
    Why another frontend framework? — 7
        A trending project — 8
        Compatibility requirements — 9
    One-minute setup — 9
    Creating an app — 10
        Vue devtools — 11
    Templates make your DOM dynamic — 13
        Displaying text — 13
        Adding basic interactivity with directives — 14
    Summary — 16
Chapter 2: Project 1 - Markdown Notebook — 17
    A basic note editor — 18
        Setting up the project — 19
        The note editor — 20
        The preview pane — 21
            Computed property — 21
            Text interpolation escaping — 22
            Displaying HTML — 23
        Saving the note — 24
            Watching changes — 25
            Using a method — 28
            Accessing the Vue instance — 28
        Loading the saved note — 29
            Lifecycle hooks — 30
            Initializing directly in the data — 31
    Multiple notes — 32
        The note list — 32
            A method to create a new note — 33
            Button and click events with v-on — 34
            Binding attributes with v-bind — 35
            Displaying a list with v-for — 37
        Selecting a note — 39
            The current note — 40
            Dynamic CSS classes — 41

Table of Contents

Conditional templates with v-if	42
Saving the notes with the deep option	44
Saving the selection	46
The note toolbar with extras inside	47
Renaming the note	47
Deleting the note	49
Favorite notes	50
The status bar	53
Created date with a filter	54
Text stats	56
Summary	**58**
Chapter 3: Project 2 - Castle Duel Browser Game	**59**
Rules of the game	**59**
Setting up the project	**63**
The calm before the storm	**64**
The template option	64
The app state	64
The almighty components	67
Building the user interface	**67**
Our first component - the top bar	68
Adding some gameplay data to the state	68
Defining and using the components	69
Parent-to-child communication with Props	71
Props in our template	72
Displaying a card	73
Listening to native events on components	77
Child-to-parent communication with custom events	77
The hand	79
Animating the hand with transitions	82
A prettier animation	86
Playing a card	88
Animating the card list	89
The key special attribute	90
The CSS transitions	92
The overlays	93
Content distribution with slots	94
The 'player turn' overlay	96
The 'last play' overlay	97
The 'game over' overlay	97
Dynamic component	98
The overlay animation	101
Key attribute	101
The overlay background	102

Game world and scenery	102
The castles	103
Castle banners	104
Food and health bubbles	106
Banner bars	108
Animating a value	109
The animated clouds	111
The animation	113
Gameplay	115
Drawing cards	116
The initial hand	116
The hand	117
Playing a card	117
No cheating allowed	118
Removing the card from the hand	119
Waiting for the card transition to end	120
Applying the card effect	121
The next turn	122
New turn	122
Overlay close actions	124
Game Over!	125
Summary	125
Chapter 4: Advanced Project Setup	**127**
Setting up our development environment	127
Installing vue-cli, the official command-line tool	128
Code editors	128
Our first full-blown Vue application	128
Scaffolding the project	129
Creating the app	130
Running our application	131
Render functions	132
Configuring babel	133
Babel Vue preset	133
Polyfills	134
Updating the dependencies	134
Updating manually	135
Updating automatically	135
Updating Vue	136
Building for production	136
Single-File Components	136
Template	138
Using Pug	139

Script	139
JSX	140
Style	141
Scoped styles	142
Adding preprocessors	143
Sass	144
Less	144
Stylus	145
Components inside components	145
Summary	**148**
Chapter 5: Project 3 - Support Center	**149**
General app structure	149
Setting up the project	150
Routing and pages	151
Vue plugins	151
Our first routes with vue-router	152
Layouts with router-view	152
Creating routes	154
The router object	156
Router modes	157
Creating a navigation menu	158
Router links	159
Active class	161
FAQ - Consuming an API	162
Server setup	162
Using fetch	163
Loading animation	167
Extending Vue with our own plugin	169
Creating a plugin	169
Plugin options	170
Fetch method	171
Reusing code with mixins	172
Fetching remote data	174
Loading management	176
Error management	177
Support tickets	179
User authentication	179
Storing the user in a centralized state	180
Another plugin	180
Login forms	181
Smart form	181
Form input component	184
Customizing v-model	189
Login component	189

Table of Contents

Style children of scoped elements	194
Improving our fetch plugin	196
Sign up operation	197
Login operation	198
User menu	199
Logout method	199
Private routes with navigation guards	200
Route meta properties	201
Router navigation guards	202
Redirecting to the wanted route	204
Initializing user authentication	205
Guest routes	205
Displaying and adding tickets	**206**
Tickets list	206
Session expiration	208
Nested routes	210
Fixing our navigation guard	213
Sending a form	214
Form textarea	215
Binding attributes	216
User actions	217
Backup user input	218
Advanced routing features	**221**
Dynamic routes with parameters	222
Dynamic remote data	223
The dynamic route	225
Not found page	229
Transitions	230
Scrolling behavior	230
Summary	**232**
Chapter 6: Project 4 - Geolocated Blog	**233**
Google Auth and state management	**234**
Project setup	234
Creating the app	235
Some routing	237
State management with Vuex	239
Why do I need this?	239
The Vuex Store	241
The state is the source of truth	243
Mutations update the state	245
Strict mode	246
Time-travel debugging	247
Getters compute and return data	248
Actions for store operations	249
Mapping helpers	250

[v]

User state	252
Setting up Google OAuth	252
Login button	254
User in the store	256
Adapting the router	257
Adapting the fetch plugin	258
Check the user session on start	258
The profile picture	259
Synchronizing the store and the router	260
Embedding Google Maps	**260**
Installation	260
Getting the API key	260
Installing the library	261
Adding a map	262
Connecting the BlogMap and the store	263
Vuex modules	263
Namespaced module	264
Accessing global elements	266
BlogMap module and component	266
Mutations	266
Actions	267
Mapping in the component	267
User position	268
Centering on the user	269
Blog posts and comments	**270**
Posts store module	270
Rendering functions and JSX	272
Writing the view in JavaScript with render functions	272
Dynamic templates	273
Data objects	274
Virtual DOM	277
What is JSX?	278
Blog content structure (in JSX!)	279
No content	282
Creating a post	282
Draft store actions	282
Blog Map changes	283
Click handler	284
Ghost marker	285
Post form	286
Making the request	289
Fetching posts	290
Store action	290
Fetch posts action	290
Action dispatching	292

Displaying markers	293
Login and logout	294
Logout	295
Login	296
Selecting a post	297
Post details	297
Store changes for post selection and sending	297
Post Content component	298
Location info and scoped slots	300
Scoped slots to pass data to the parent	300
Implementing of the component	302
Comments - functional components	304
Store changes for comments	304
Functional component	305
Summary	309
Chapter 7: Project 5 - Online Shop and Scaling Up	**311**
Advanced development workflow	312
Setting up the project	313
Generating a quick development API	313
Launching the app	314
Auto-prefixing CSS with PostCSS	315
Targeting specific browsers with browserslist	316
Improving code quality and style with ESLint	317
Configuring ESLint	318
Customizing the rules	319
Running ESLint	319
ESLint inside Webpack	320
Unit testing with Jest	323
Configuring Jest	323
Babel configuration for Jest	324
Our first unit test	325
ESLint and Jest globals	326
Jest snapshots	327
Updating the snapshots	328
Complementary topics	329
Internationalization and code-splitting	329
Code-splitting with dynamic imports	330
Automatically loading the user locale	332
Changing Language page	334
Server-side rendering	335
Universal App Structure	336
Client entry	338
Server entry	339
State management	339

Table of Contents

Restoring the Vuex state on the client	341
Webpack configuration	342
Client configuration	343
Server configuration	343
Server-side setup	344
Page template	345
Express server	345
Creating and updating the renderer	346
Rendering the Vue app	347
Running our SSR app	347
Unnecessary fetch	348
Production build	349
Additional configuration	349
Extracting the style into CSS files	349
Production express server	350
New npm scripts	351
Summary	353
Chapter 8: Project 6 - Real-time Dashboard with Meteor	**355**
Setting up the project	356
What is Meteor?	357
Installing Meteor	357
Creating the project	358
Our first Vue Meteor app	359
Routing	360
Production measures	362
Meteor collections integration	362
Setting up data	362
Adding a collection	362
Adding a Meteor method	363
Simulating measures	364
Inspecting the data	365
Dashboard and reporting	366
Progress bars library	366
Meteor publication	366
Creating the Dashboard component	367
Indicators	369
Listing the measures	371
Summary	373
Index	**375**

[viii]

Preface

Relatively new as a UI library, Vue is a very serious challenger to current leading libraries such as Angular and React. It has a lot to offer--it is simple, flexible, and very fast, yet it still provides all the features necessary to build a full-blown modern web app.

Its progressive nature makes it easy to get started with, and then you can use more advanced features to scale your app up. Vue also have a rich ecosystem surrounding it, including official first-party libraries for routing and state management, bootstrapping, and unit-testing. Vue even supports server-side rendering out of the box!

All this is possible thanks to an amazing community and an awesome core team that drive innovation on the web and make Vue a sustainable open source project.

To help you learn Vue and build apps with it, this book is structured as a series of six guides. Each guide is a concrete project, in which you will build a real application by yourself. This means you will have six Vue apps up and running by the end!

Just like Vue, the projects are progressive and introduce new topics step by step to make your learning experience easier. The first projects don't require extensive configuration or build tools, so you can make concrete apps right away. Then, more advanced topics will be progressively added to the project so that you will have a complete skill set by the end of the book.

What this book covers

Chapter 1, *Getting Started with Vue*, covers how to create a basic Vue app with a dynamic template and basic interactivity, thanks to directives.

Chapter 2, *Project 1 - Markdown Notebook*, explores the creation of a complete Vue app with features such as computed properties, methods, life cycle hooks, list displays, DOM events, dynamic CSS, template conditionals, and filter formatting.

Chapter 3, *Project 2 - Castle Duel Browser Game*, explains the creation of a browser card game structured as a tree of reusable components that communicate with each other. It also features animations and dynamic SVG graphics.

Chapter 4, *Advanced Project Setup*, focuses on how to use the official Vue command-line tool to bootstrap a full blown project with webpack, babel, and more build tools. It also covers the Single-File Component format, allowing readers to create components as building blocks.

Chapter 5, *Project 3 - Support Center*, takes you through how to structure a multipage app with the official routing library--nested routes, dynamic parameters, navigation guards, and such. The project also features a custom user login system.

Chapter 6, *Project 4 - Geolocated Blog*, walks through the creation of an app featuring Google OAuth login and the Google Maps API. This chapter also covers the important topic of state management using the official VueX library, plus fast functional components.

Chapter 7, *Project 5 - Online Shop and Scaling up*, outlines advanced development techniques such as checking code quality with ESLint, unit testing Vue components with Jest, translating an app into multiple languages, and improving speed and SEO with server-side rendering.

Chapter 8, *Project 6 - Real-time Dashboard with Meteor*, teaches you how to use Vue in a Meteor app in order to take advantage of the real-time capabilities of this full-stack framework.

What you need for this book

To follow this book, you will only need a text or code editor (Visual Studio Code and Atom are recommended) and a web browser (preferably the latest version of Firefox or Chrome for the development tools).

Who this book is for

If you are a web developer who now wants to create rich and interactive professional applications using Vue.js, then this book is for you. Prior knowledge of JavaScript is assumed. Familiarity with HTML, Node.js, and tools such as npm and webpack will be helpful, but not necessary.

Conventions

In this book, you will find a number of styles of text that distinguish between different kinds of information. Here are some examples of these styles, and an explanation of their meaning.

Code words in text are shown as follows: "We can select HTML elements through the use of the `d3.select` function."

A block of code is set as follows:

```
class Animal
{
public:
virtual void Speak(void) const //virtual in the base class
{
   //Using the Mach 5 console print
   M5DEBUG_PRINT("...\n");
}
```

New terms and **important words** are shown in bold. Words that you see on the screen, in menus or dialog boxes for example, appear in the text like this: "Clicking the **Next** button moves you to the next screen."

> Warnings or important notes appear in a box like this.

> Tips and tricks appear like this.

Reader feedback

Feedback from our readers is always welcome. Let us know what you think about this book-what you liked or may have disliked. Reader feedback is important for us to develop titles that you really get the most out of.

To send us general feedback, simply send an e-mail to `feedback@packtpub.com`, and mention the book title via the subject of your message.

Preface

If there is a topic that you have expertise in and you are interested in either writing or contributing to a book, see our author guide on www.packtpub.com/authors.

Customer support

Now that you are the proud owner of a Packt book, we have a number of things to help you to get the most from your purchase.

Downloading the example code

You can download the example code files for this book from your account at http://www.packtpub.com. If you purchased this book elsewhere, you can visit http://www.packtpub.com/support and register to have the files e-mailed directly to you.

You can download the code files by following these steps:

1. Log in or register to our website using your e-mail address and password.
2. Hover the mouse pointer on the **SUPPORT** tab at the top.
3. Click on **Code Downloads & Errata**.
4. Enter the name of the book in the **Search** box.
5. Select the book for which you're looking to download the code files.
6. Choose from the drop-down menu where you purchased this book from.
7. Click on **Code Download**.

You can also download the code files by clicking on the **Code Files** button on the book's webpage at the Packt Publishing website. This page can be accessed by entering the book's name in the **Search** box. Please note that you need to be logged in to your Packt account.

Once the file is downloaded, please make sure that you unzip or extract the folder using the latest version of:

- WinRAR / 7-Zip for Windows
- Zipeg / iZip / UnRarX for Mac
- 7-Zip / PeaZip for Linux

The code bundle for the book is also hosted on GitHub at https://github.com/PacktPublishing/Vue-js-2-Web-Development-Projects. We also have other code bundles from our rich catalog of books and videos available at https://github.com/PacktPublishing/. Check them out!.

Downloading the color images of this book

We also provide you with a PDF file that has color images of the screenshots/diagrams used in this book. The color images will help you better understand the changes in the output. You can download this file from `https://www.packtpub.com/sites/default/files/downloads/Vuejs2WebDevelopmentProjects_ColorImages.pdf`.

Errata

Although we have taken every care to ensure the accuracy of our content, mistakes do happen. If you find a mistake in one of our books-maybe a mistake in the text or the code-we would be grateful if you could report this to us. By doing so, you can save other readers from frustration and help us improve subsequent versions of this book. If you find any errata, please report them by visiting `http://www.packtpub.com/submit-errata`, selecting your book, clicking on the **Errata Submission Form** link, and entering the details of your errata. Once your errata are verified, your submission will be accepted and the errata will be uploaded to our website or added to any list of existing errata under the Errata section of that title.

To view the previously submitted errata, go to `https://www.packtpub.com/books/content/support` and enter the name of the book in the search field. The required information will appear under the **Errata** section.

Piracy

Piracy of copyrighted material on the Internet is an ongoing problem across all media. At Packt, we take the protection of our copyright and licenses very seriously. If you come across any illegal copies of our works in any form on the Internet, please provide us with the location address or website name immediately so that we can pursue a remedy.

Please contact us at `copyright@packtpub.com` with a link to the suspected pirated material.

We appreciate your help in protecting our authors and our ability to bring you valuable content.

Questions

If you have a problem with any aspect of this book, you can contact us at `questions@packtpub.com`, and we will do our best to address the problem.

1
Getting Started with Vue

Vue (https://vuejs.org/) is a JavaScript library focused on building web user interfaces. In this chapter, we will meet the library and after a brief introduction, we will start creating a web app, laying the ground for the different projects we will build together in this book.

Why another frontend framework?

Vue is a relative newcomer in the JavaScript frontend landscape, but a very serious challenger to the current leading libraries. It is simple, flexible, and very fast, while still providing a lot of features and optional tools that can help you build a modern web app efficiently. Its creator, *Evan You*, calls it the **progressive framework**:

- Vue is incrementally adoptable, with a core library focused on user interfaces that you can use in existing projects
- You can make small prototypes all the way up to large and sophisticated web applications
- Vue is approachable--the beginners can pick up the library easily, and the confirmed developers can be productive very quickly

Vue roughly follows a Model-View-ViewModel architecture, which means the View (the user interface) and the Model (the data) are separated, with the ViewModel (Vue) being a mediator between the two. It handles the updates automatically and has been already optimized for you. Therefore, you don't have to specify when a part of the View should update because Vue will choose the right way and time to do so.

Getting Started with Vue

The library also takes inspiration from other similar libraries such as React, Angular, and Polymer. The following is an overview of its core features:

- A reactive data system that can update your user interface automatically, with a lightweight virtual-DOM engine and minimal optimization efforts, is required
- Flexible View declaration--artist-friendly HTML templates, JSX (HTML inside JavaScript), or hyperscript render functions (pure JavaScript)
- Composable user interfaces with maintainable and reusable components
- Official companion libraries that come with routing, state management, scaffolding, and more advanced features, making Vue a non-opinionated but fully fleshed out frontend framework

A trending project

Evan You started working on the first prototype of Vue in 2013, while working at Google, using Angular. The initial goal was to have all the cool features of Angular, such as data binding and data-driven DOM, but without the extra concepts that make this framework opinionated and heavy to learn and use.

The first public release was published on February 2014 and had immediate success the very first day, with HackerNews frontpage, `/r/javascript` at the top spot and 10k unique visits on the official website.

The first major version 1.0 was reached in October 2015, and by the end of that year, the npm downloads rocketed to 382k ytd, the GitHub repository received 11k stars, the official website had 363k unique visitors, and the popular PHP framework Laravel had picked Vue as its official frontend library instead of React.

The second major version, 2.0, was released in September 2016, with a new virtual DOM-based renderer and many new features such as server-side rendering and performance improvements. This is the version we will use in this book. It is now one of the fastest frontend libraries, outperforming even React according to a comparison refined with the React team (`https://vuejs.org/v2/guide/comparison`). At the time of writing this book, Vue was the second most popular frontend library on GitHub with 72k stars, just behind React and ahead of Angular 1 (`https://github.com/showcases/front-end-javascript-frameworks`).

The next evolution of the library on the roadmap includes more integration with Vue-native libraries such as Weex and NativeScript to create native mobile apps with Vue, plus new features and improvements.

Today, Vue is used by many companies such as Microsoft, Adobe, Alibaba, Baidu, Xiaomi, Expedia, Nintendo, and GitLab.

Compatibility requirements

Vue doesn't have any dependency and can be used in any ECMAScript 5 minimum-compliant browser. This means that it is not compatible with Internet Explorer 8 or less, because it needs relatively new JavaScript features such as `Object.defineProperty`, which can't be polyfilled on older browsers.

In this book, we are writing code in JavaScript version ES2015 (formerly ES6), so for the first few chapters, you will need a modern browser to run the examples (such as Edge, Firefox, or Chrome). At some point, we will introduce a compiler called *Babel* that will help us make our code compatible with older browsers.

One-minute setup

Without further ado, let's start creating our first Vue app with a very quick setup. Vue is flexible enough to be included in any web page with a simple `script` tag. Let's create a very simple web page that includes the library, with a simple `div` element and another `script` tag:

```html
<html>
<head>
  <meta charset="utf-8">
  <title>Vue Project Guide setup</title>
</head>
<body>

  <!-- Include the library in the page -->
  <script src="https://unpkg.com/vue/dist/vue.js"></script>

  <!-- Some HTML -->
  <div id="root">
    <p>Is this an Hello world?</p>
  </div>
```

Getting Started with Vue

```
    <!-- Some JavaScript -->
    <script>
    console.log('Yes! We are using Vue version', Vue.version)
    </script>

  </body>
</html>
```

In the browser console, we should have something like this:

```
Yes! We are using Vue version 2.0.3
```

As you can see in the preceding code, the library exposes a `Vue` object that contains all the features we need to use it. We are now ready to go.

Creating an app

For now, we don't have any Vue app running on our web page. The whole library is based on **Vue instances**, which are the mediators between your View and your data. So, we need to create a new Vue instance to start our app:

```
// New Vue instance
var app = new Vue({
  // CSS selector of the root DOM element
  el: '#root',
  // Some data
  data () {
    return {
      message: 'Hello Vue.js!',
    }
  },
})
```

The Vue constructor is called with the `new` keyword to create a new instance. It has one argument--the option object. It can have multiple attributes (called options), which we will discover progressively in the following chapters. For now, we are using only two of them.

With the `el` option, we tell Vue where to add (or "mount") the instance on our web page using a CSS selector. In the example, our instance will use the `<div id="root">` DOM element as its root element. We could also use the `$mount` method of the Vue instance instead of the `el` option:

```
var app = new Vue({
  data () {
```

[10]

```
    return {
      message: 'Hello Vue.js!',
    }
  },
})
// We add the instance to the page
app.$mount('#root')
```

> 💡 **TIP** Most of the special methods and attributes of a Vue instance start with a dollar character.

We will also initialize some data in the `data` option with a `message` property that contains a string. Now the Vue app is running, but it doesn't do much, yet.

> ℹ️ You can add as many Vue apps as you like on a single web page. Just create a new Vue instance for each of them and mount them on different DOM elements. This comes in handy when you want to integrate Vue in an existing project.

Vue devtools

An official debugger tool for Vue is available on Chrome as an extension called **Vue.js devtools**. It can help you see how your app is running to help you debug your code. You can download it from the Chrome Web Store (`https://chrome.google.com/webstore/search/vue`) or from the Firefox addons registry (`https://addons.mozilla.org/en-US/firefox/addon/vue-js-devtools/?src=ss`).

For the Chrome version, you need to set an additional setting. In the extension settings, enable **Allow access to file URLs** so that it can detect Vue on a web page opened from your local drive:

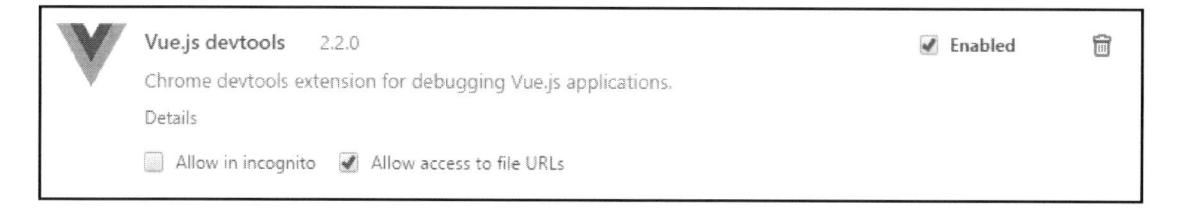

V	Vue.js devtools 2.2.0	✓ Enabled	🗑
	Chrome devtools extension for debugging Vue.js applications.		
	Details		
	☐ Allow in incognito ✓ Allow access to file URLs		

Getting Started with Vue

On your web page, open the Chrome Dev Tools with the *F12* shortcut (or *Shift + command + c* on OS X) and search for the **Vue** tab (it may be hidden in the **More tools...** dropdown). Once it is opened, you can see a tree with our Vue instance named **Root** by convention. If you click on it, the sidebar displays the properties of the instance:

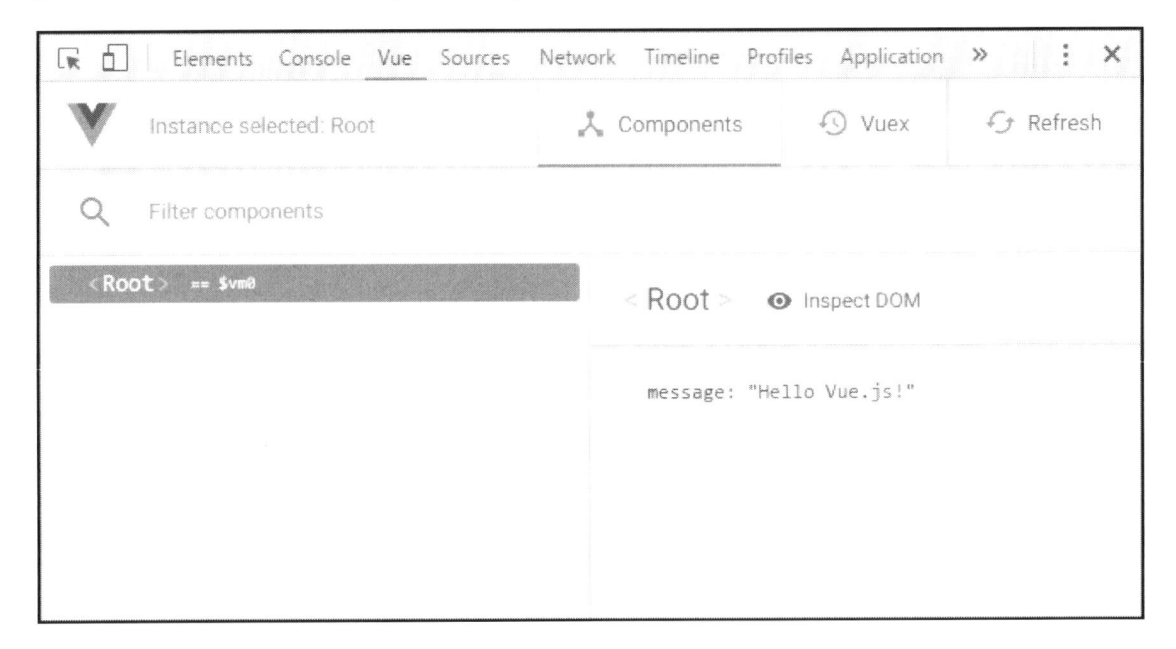

| Elements | Console | Vue | Sources | Network | Timeline | Profiles | Application |

Instance selected: Root — Components — Vuex — Refresh

Filter components

`<Root>` == $vm0

`<Root>` Inspect DOM

message: "Hello Vue.js!"

> **TIP:** You can drag and drop the `devtools` tab to your liking. Don't hesitate to place it among the first tabs, as it will be hidden in the page where Vue is not in development mode or is not running at all.

You can change the name of your instance with the `name` option:

```
var app = new Vue({
  name: 'MyApp',
  // ...
})
```

This will help you see where your instance in the devtools is when you will have many more:

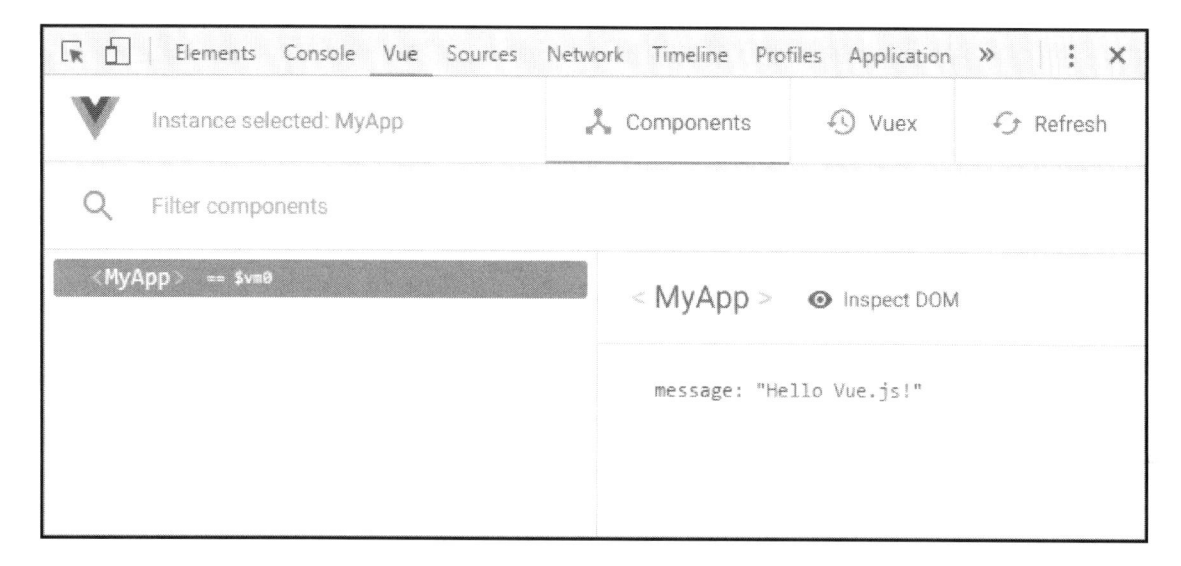

Templates make your DOM dynamic

With Vue, we have several systems at our disposal to write our View. For now, we will start with templates. A template is the easiest way to describe a View because it looks like HTML a lot, but with some extra syntax to make the DOM dynamically update very easily.

Displaying text

The first template feature we will see is the **text interpolation**, which is used to display dynamic text inside our web page. The text interpolation syntax is a pair of double curly braces containing a JavaScript expression of any kind. Its result will replace the interpolation when Vue will process the template. Replace the `<div id="root">` element with the following:

```
<div id="root">
  <p>{{ message }}</p>
</div>
```

The template in this example has a `<p>` element whose content is the result of the `message` JavaScript expression. It will return the value of the message attribute of our instance. You should now have a new text displayed on your web page--**Hello Vue.js!**. It doesn't seem like much, but Vue has done a lot of work for us here--we now have the DOM wired with our data.

To demonstrate this, open your browser console and change the `app.message` value and press *Enter* on the keyboard:

```
app.message = 'Awesome!'
```

The message has changed. This is called **data-binding**. It means that Vue is able to automatically update the DOM whenever your data changes without requiring anything from your part. The library includes a very powerful and efficient reactivity system that keeps track of all your data and is able to update what's needed when something changes. All of this is very fast indeed.

Adding basic interactivity with directives

Let's add some interactivity to our otherwise quite static app, for example, a text input that will allow the user to change the message displayed. We can do that in templates with special HTML attributes called **directives**.

> All the directives in Vue start with `v-` and follow the kebab-case syntax. That means you should separate the words with a dash. Remember that HTML attributes are case insensitive (whether they are uppercase or lowercase doesn't matter).

The directive we need here is `v-model`, which will bind the value of our `<input>` element with our `message` data property. Add a new `<input>` element with the `v-model="message"` attribute inside the template:

```
<div id="root">
  <p>{{ message }}</p>
  <!-- New text input -->
  <input v-model="message" />
</div>
```

Vue will now update the `message` property automatically when the input value changes. You can play with the content of the input to verify that the text updates as you type and the value in the devtools changes:

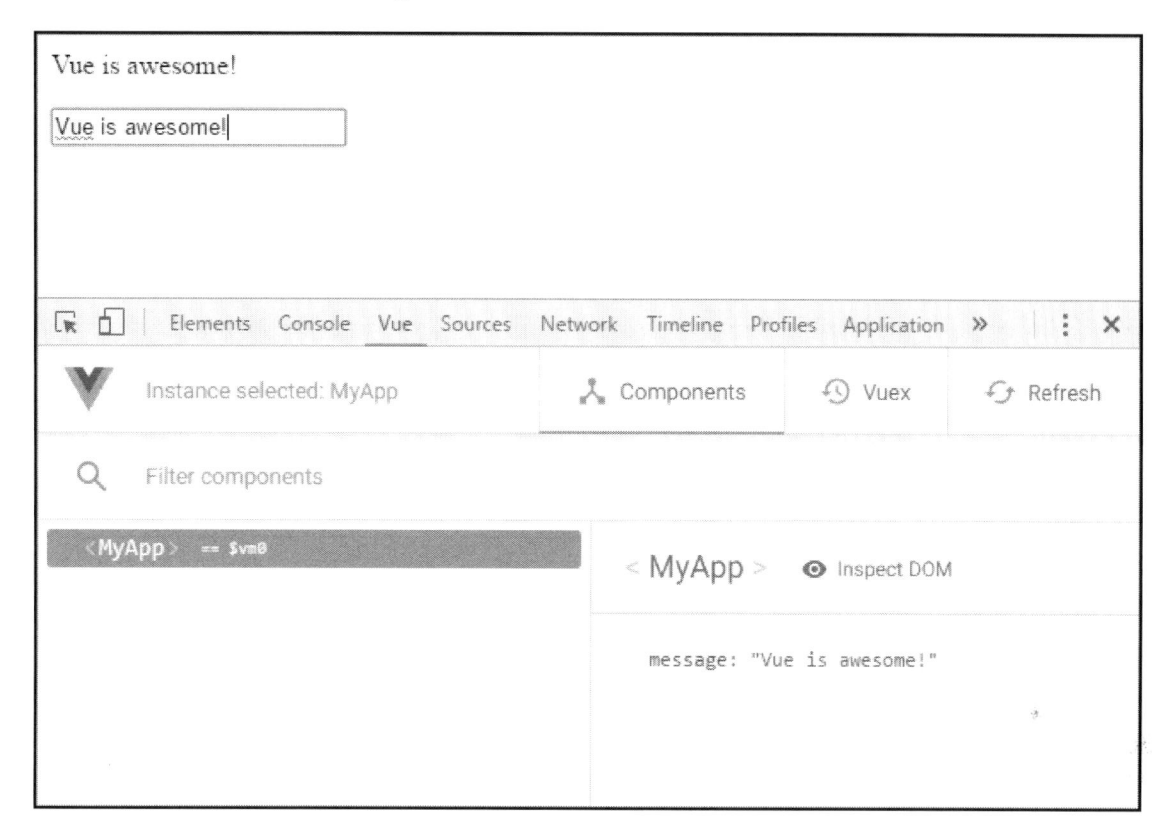

There are many more directives available in Vue, and you can even create your own. Don't worry, we will cover that in later chapters.

Summary

In this chapter, we quickly set up a web page to get started using Vue and wrote a simple app. We created a Vue instance to mount the Vue app on the page and wrote a template to make the DOM dynamic. Inside this template, we used a JavaScript expression to display text, thanks to text interpolations. Finally, we added some interactivity with an input element that we bound to our data with the `v-model` directive.

In the next chapter, we will create our first real web app with Vue--a markdown notebook. We will need more Vue superpowers to turn the development of this app into a fun and swift experience.

2
Project 1 - Markdown Notebook

The first app we will create is a markdown notebook, using several Vue features in a step-by-step manner. We will reuse what we saw in `Chapter 1`, *Getting Started with Vue*, and add more elements on top of it, such as useful directives, events for user interaction, more instance options, and filters to process values.

Before we start writing the code, let's talk about the app and review our objectives:

- The notebook app will allow the user to write notes in markdown
- The markdown will be previewed in real time
- The users will be able to add as many notes as they want
- The notes will be restored the next time the user visits the app

To do that, we will divide the user interface into three sections:

- A main section in the middle with the note editor
- A right pane, which previews the markdown of the current node
- A left pane, with the list of notes and a button to add a new one

Project 1 - Markdown Notebook

Here is what it will look like at the end of the chapter:

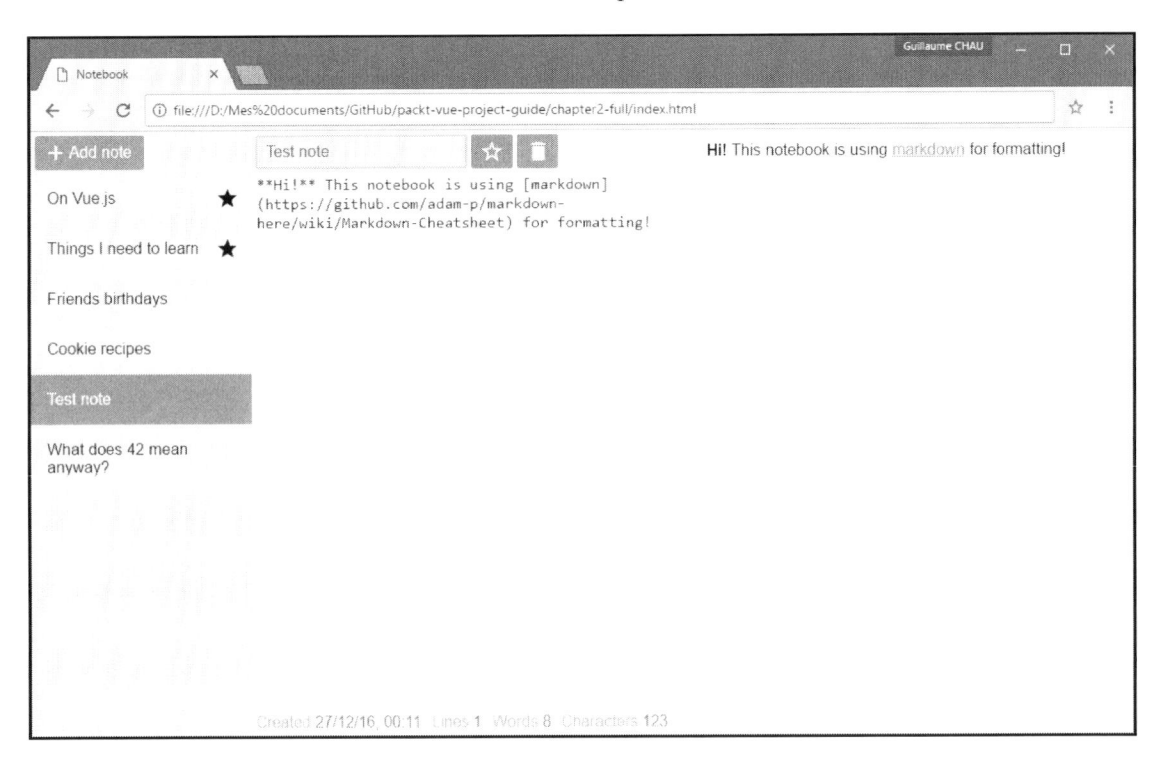

A basic note editor

We will start small with a very simple markdown note app that only displays a text editor on the left and a markdown preview on the right. Then, we will turn it into a full notebook with multiple note support.

Setting up the project

For this project, we will have a few files ready to get us started:

1. First, download *simple-notebook* project files and extract them in the same folder. Open the `index.html` file and add a `div` element with the `notebook` ID and a nested `section` element with the `main` class. You should have the following content inside the file:

```html
<html>
<head>
  <title>Notebook</title>
  <!-- Icons & Stylesheets -->
  <link href="https://fonts.googleapis.com/icon?family=Material+Icons" rel="stylesheet">
  <link rel="stylesheet" href="style.css" />
</head>
<body>
  <!-- Include the library in the page -->
  <script src="https://unpkg.com/vue/dist/vue.js"></script>

  <!-- Notebook app -->
  <div id="notebook">

    <!-- Main pane -->
    <section class="main">

    </section>

  </div>

  <!-- Some JavaScript -->
  <script src="script.js"></script>
</body>
</html>
```

Project 1 - Markdown Notebook

2. Now, open the `script.js` file to add some JavaScript. Just like you did in Chapter 1, *Getting Started with Vue*, create a Vue instance mounted on the `#notebook` element with a Vue constructor:

   ```
   // New VueJS instance
   new Vue({
     // CSS selector of the root DOM element
     el: '#notebook',
   })
   ```

3. Then, add a data property called `content` that will hold the content of your note:

   ```
   new Vue({
     el: '#notebook',

     // Some data
     data () {
       return {
         content: 'This is a note.',
       }
     },
   })
   ```

Now you are ready to create your first real Vue app.

The note editor

Now that we have our app running, let's add the text editor. We will use a simple `textarea` element and the `v-model` directive we saw in Chapter 1, *Getting Started with Vue*.

Create a `section` element and put the `textarea` inside, then add the `v-model` directive bound to our `content` property:

```
<!-- Main pane -->
<section class="main">
  <textarea v-model="content"></textarea>
</section>
```

Now, if you change the text ;inside the note editor, the value of `content` should automatically chance in the devtools.

> The `v-model` directive is not limited to text inputs. You can also use it in other form elements, such as checkboxes, radio buttons, or even custom components, as we will see later in the book.

The preview pane

To compile the note markdown into valid HTML, we will need an additional library called Marked (https://www.npmjs.com/package/marked):

1. Include the library in the page just after the `script` tag referencing Vue:

   ```
   <!-- Include the library in the page -->
   <script src="https://unpkg.com/vue/dist/vue.js"></script>
   <!-- Add the marked library: -->
   <script src="https://unpkg.com/marked"></script>
   ```

   `marked` is very easy to use--just call it with the markdown text, and it will return the corresponding HTML.

2. Try the library with some markdown text:

   ```
   const html = marked('**Bold** *Italic* [link](http://vuejs.org/)')
   console.log(html)
   ```

   You should have the following output in the browser console:

   ```
   <p><strong>Bold</strong> <em>Italic</em>
   <a href="http://vuejs.org/">link</a></p>
   ```

Computed property

A very powerful feature of Vue is the **computed property**. It allows us to define new properties that combine any amount of properties and use transformations, such as converting a markdown string into HTML--that's why its value is defined by a function. A computed property has the following features:

- The value is cached so that the function doesn't rerun if it's not necessary, preventing useless computation
- It is automatically updated as needed when a property used inside the function has changed

- A computed property can be used exactly like any property (and you can use computed properties inside other computed properties)
- It is not computed until it is really used somewhere in the app

This will help us automatically convert the note markdown into valid HTML, so we can display a preview in real time. We just need to declare our computed property in the `computed` option:

```
// Computed properties
computed: {
  notePreview () {
    // Markdown rendered to HTML
    return marked(this.content)
  },
},
```

Text interpolation escaping

Let's try to display our note in a new pane using a text interpolation:

1. Create an `<aside>` element with the `preview` class, which displays our `notePreview` computed property:

   ```
   <!-- Preview pane -->
   <aside class="preview">
     {{ notePreview }}
   </aside>
   ```

   We should now have the preview pane displaying our note on the right side of the app. If you type some text in the note editor, you should see the preview updating automatically. However, there is an issue with our app, which arises when you use markdown formatting.

2. Try making your text bold by surrounding it with `**`, as follows:

   ```
   I'm in **bold**!
   ```

   Our computed property should return this in valid HTML, and we should have some bold text rendered in our preview pane. Instead, we can see the following:

```
I'm in <strong>bold</strong>!
```

[22]

We have just discovered that the text interpolation automatically escapes the HTML tags. This is to prevent injection attacks and improve the security of our app. Fortunately, there is a way to display some HTML, as we will see in a moment. However, this forces you to think about using it to include potentially harmful dynamic content.

For example, you create a comment system, where any user can write some text to comment on your app pages. What if someone writes some HTML in their comment, which is then displayed in the page as valid HTML? They could add some malicious JavaScript code, and all the visitors of your app would be vulnerable. It's called a cross-site scripting attack, or an XSS attack. That's why text interpolation always escapes HTML tags.

> **TIP**: It is not recommended to use `v-html` on content created by the users of the application. They could write malicious JavaScript code inside a `<script>` tag that would be executed. However, with normal text interpolation, you would be safe because the HTML would not be executed.

Displaying HTML

Now that we know that text interpolations can't render HTML for security reasons, we will need another way to render dynamic HTML--the `v-html` directive. Like the `v-model` directive we saw in Chapter 1, *Getting Started with Vue*, this is a special attribute that adds a new feature to our template. This one is able to render any valid HTML string into our app. Just pass the string as the value, as follows:

```
<!-- Preview pane -->
<aside class="preview" v-html="notePreview">
</aside>
```

Now, the markdown preview should work correctly, and the HTML is dynamically inserted in our page.

> **TIP**: Any content inside our `aside` element will be replaced by the value of the `v-html` directive. You can use this to put placeholder contents inside.

Project 1 - Markdown Notebook

Here is the result you should have:

> There is an equivalent directive for text interpolation, `v-text`, which behaves like `v-html`, but escapes the HTML tags just like classic text interpolations.

Saving the note

For now, if you close or refresh the app, your note will be lost. It would be a good idea to save and load it the next time we open the app. To achieve this, we will use the standard `localStorage` API provided by most browsers.

Watching changes

We would like to save our note as soon as its content changes. That's why we need something that is called when our `content` data property changes, such as **watchers**. Let's add some watchers to our application!

1. Add a new `watch` option to the Vue instance.

    This option is a dictionary with the keys being the name of the watched properties and the value being a watching option object. This object has to have a `handler` property, which is either a function or the name of a method. The handler will receive two arguments--the new value and the old value of the property being watched.

    Here is an example with a simple handler:

    ```
    new Vue({
      // ...

      // Change watchers
      watch: {
        // Watching 'content' data property
        content: {
          handler (val, oldVal) {
            console.log('new note:', val, 'old note:', oldVal)
          },
        },
      },
    })
    ```

    Now, when you type in the note editor, you should get the following message in the browser console:

    ```
    new note: This is a **note**! old note: This is a **note**
    ```

    This will be very helpful in saving the note whenever it changes.

    There are two other options you can use alongside `handler`:

    - `deep` is a Boolean that tells Vue to watch for changes recursively inside nested objects. This is not useful here, as we only watch a string.
    - `immediate` is also a Boolean that forces the handler to be called immediately instead of waiting for the first change. In our case, this will not have a meaningful impact, but we can try it to note its effects.

Project 1 - Markdown Notebook

> **TIP:** The default value of these options is `false`, so if you don't need them, you can skip them entirely.

2. Add the immediate option to the watcher:

```
content: {
  handler (val, oldVal) {
    console.log('new note:', val, 'old note:', oldVal)
  },
  immediate: true,
},
```

As soon as you refresh the app, you should see the following message pop up in the browser console:

```
new note: This is a **note** old note: undefined
```

Unsurprisingly, the old value of the note was `undefined`, because the watcher handler was called when the instance was created.

3. We don't really need this option here, so go ahead and delete it:

```
content: {
  handler (val, oldVal) {
    console.log('new note:', val, 'old note:', oldVal)
  },
},
```

Since we are not using any option, we can use a shorter syntax by skipping the object containing the `handler` option:

```
content (val, oldVal) {
  console.log('new note:', val, 'old note:', oldVal)
},
```

> **TIP:** This is the most common syntax for watchers when you don't need other options, such as `deep` or `immediate`.

[26]

4. Let's save our note. Use the `localStorage.setItem()` API to store the note content:

```
content (val, oldVal) {
  console.log('new note:', val, 'old note:', oldVal)
  localStorage.setItem('content', val)
},
```

To check whether this worked, edit the note and open the browser devtools in the **Application** or **Storage** tab (depending on your browser) you should find a new entry under the **Local Storage** section:

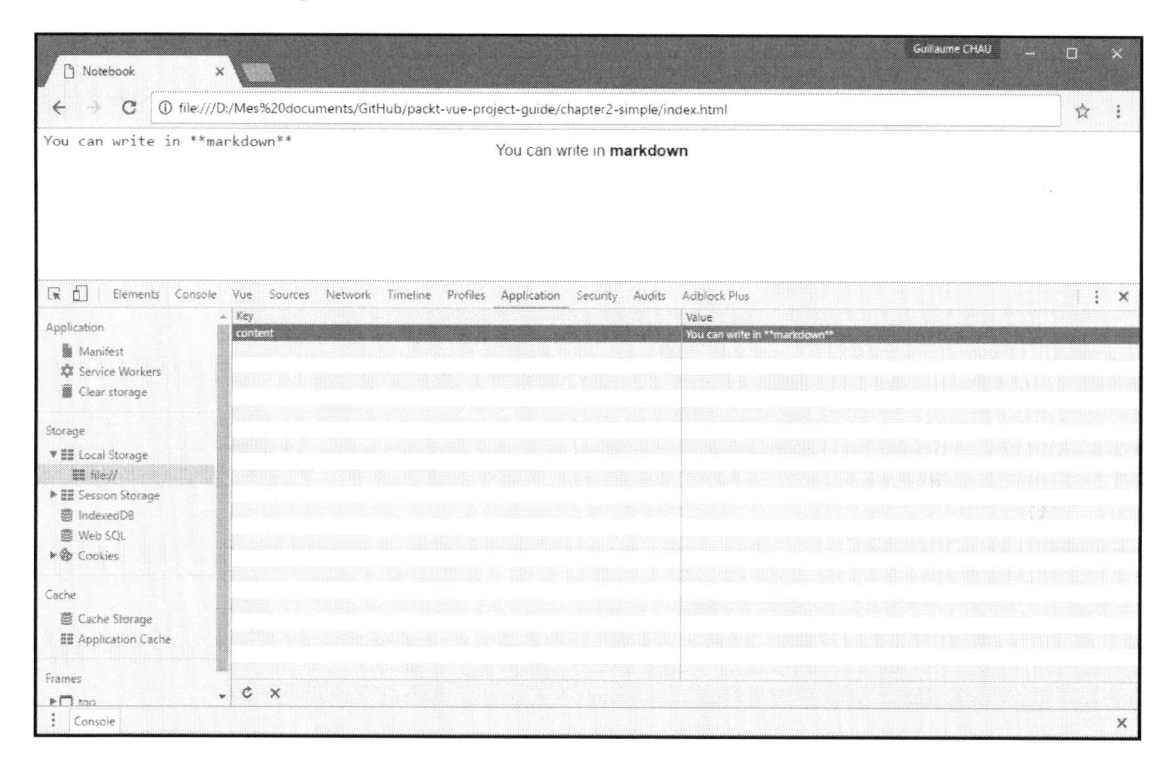

Project 1 - Markdown Notebook

Using a method

There is a good coding principle that says *Don't Repeat Yourself*, and we really should follow it. That's why we can write some logic in reusable functions called **methods**. Let's move our saving logic into one:

1. Add a new `methods` option to the Vue instance and use the `localStorage` API there:

   ```
   new Vue({
     // ...

     methods: {
       saveNote (val) {
         console.log('saving note:', val)
         localStorage.setItem('content', val)
       },
     },
   })
   ```

2. We can now use the method name in the `handler` option of our watcher:

   ```
   watch: {
     content: {
       handler: 'saveNote',
     },
   },
   ```

Alternatively, we can use it with the shorter syntax:

```
watch: {
  content: 'saveNote',
},
```

Accessing the Vue instance

Inside the methods, we can access the Vue instance with the `this` keyword. For example, we could call another method:

```
methods: {
  saveNote (val) {
    console.log('saving note:', val)
    localStorage.setItem('content', val)
    this.reportOperation('saving')
  },
```

```
  reportOperation (opName) {
    console.log('The', opName, 'operation was completed!')
  },
},
```

Here, the `saveNote` method will be called from the `contentChanged` method.

We can also access the other properties and special functions of our Vue instance through `this`. We could remove the `saveNote` argument and access the `content` data property directly:

```
methods: {
  saveNote () {
    console.log('saving note:', this.content)
    localStorage.setItem('content', this.content)
  },
},
```

This also works in the watcher handler we created in the *Watching changes* section:

```
watch: {
  content (val, oldVal) {
    console.log('new note:', val, 'old note:', oldVal)
    console.log('saving note:', this.content)
    localStorage.setItem('content', this.content)
  },
},
```

> Basically, you can access the Vue instance with `this` in any function bound to it: methods, handlers, and other hooks.

Loading the saved note

Now that we save the note content each time it changes, we will need to restore it when the app is reopened. We will use the `localStorage.getItem()` API for that. Add the following line at the end of your JavaScript file:

```
console.log('restored note:', localStorage.getItem('content'))
```

Project 1 - Markdown Notebook

When you refresh your app, you should see the saved note content printed in the browser console.

Lifecycle hooks

The first way that comes to mind to restore our note content into the Vue instance is to set the content data property when the instance is created.

Each Vue instance follows a precise lifecycle with several steps--it will be created, mounted on the page, updated, and finally, destroyed. For example, during the creating step, Vue will make the instance data reactive.

> Hooks are a specific set of functions that are automatically called at some point in time. They allow us to customize the logic of the framework. For example, we can call a method when a Vue instance is created.

We have multiple hooks at our disposal to execute logic when, or just before, each of these steps occurs:

- `beforeCreate`: This is called when the Vue instance object is created (for example, with `new Vue({})`), but before Vue has done anything with it.
- `created`: This is called after the instance is ready and fully operating. Note that, at this point, the instance is not in the DOM yet.
- `beforeMount`: This is called just before the instance is added (or mounted) on the web page.
- `mounted`: This is called when the instance is on the page and visible in the DOM.
- `beforeUpdate`: This is called when the instance needs to be updated (generally, when a data or computed property has changed).
- `updated`: This is called after the data changes are applied to the template. Note that the DOM may not be up to date yet.
- `beforeDestroy`: This is called just before the instance is torn down.
- `destroyed`: This is called when the instance is fully removed.

For now, we will only use the `created` hook to restore the note content. To add a lifecycle hook, just add a function with the corresponding name into the Vue instance options:

```
new Vue({
  // ...

  // This will be called when the instance is ready
  created () {
    // Set the content to the stored value
    // or to a default string if nothing was saved
    this.content = localStorage.getItem('content') || 'You can write in **markdown**'
  },
})
```

Now, when you refresh the app, the ;created hook will be automatically called when the instance is created. This will set the `content` data property value to the result of the restoration or to `'You can write in **markdown**'` if the result was falsy, in case we didn't have anything saved before.

> **TIP**
> In JavaScript, a value is falsy when equal to `false`, 0, an empty string, `null`, `undefined`, or `NaN` (not a number). Here, the `localStorage.getItem()` function will return `null` if the corresponding key doesn't exist in the browser local storage data.

The watcher we set up is also called, so the note is saved, and you should see something similar to this in the browser console:

```
new note: You can write in **markdown** old note: This is a note
saving note: You can write in **markdown**
The saving operation was completed!
```

We can see that when the created hook is called, Vue has already set the data properties and their initial values (here, *This is a note*).

Initializing directly in the data

The other way is to initialize the `content` data property with the restored value directly:

```
new Vue({
  // ...
  data () {
    return {
      content: localStorage.getItem('content') || 'You can write in **markdown**',
```

[31]

```
    }
  },
  // ...
})
```

With the preceding code, the watcher handler will not be called because we initialize the `content` value instead of changing it.

Multiple notes

A notebook with only one note is not that useful, so let's turn it into a multiple note one. We will add a new side panel on the left with the list of notes, plus a few extra elements, such as a text field to rename the notes and a favorite toggle button.

The note list

We will now lay the groundwork for the side pane containing the list of notes:

1. Add a new `aside` element with the `side-bar` class before the main section:

    ```
    <!-- Notebook app -->
    <div id="notebook">

      <!-- Sidebar -->
      <aside class="side-bar">
        <!-- Here will be the note list -->
      </aside>

      <!-- Main pane -->
      <section class="main">
    ...
    ```

2. Add a new data property called `notes`--it will be the array containing all of our notes:

    ```
    data () {
      return {
        content: ...
        // New! A note array
        notes: [],
      }
    },
    ```

A method to create a new note

Each of our notes will be an object with the following data:

- id: This will be the note unique identifier
- title: This ;will contain the name of the note displayed in the list
- content: This ;will be the note markdown content
- created: This ;will be the date the note was created
- favorite: This ;will be a Boolean that allows for marking a note that will be displayed at the top of the list as favorite

Let's add a method that will create a new note and call it addNote, which will create a new note object with a default value:

```
methods:{
  // Add a note with some default content and select it
  addNote () {
    const time = Date.now()
    // Default new note
    const note = {
      id: String(time),
      title: 'New note ' + (this.notes.length + 1),
      content: '**Hi!** This notebook is using [markdown](https://github.com/adam-p/markdown-here/wiki/Markdown-Cheatsheet) for formatting!',
      created: time,
      favorite: false,
    }
    // Add to the list
    this.notes.push(note)
  },
}
```

We take the current time (which means the number of milliseconds elapsed since 1 January 1970 00:00:00 UTC), which will be a perfect way to have a unique identifier on each note. We also set default values, such as a title and some content, plus the created date and the favorite ;Boolean. Finally, we add the note to the notes array property.

Button and click events with v-on

Now, we will need a button to call this method. Create a new button element inside a `div` element with the toolbar class:

```
<aside class="side-bar">
  <!-- Toolbar -->
  <div class="toolbar">
    <!-- Add note button -->
    <button><i class="material-icons">add</i> Add note</button>
  </div>
</aside>
```

To call the `addNote` method when the user clicks on the button, we will need a new directive--`v-on`. The value will be the function called when the event is caught, but it also expects an argument to know which event to listen to. However, how do we pass the argument to the directive, you might ask? It's quite simple! Add a `:` character after the directive name, followed by the argument. Here is an example:

```
<button v-directive:argument="value">
```

In our case, we are using the `v-on` directive with the event name as the argument, and more specifically, the `click` event. It should look like this:

```
<button v-on:click="callback">
```

Our button should call the `addNote` method when it is clicked on, so go ahead and modify the button we added earlier:

```
<button v-on:click="addNote"><i class="material-icons">add</i> Add note</button>
```

There is an optional special shortcut for the `v-on` directive--the `@` character that allows you to rewrite the preceding ;code to the following:

```
<button @click="addNote"><i class="material-icons">add</i> Add note</button>
```

Now that our button is ready, try adding a few notes. We don't see them in the app yet, but you can open the devtools and note the note list change:

Binding attributes with v-bind

It would be helpful if a tooltip showed the number of notes we already had on the "Add note" button, wouldn't it? At least we can introduce another useful directive!

The tooltips are added with the title HTML attribute. Here is an example:

```
<button title="3 note(s) already">
```

Here, it is only a static text, though, and we would like to make it dynamic. Thankfully, there is a directive that allows us to bind a JavaScript expression to an attribute--v-bind. Like the v-on directive, it expects an argument, which is the name of the target attribute.

We can rewrite the preceding example with a JavaScript expression as follows:

```
<button v-bind:title="notes.length + ' note(s) already'">
```

Project 1 - Markdown Notebook

Now, if you leave the mouse cursor over the button, you will get the number of notes:

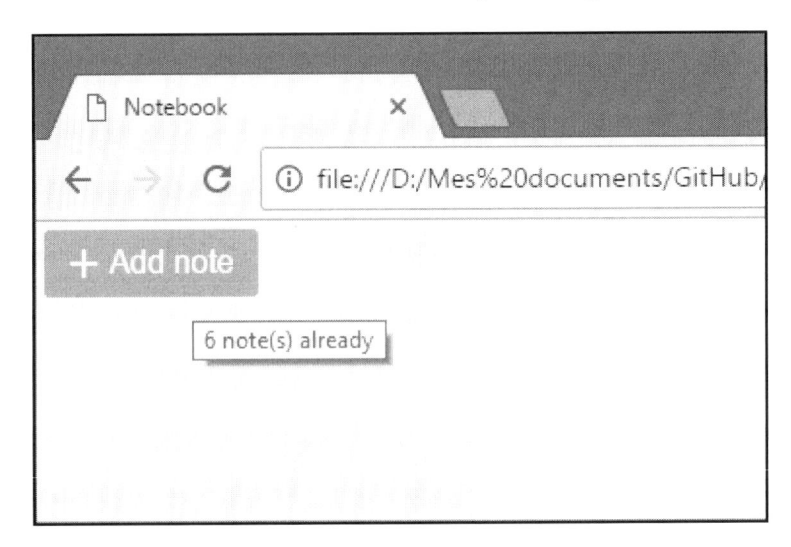

Like the `v-on` directive, `v-bind` has a special shortcut syntax (both are the most used directives)--you can just skip the `v-bind` part and only put the `:` character with the attribute name. The example would look like this:

```
<button :title="notes.length + ' note(s) already'">
```

> **TIP**
> JavaScript expressions bound with `v-bind` will re-evaluate automatically when needed and update the value of the corresponding attribute.

We could also move the expression to a computed property and use it instead. The computed property could be as follows:

```
computed: {
  ...

  addButtonTitle () {
    return notes.length + ' note(s) already'
  },
},
```

Then, we would rewrite the bound attribute, as follows:

```
<button :title="addButtonTitle">
```

Displaying a list with v-for

We will now display the list of notes below the toolbar.

1. Just below the toolbar, add a new `div` element with the ;notes class:

```
<aside class="side-bar">
  <div class="toolbar">
    <button @click="addNote"><i class="material-icons">add</i>
    Add note</button>
  </div>
  <div class="notes">
    <!-- Note list here -->
  </div>
</aside>
```

Now, we want to display a list of multiple div elements, one for each note. To achieve this, we need the `v-for` directive. It takes a special expression as the value, in the form of `item of items`, that will iterate over the `items` array or object and expose an `item` value for this part of the template. Here is an example:

```
<div v-for="item of items">{{ item.title }}</div>
```

You can also use the `in` keyword instead of `of`:

```
<div v-for="item in items">{{ item.title }}</div>
```

Imagine that we have the following array:

```
data () {
  return {
    items: [
      { title: 'Item 1' },
      { title: 'Item 2' },
      { title: 'Item 3' },
    ]
  }
}
```

[37]

The final rendered DOM will look like this:

```
<div>Item 1</div>
<div>Item 2</div>
<div>Item 3</div>
```

> As you can see, the element on which you put the `v-for` directive is repeated in the DOM.

2. Let's go back to our notebook and display the notes in the side pane. We store them in the notes data property, so we need to iterate over it:

```
<div class="notes">
  <div class="note" v-for="note of notes">{{note.title}}</div>
</div>
```

We should now have the notes list displayed below the button:

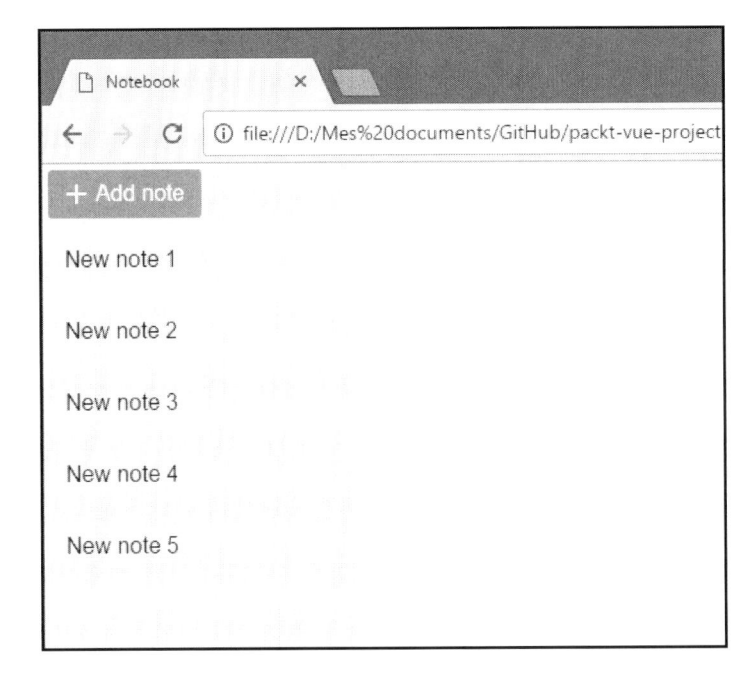

Chapter 2

Add a few more notes using the button, and you should see that the list is updating automatically!

Selecting a note

When a note is selected, it becomes the context of the middle and right panes of the app--the text editor modifies its content, and the preview pane displays its formatted markdown. Let's implement this behavior!

1. Add a new data property called `selectedId` that will hold the ID of the selected note:

   ```
   data () {
     return {
       content: localStorage.getItem('content') || 'You can write in
       **markdown**',
       notes: [],
       // Id of the selected note
       selectedId: null,
     }
   },
   ```

   > **TIP**: We could have created a `selectedNote` property instead, holding the note object, but it would have made the saving logic more complex, with no benefit.

2. We need a new method that will be called when we click on a note in the list to select ID. Let's call it `selectNote`:

   ```
   methods: {
     ...

     selectNote (note) {
       this.selectedId = note.id
     },
   }
   ```

[39]

3. Like we did for the add note button, we will listen for the `click` event with the `v-on` directive on each note item in the list:

```
<div class="notes">
  <div class="note" v-for="note of notes"
  @click="selectNote(note)">{{note.title}}</div>
</div>
```

Now, you should see the ;updated `selectedId` data property when you click on a note.

The current note

Now that we know which note is currently selected, we can replace the old `content` data property we created at the beginning. It would be very useful to have a computed property to easily access the selected note, so we will create one now:

1. Add a new computed property called `selectedNote` that returns the note with an ID that matches our `selectedId` property:

```
computed: {
  ...

  selectedNote () {
    // We return the matching note with selectedId
    return this.notes.find(note => note.id === this.selectedId)
  },
}
```

> `note => note.id === this.selectedId` is an arrow function from the ES2015 JavaScript version. Here, it takes a `note` argument and returns the result of the `note.id === this.selectedId` expression.

We need to replace the old `content` data property with `selectedNote.content` in our code.

2. Start by modifying the editor in the template:

```
<textarea v-model="selectedNote.content"></textarea>
```

3. Then, change the `notePreview` computed property to now use `selectedNote`:

   ```
   notePreview () {
     // Markdown rendered to HTML
     return this.selectedNote ? marked(this.selectedNote.content) :
   ''
   },
   ```

Now, the text editor and the preview pane will display the selected note when you click on it in the list.

You can safely remove the `content` data property, its watcher, and the `saveNote` method, which are no longer used in the app.

Dynamic CSS classes

It would be nice to add a `selected` CSS class when a note is the selected one in the note list (for example, to display a different background color). Thankfully, Vue has a very useful trick to help us achieve this--the `v-bind` directive (the `:` character being its shorthand) has some magic to make the manipulation of CSS classes easier. Instead of passing a string, you can pass an array of strings:

```
<div :class="['one', 'two', 'three']">
```

We will get the following in the DOM:

```
<div class="one two three">
```

However, the most interesting feature is that you can pass an object whose keys are the class names and whose values are Booleans that determine whether or not each class should be applied. Here is an example:

```
<div :class="{ one: true, two: false, three: true }">
```

This object notation will produce the following HTML:

```
<div class="one three">
```

In our case, we want to apply the selected class only if the note is the selected one. So, we will simply write as follows:

```
<div :class="{ selected: note === selectedNote }">
```

The note list should now look like this:

```
<div class="notes">
  <div class="note" v-for="note of notes" @click="selectNote(note)"
   :class="{selected: note === selectedNote}">{{note.title}}</div>
</div>
```

> **TIP**: You can combine a static `class` attribute with a dynamic one. It is recommended that you put the nondynamic classes into the static attribute because Vue will optimize the static values.

Now, when you click on a note in the list to select it, its background will change color:

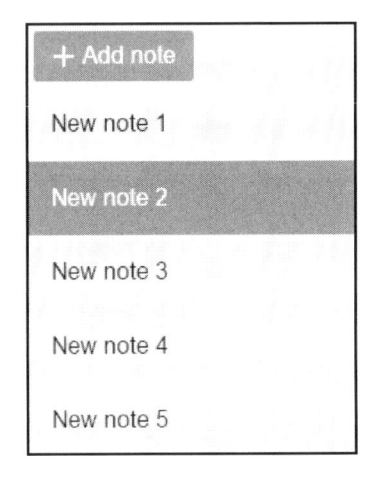

Conditional templates with v-if

We need one last thing before testing our change; the main and preview panes shouldn't be displayed if no note is selected--it would not make sense for the user to have an empty editor and preview pane pointing to nothing, and it would make our code crash since `selectedNote` would be `null`. Thankfully, the `v-if` directive can dynamically take parts out of the template when we want. It works just like the JavaScript `if` keyword, with a condition.

Chapter 2

In this example, the `div` element will not be in the DOM at all while the `loading` property is falsy:

```
<div v-if="loading">
  Loading...
</div>
```

There are also two other useful directives, `v-else` and `v-else-if`, that will work as you might have expected:

```
<div v-if="loading">
  Loading...
</div>

<div v-else-if="processing">
  Processing
</div>

<div v-else>
  Content here
</div>
```

Back in our app, add the `v-if="selectedNote"` condition to both the main and preview panes so that they are not added to the DOM until a note is selected:

```
<!-- Main pane -->
<section class="main" v-if="selectedNote">
  ...
</section>

<!-- Preview pane -->
<aside class="preview" v-if="selectedNote" v-html="notePreview">
</aside>
```

The repetition here is a bit unfortunate, but Vue has us covered. You can surround both elements with a special `<template>` tag that acts like braces in JavaScript:

```
<template v-if="selectedNote">
  <!-- Main pane -->
  <section class="main">
    ...
  </section>

  <!-- Preview pane -->
  <aside class="preview" v-html="notePreview">
  </aside>
</template>
```

[43]

At this point, the app should look like this:

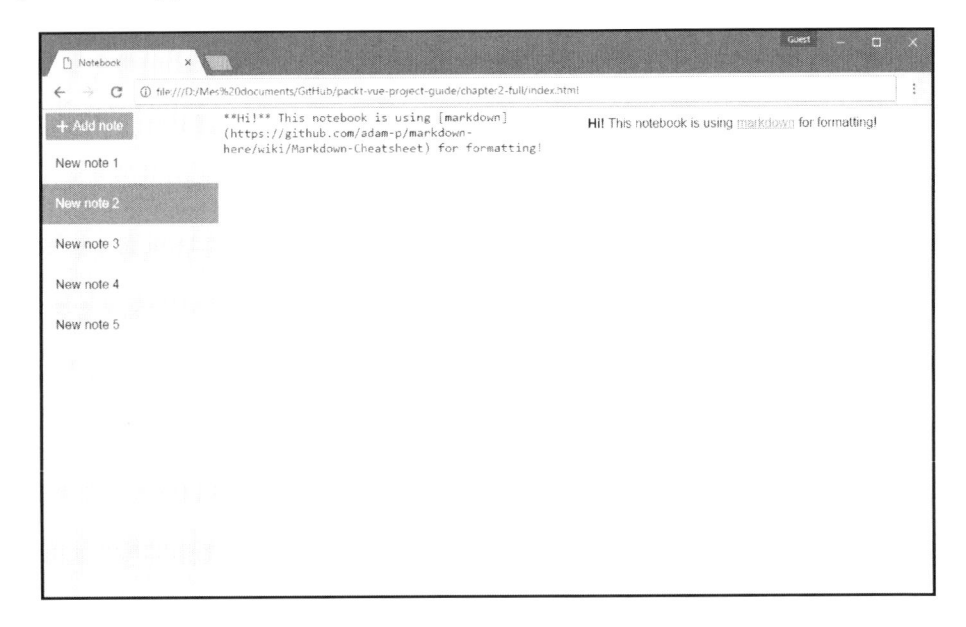

> The `<template>` tag will not be present in the DOM; it is more like a ghost element that is useful to regroup real elements together.

Saving the notes with the deep option

Now, we would like to save and restore the notes between sessions, just like we did for the note content:

1. Let's create a new `saveNotes` method. Since we can't save an array of objects directly into the `localStorage` API (it only accepts strings), we need to convert it to JSON first with `JSON.stringify`:

    ```
    methods: {
      ...
      saveNotes () {
        // Don't forget to stringify to JSON before storing
        localStorage.setItem('notes', JSON.stringify(this.notes))
    ```

```
        console.log('Notes saved!', new Date())
      },
    },
```

Like we did for the previous `content` property, we will watch the `notes` data property for changes to trigger the `saveNotes` method.

2. Add a watcher in the watch option:

    ```
    watch: {
      notes: 'saveNotes',
    }
    ```

    Now, if you try to add a few tasks, you should see something like this in your console:

    ```
    Notes saved! Mon Apr 42 2042 17:40:23 GMT+0100 (Paris, Madrid)
    Notes saved! Mon Apr 42 2016 17:42:51 GMT+0100 (Paris, Madrid)
    ```

3. Change the initialization of the `notes` property in the `data` hook to load the stored list from `localStorage`:

    ```
    data () {
      return {
        notes: JSON.parse(localStorage.getItem('notes')) || [],
        selectedId: null,
      }
    },
    ```

The newly added notes should be restored when you refresh the page. However, if you try to change the content of one note, you will notice that it doesn't trigger the `notes` watcher, and thus, the notes are not saved. This is because, by default, the watchers are only watching the direct changes to the target object--assignment of a simple value, adding, removing, or moving an item in an array. For example, the following operations will be detected by default:

```
// Assignment
this.selectedId = 'abcd'

// Adding or removing an item in an array
this.notes.push({...})
this.notes.splice(index, 1)

// Sorting an array
this.notes.sort(...)
```

However, all the other operations, like these, will not trigger the watcher:

```
// Assignment to an attribute or a nested object
this.myObject.someAttribute = 'abcd'
this.myObject.nestedObject.otherAttribute = 42

// Changes made to items in an array
this.notes[0].content = 'new content'
```

In this case, you will need to add the `deep` option to the watcher:

```
watch: {
  notes: {
    // The method name
    handler: 'saveNotes',
    // We need this to watch each note's properties inside the array
    deep: true,
  },
}
```

That way, Vue will also watch the objects and attributes recursively inside our `notes` array. Now, if you type into the text editor, the notes list should be saved--the `v-model` directive will modify the `content` property of the selected note, and with the `deep` option, the watcher will be triggered.

Saving the selection

It would be very handy if our app could select the note that was selected last time. We just need to store and load the `selectedId` data property used to store the ID of the selected note. That's right! Once more, we will use a watcher to trigger the save:

```
watch: {
  ...

  // Let's save the selection too
  selectedId (val) {
    localStorage.setItem('selected-id', val)
  },
}
```

[46]

Also, we will restore the value when the property is initialized:

```
data () {
  return {
    notes: JSON.parse(localStorage.getItem('notes')) || [],
    selectedId: localStorage.getItem('selected-id') || null,
  }
},
```

It's ready! Now, when you refresh the app, it should look exactly how you left it, with the same note selected.

The note toolbar with extras inside

Some features are still missing from our app, such as deleting or renaming the selected note. We will add these in a new toolbar, just above the note text editor. Go ahead and create a new `div` element with the `toolbar` class ;inside the main section:

```
<!-- Main pane -->
<section class="main">
  <div class="toolbar">
    <!-- Our toolbar is here! -->
  </div>
  <textarea v-model="selectedNote.content"></textarea>
</div>
```

We will add three new features in this toolbar:

- Renaming the note
- Deleting the note
- Marking the note as favorite

Renaming the note

This first toolbar feature is also the easiest. It only consists of a text input bound to the `title` property of the selected note with the `v-model` directive.

Project 1 - Markdown Notebook

In the toolbar `div` element we just created, add this `input` element with the `v-model` directive and a `placeholder` to inform the user of its function:

```
<input v-model="selectedNote.title" placeholder="Note title" />
```

You should have a functional rename field above the text editor and see the note name change automatically in the note list as you type:

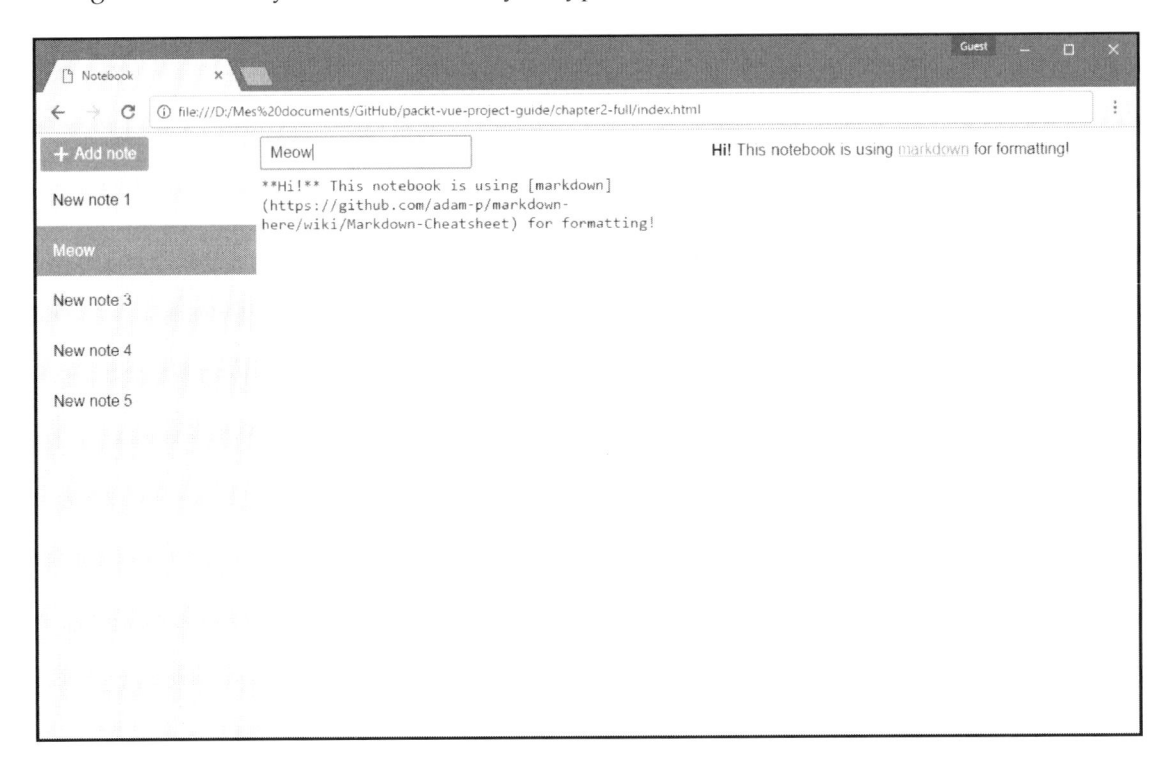

> Since we set the `deep` option on the `notes` watcher, the note list will be saved whenever you change the name of the selected note.

Deleting the note

This second feature is a bit more complicated because we need a new method:

1. Add a `button` element after the rename text input:

   ```
   <button @click="removeNote" title="Remove note"><i
   class="material-icons">delete</i></button>
   ```

   As you can see, we listen to the `click` event with the `v-on` shorthand (the `@` character) that calls the `removeNote` method that we will create very soon. Also, we put an appropriate icon as the button content.

2. Add a new `removeNote` method that asks the user for confirmation and then removes the currently selected note from the `notes` array using the `splice` standard array method:

   ```
   removeNote () {
     if (this.selectedNote && confirm('Delete the note?')) {
       // Remove the note in the notes array
       const index = this.notes.indexOf(this.selectedNote)
       if (index !== -1) {
         this.notes.splice(index, 1)
       }
     }
   }
   ```

Now, if you try deleting the current note, you should note that the following three things happen:

- The note is removed from the note list on the left
- The text editor and the preview pane are hidden
- The note list has been saved according to the browser console

Project 1 - Markdown Notebook

Favorite notes

The last toolbar feature is the most complex. We want to reorder the note list with the favorite notes first. To do that, each note has a `favorite` Boolean property that will be toggled with a button. In addition to that, a star icon will be displayed in the note list to make it obvious which notes are favorite and which ones are not:

1. Start by adding another button to the toolbar before the Remove note ;button:

   ```
   <button @click="favoriteNote" title="Favorite note"><i
   class="material-icons">{{ selectedNote.favorite ? 'star' :
   'star_border' }}</i></button>
   ```

   Once again, we use the `v-on` shorthand to call the `favoriteNote` method we will create next. We will also display an icon, depending on the value of the `favorite` property of the selected note--a full star if it is `true`, or an outlined one if it is not.

   The final result will look like this:

   On the left, there is a button for when the note is not favorite, and on the right, for when it is, after clicking on it.

2. Let's create a very simple `favoriteNote` method that only invert the value of the `favorite` ;Boolean property on the selected note:

   ```
   favoriteNote () {
     this.selectedNote.favorite = !this.selectedNote.favorite
   },
   ```

   We can rewrite this with the XOR operator:

   ```
   favoriteNote () {
     this.selectedNote.favorite = this.selectedNote.favorite ^ true
   },
   ```

   This can be nicely shortened, as follows:

   ```
   favoriteNote () {
     this.selectedNote.favorite ^= true
   },
   ```

Chapter 2

Now, you should be able to toggle the favorite button, but it doesn't have any real effect yet.

We need to sort the note list in two ways--first, we sort all the notes by their creation date, then we sort them so that the favorite ones are put at the start. Thankfully, we have a very convenient standard array method for that--`sort`. It takes one argument, which is a function with two parameters--two items to be compared. The result is a number, as follows:

- `0`, if the two items are in an equivalent position
- `-1`, if the first item should be before the second one
- `1`, if the first item should be after the second one

> **TIP**
> You are not limited to the `1` number, since you can return any arbitrary number, positive or negative. For example, if you return `-42`, it will be the same as `-1`.

The first sorting operation will be achieved with this simple subtracting code:

```
sort((a, b) => a.created - b.created)
```

Here, we compare two notes on their creation date that we stored as a number of milliseconds, thanks to `Date.now()`. We just subtract them so that we get a negative number if `b` was created after `a`, or a positive number if `a` was created after `b`.

The second sort is done with two ternary operations:

```
sort((a, b) => (a.favorite === b.favorite)? 0 : a.favorite? -1 : 1)
```

If both notes are favorite, we don't change their position. If `a` is favorite, we return a negative number to put it before `b`. In the other case, we return a positive number, so `b` is put before `a` in the list.

The best way is to create a computed property called `sortedNotes`, which will get updated and cached automatically by Vue.

[51]

3. Create the new `sortedNotes` computed property:

```
computed: {
  ...

  sortedNotes () {
    return this.notes.slice()
      .sort((a, b) => a.created - b.created)
      .sort((a, b) => (a.favorite === b.favorite) ? 0
        : a.favorite? -1
        : 1)
  },
}
```

> **TIP**: Since `sort` modifies the source array directly, we should create a copy of it with the `slice` method. This will prevent unwanted triggers of the `notes` watcher.

Now, we can simply swap `notes` with `sortedNotes` in the `v-for` directive used to display the list--it will now sort the notes automatically as we expected:

```
<div v-for="note of sortedNotes">
```

We can also use the `v-if` directive we introduced earlier to display a star icon only if the note is favorite:

```
<i class="icon material-icons" v-if="note.favorite">star</i>
```

4. Modify the note list with the preceding changes:

```
<div class="notes">
  <div class="note" v-for="note of sortedNotes"
    :class="{selected: note === selectedNote}"
    @click="selectNote(note)">
    <i class="icon material-icons" v-if="note.favorite">
    star</i>
    {{note.title}}
  </div>
</div>
```

The app should now look as follows:

[52]

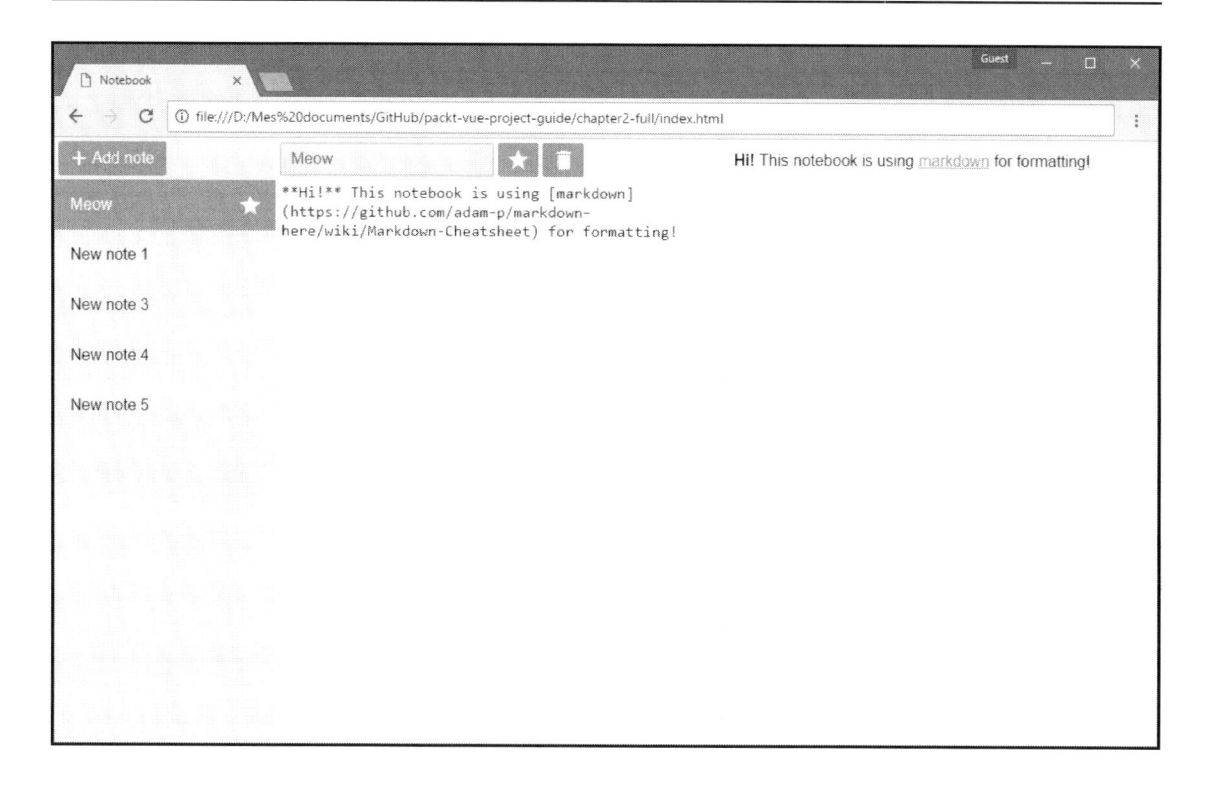

The status bar

The last section we will add to our app is a status bar, displayed at the bottom of the text editor, with some useful info--the date the note was created, with the lines, words, and characters count.

Create a new `div` element with the `toolbar` and `status-bar` classes and place it after the `textarea` element:

```
<!-- Main pane -->
<section class="main">
  <div class="toolbar">
    <!-- ... -->
  </div>
  <textarea v-model="selectedNote.content"></textarea>
  <div class="toolbar status-bar">
    <!-- The new status bar here! -->
  </div>
</section>
```

Project 1 - Markdown Notebook

Created date with a filter

We will now display the creation date of the selected note in the status bar.

1. In the status bar `div` element, create a new `span` element as follows:

   ```
   <span class="date">
     <span class="label">Created</span>
     <span class="value">{{ selectedNote.created }}</span>
   </span>
   ```

   Now, if you look at the result displayed in your browser, you should see the number of milliseconds representing the date the note was created:

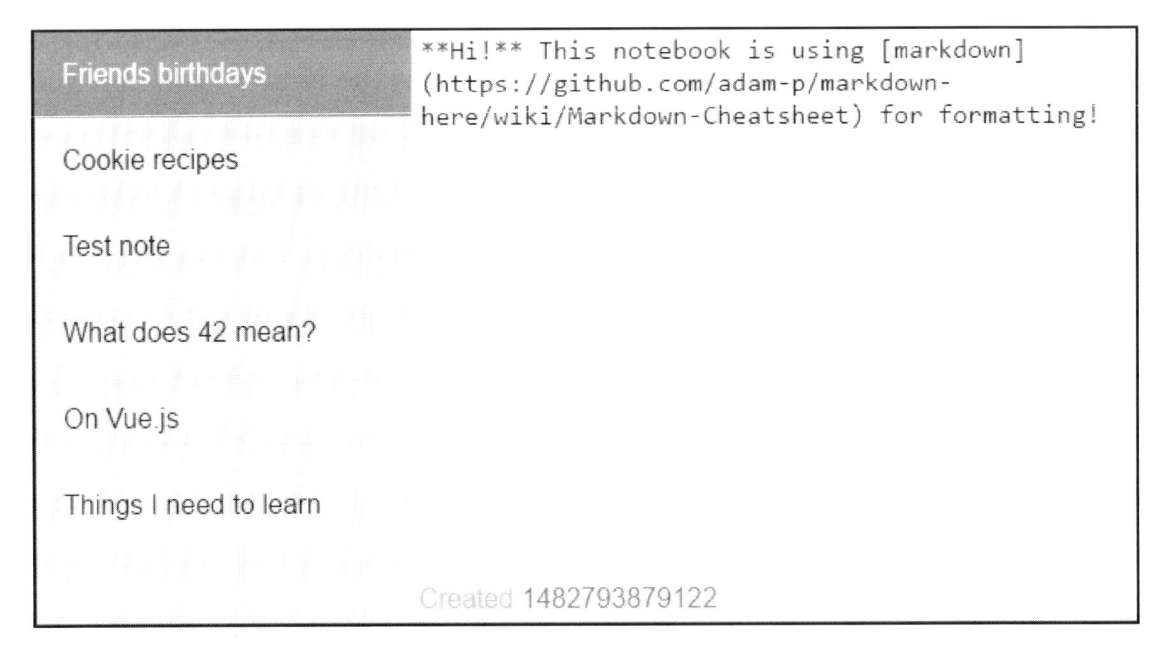

   [Screenshot showing notes list with "Friends birthdays" selected, note content "**Hi!** This notebook is using [markdown](https://github.com/adam-p/markdown-here/wiki/Markdown-Cheatsheet) for formatting!" and status bar "Created 1482793879122"]

   This is not user-friendly at all!

   We need a new library to help us format the date into a more readable result-- `momentjs`, which is a very popular time and date manipulation library.

2. Include it in the page like we did for the `marked` library:

   ```
   <script src="https://unpkg.com/moment"></script>
   ```

[54]

Chapter 2

To format a date, we will first create a `moment` object, and then we will use the `format` method like in the following:

```
moment(time).format('DD/MM/YY, HH:mm')
```

Now is the time to introduce one last feature of Vue for this chapter--the **filters**. These are functions that are used inside templates to easily process data before it is displayed or passed to an attribute. For example, we could have an uppercase filter to transform a string into uppercase letters or a currency filter to convert currencies on the fly in a template. The function takes one argument--the value to be processed by the filter. It returns the processed value.

So, we will create a new `date` filter that will take a date time and will format it to a human-readable format.

3. Register this filter with the `Vue.filter` global method (outside of the Vue instance creation code, for example, at the beginning of the file):

```
Vue.filter('date', time => moment(time)
  .format('DD/MM/YY, HH:mm'))
```

Now, we can use this `date` filter in our template to display dates. The syntax is the JavaScript expression like we used before, followed by a pipe operator and the name of the filter:

```
{{ someDate | date }}
```

If `someDate` contains a date, it will output something like this in the DOM, respecting the `DD/MM/YY, HH:mm` format we defined before:

```
12/02/17, 12:42
```

4. Change the stat template into this:

```
<span class="date">
  <span class="label">Created</span>
  <span class="value">{{ selectedNote.created | date }}</span>
</span>
```

[55]

Project 1 - Markdown Notebook

We should have the date nicely formatted and displayed in our app:

Text stats

The last stats we can display are more "writer-oriented"--the lines, words, and characters count:

1. Let's create three new computed properties for each counter, with some Regular Expressions to get the job done:

   ```
   computed: {
     linesCount () {
       if (this.selectedNote) {
         // Count the number of new line characters
         return this.selectedNote.content.split(/\r\n|\r|\n/).length
       }
     },
     wordsCount () {
       if (this.selectedNote) {
         var s = this.selectedNote.content
         // Turn new line cahracters into white-spaces
         s = s.replace(/\n/g, ' ')
         // Exclude start and end white-spaces
   ```

Chapter 2

```
      s = s.replace(/(^\s*)|(\s*$)/gi, '')
      // Turn 2 or more duplicate white-spaces into 1
      s = s.replace(/\s\s+/gi, ' ')
      // Return the number of spaces
      return s.split(' ').length
    }
  },

  charactersCount () {
    if (this.selectedNote) {
      return this.selectedNote.content.split('').length
    }
  },
}
```

> **TIP**: Here, we added some conditions to prevent the code from running if no note is currently selected. This will avoid crashes if you use the Vue devtools to inspect the app in this case, because it will try to compute all the properties.

2. You can now add three new stat `span` elements with the corresponding computed properties:

```
<span class="lines">
  <span class="label">Lines</span>
  <span class="value">{{ linesCount }}</span>
</span>
<span class="words">
  <span class="label">Words</span>
  <span class="value">{{ wordsCount }}</span>
</span>
<span class="characters">
  <span class="label">Characters</span>
  <span class="value">{{ charactersCount }}</span>
</span>
```

Project 1 - Markdown Notebook

The final status bar should look like this:

```
Friends birthdays        **Hi!** This notebook is using [markdown]
                         (https://github.com/adam-p/markdown-
                         here/wiki/Markdown-Cheatsheet) for formatting!
Cookie recipes

Test note

What does 42 mean?

On Vue.js

Things I need to learn

                         Created 27/12/16, 00:11  Lines 1  Words 8  Characters 123
```

Summary

In this chapter, we created our first real Vue app, with several useful functions, like a real-time markdown preview, a note list, and the local persistence of the notes. We introduced different Vue features, such as the computed properties that are automatically updated and cached as needed, the methods to reuse logic inside functions, the watchers to trigger code when properties change, lifecycle hooks to execute code when the Vue instance is created, and the filters to easily process expressions in our template. We also used a lot of Vue directives inside our template, such as ;v-model to bind form inputs, v-html to display dynamic HTML from our JavaScript properties, v-for to repeat elements and display lists, v-on (or @) to listen to events, v-bind (or :) to dynamically bind HTML attributes to JavaScript expressions or to apply CSS classes dynamically, and v-if to include or not template parts, depending on JavaScript expressions. We saw all of these features come together to build a fully functional web application, with Vue superpower helping us to get the work done without getting in the way.

In the next chapter, we will start a new project--a card-based browser game. We will introduce some new Vue features and will keep reusing all we know to continue building better and prettier web apps.

3
Project 2 - Castle Duel Browser Game

In this chapter, we will create an entirely different app--a browser game. It will consist of two players, each commanding an impressive castle and trying to destroy the other one by bringing either the opponent's food or damage levels to zero with the help of action cards.

In this project and in the following ones, we will split our app into reusable components. This is the heart of the framework, and all its API is built around this idea. We will see how to define and use components and how to make them communicate with each other. The result will be a better structure for our app.

Rules of the game

Here are the rules we will implement in the game:

- Two players play turn by turn
- Each player starts the game with 10 health, 10 food, and a 5-card hand
- The players can't have more than 10 health and 10 food
- A player loses when their food or health reaches zero
- Both the players can lose in a draw
- During one player's turn, each player's only possible action is to play a card, which is then put in the discard pile
- Each player draws a card from the draw pile at the beginning of the turn (except for their first turn)
- Thanks to the two preceding rules, each player has exactly five cards in their hand when they start their turn

Project 2 - Castle Duel Browser Game

- If the draw pile is empty when the player draws a card, the draw pile is refilled with the discard pile
- Cards can modify the health and food of the player or their opponent
- Some cards can also make a player skip their turn

The gameplay is built around the facts that players must play one and only one card each turn and that most of the cards will have a negative effect on them (the most common one being losing food). You have to think of your strategy before playing.

The app will consists of two layers--the world, where game objects (such as the scenery and the castles) are drawn, and the user interface.

The world will have two castles facing each other, a ground, and a sky, with multiple animated clouds; each castle will feature two banners--the green one being the player food, and the red one being the player health--with a little bubble displaying the amount of food or health remaining:

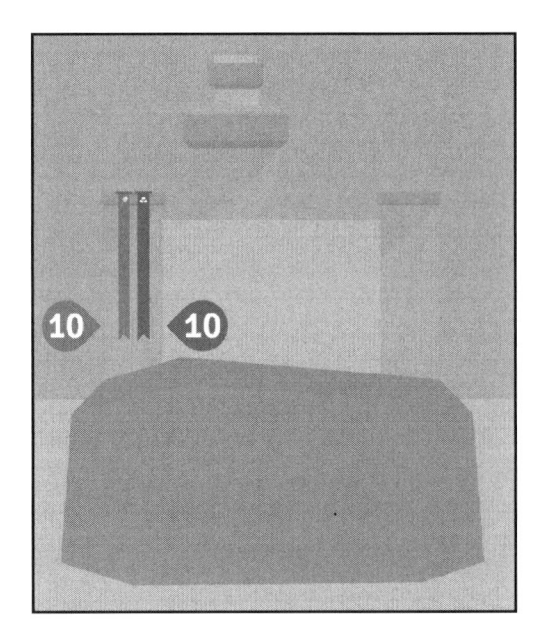

For the UI, there will be a bar at the top, with a turn counter and the names of the two players. At the bottom of the screen, the hand will display the cards of the current player.

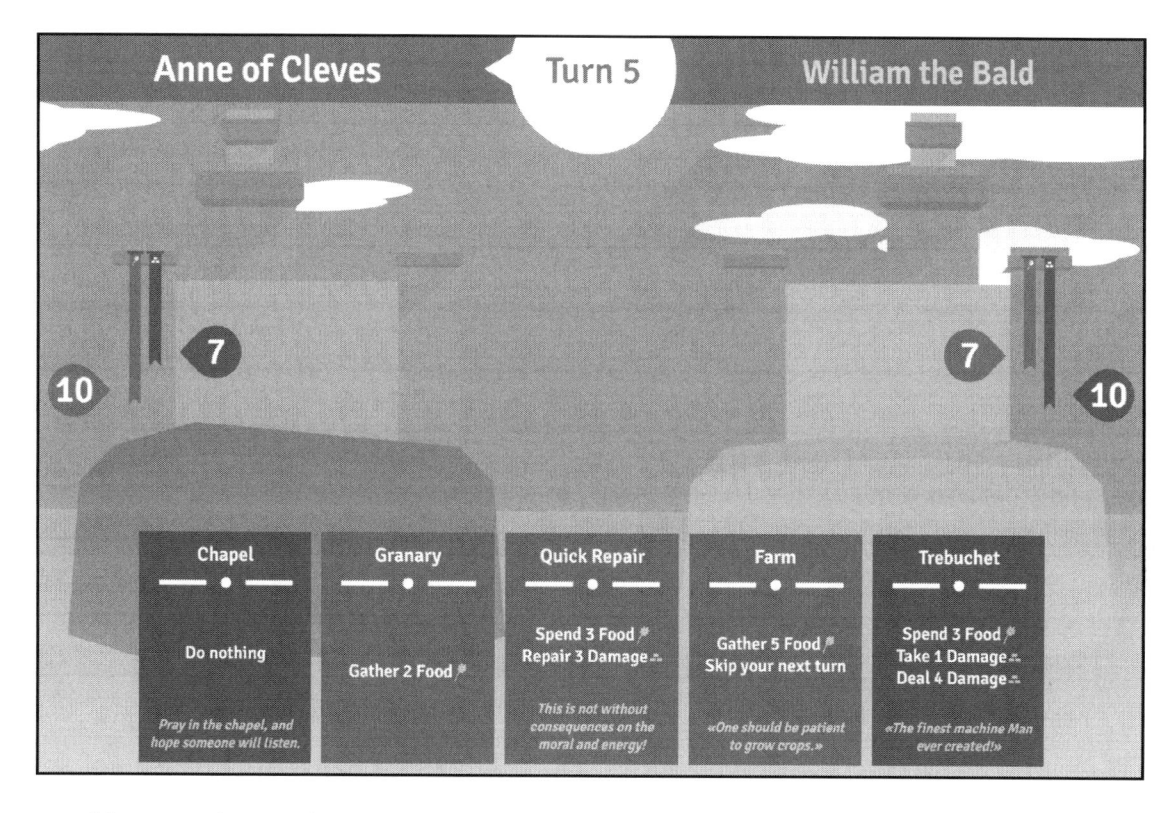

In addition to these, a few overlays will be periodically shown, hiding the hand. One will show the name of the player going next:

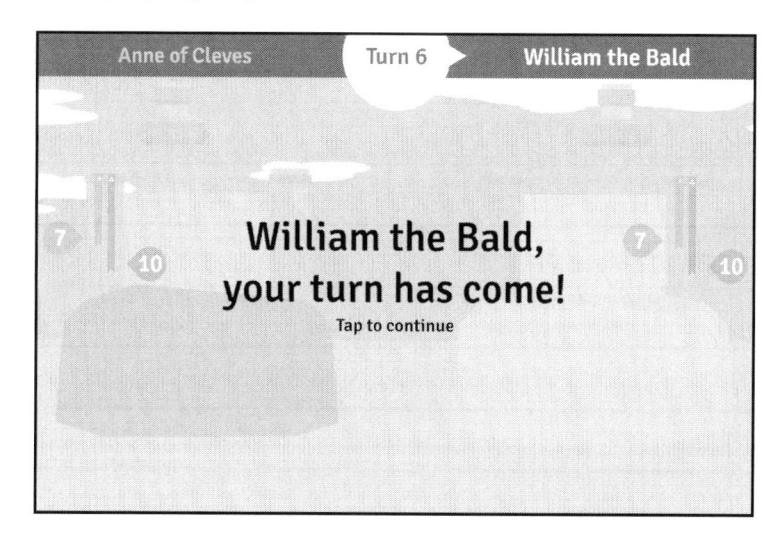

Project 2 - Castle Duel Browser Game

It will be followed by another overlay displaying the card that was played last turn by the opponent. This will allow the game to be played on the same screen (for example, a tablet).

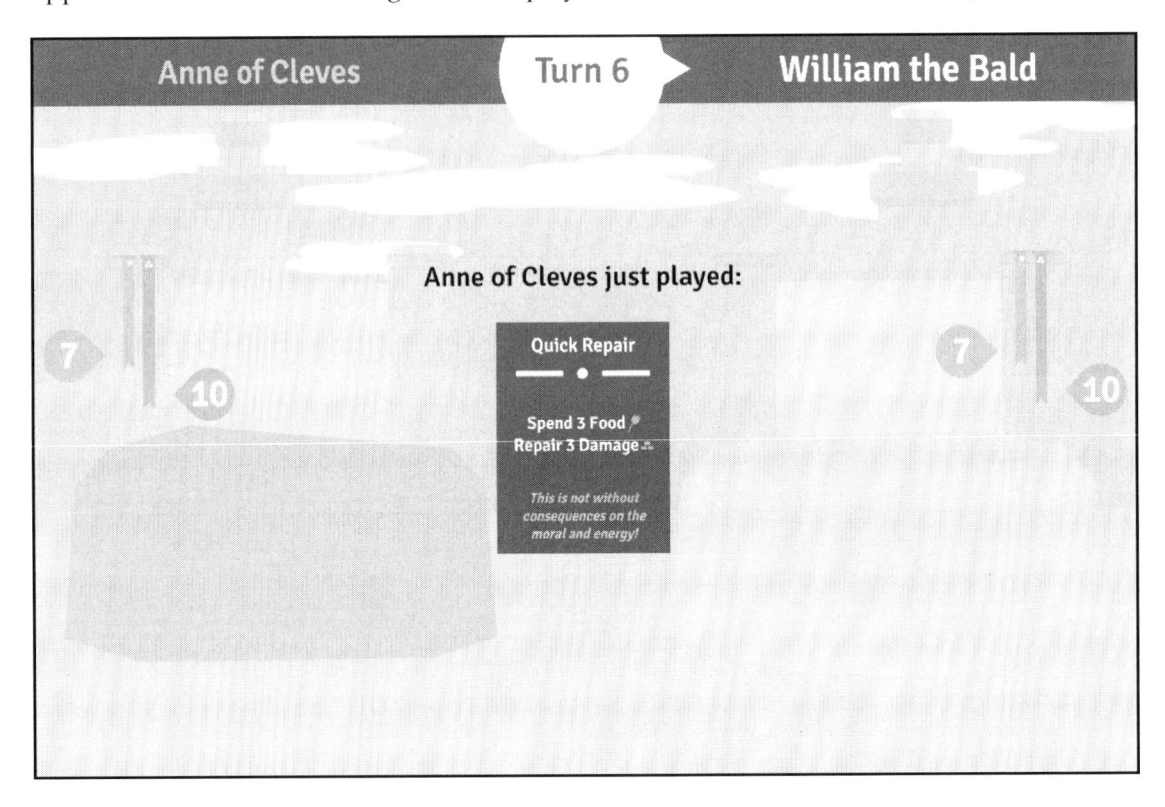

![Screenshot showing game overlay with "Anne of Cleves" on left, "Turn 6" in center, "William the Bald" on right. Center displays "Anne of Cleves just played: Quick Repair - Spend 3 Food, Repair 3 Damage. This is not without consequences on the moral and energy!"]

The third overlay will be only shown when the game is over, displaying whether the players have won or lost. Clicking on this overlay will reload the page, allowing the players to start a new game.

Chapter 3

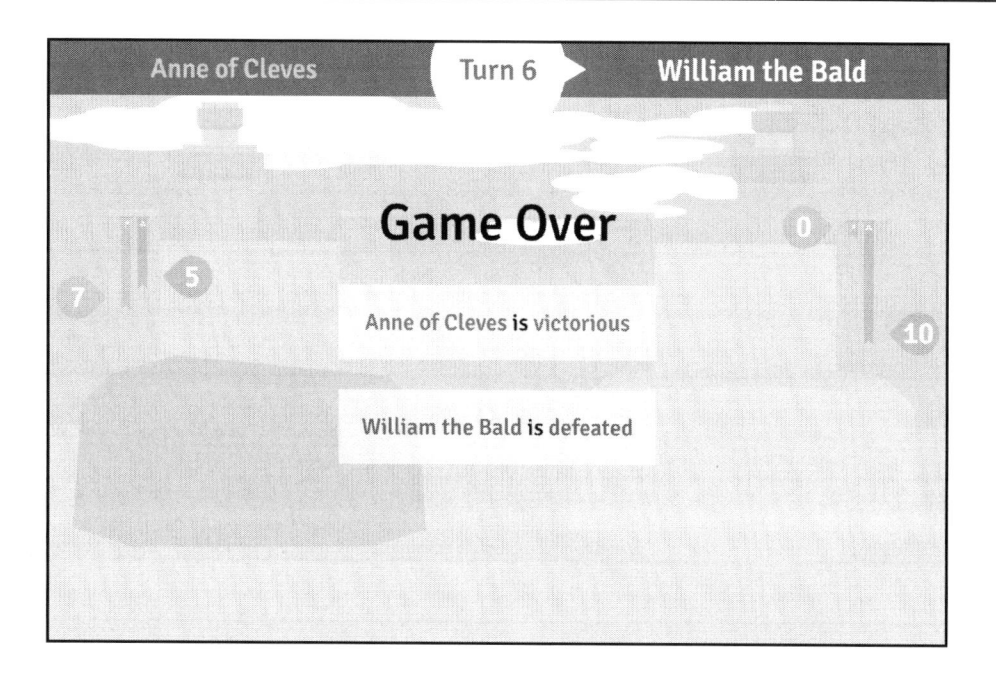

Setting up the project

Download the `chapter 2` files and extract the project setup into an empty folder. You should have the following content:

- `index.html`: The web page
- `style.css`: The CSS file
- `svg`: Contains all the SVG images of the game
- `cards.js`: With all the cards data ready to use
- `state.js`: Where we will consolidate the main data properties of the game
- `utils.js`: Where we will write useful functions
- `banner-template.svg`: We will use the content of this file later

We will start with our main JavaScript file--create a new file called `main.js`.

Open the `index.html` file and add a new script tag referencing the new file, just after the `state.js` one:

```
<!-- Scripts -->
<script src="utils.js"></script>
```

```
<script src="cards.js"></script>
<script src="state.js"></script>
<script src="main.js"></script>
```

Let's create the main instance of our app in the `main.js` file:

```
new Vue({
  name: 'game',
  el: '#app',
})
```

We are now ready to go!

The calm before the storm

In this section, we will introduce a few new Vue features that will help us build the game, such as components, props, and event emitting!

The template option

If you look in the `index.html` file, you will see that the `#app` element is already there and empty. In fact, we won't write anything inside. Instead, we will use the template option directly on the definition object. Let's try it with a dumb template:

```
new Vue({
  name: 'game',
  el: '#app',

  template: `<div id="#app">
    Hello world!
  </div>`,
})
```

Here, we used the new JavaScript strings, with the ` character (back quote). It allows us, among other things, to write text spanning multiple lines, without having to write verbose string concatenations.

Now if you open the app, you should see the `'Hello world!'` text displayed. As you guessed, we won't inline the template in the `#app` element going forward.

The app state

As explained before, the `state.js` file will help us consolidate the main data of our application in one place. That way, it will be easier to write game logic functions without polluting the definition object with a lot of methods.

1. The `state.js` file declares a state variable that we will use as the data of our app. We can use it directly as the data option, as follows:

   ```
   new Vue({
     // ...
     data: state,
   })
   ```

   Now, if you open the devtools, you should see the only data property already declared in the state object:

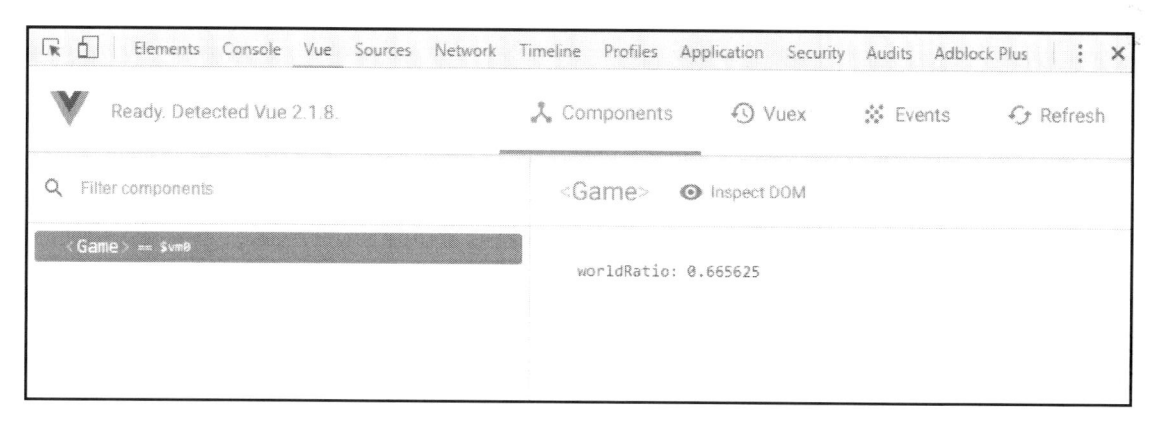

   The world ratio is a number representing how much we should scale the game objects to fit in the window. For example, `.6` means that the world should scale at 60% of its original size. It is computed with the `getWorldRatio` function in the `utils.js` file.

   There is one thing missing, though--it is not recomputed when the window is resized. This is something we have to implement ourselves. After the Vue instance constructor, add an event listener to the window object to detect when it is resized.

2. Inside the handler, update the `worldRatio` data property of the state. You can also display `worldRatio` in the template:

```
new Vue({
  name: 'game',
  el: '#app',

  data: state,

  template: `<div id="#app">
    {{ worldRatio }}
  </div>`,
})

// Window resize handling
window.addEventListener('resize', () => {
  state.worldRatio = getWorldRatio()
})
```

Try resizing your browser window horizontally--the `worldRatio` data property is updated in the Vue app.

But wait! We are modifying the state object, not the Vue instance...

You are right! However, we have set the Vue instance `data` property with the `state` object. This means Vue has set up reactivity on it, and we can change its attributes to update our app, as we will see in a second.

3. To ensure that `state` is the app's reactive data, try comparing the instance data object and the global state object:

```
new Vue({
  // ...
  mounted () {
    console.log(this.$data === state)
  },
})
```

These are the same objects we set with the data option. So when you do:

```
this.worldRatio = 42
```

You are also doing this:

```
this.$data.worldRatio = 42
```

[66]

This is, in fact, the same as follows:

```
state.worldRatio = 42
```

This will be useful in the gameplay function that will use the state object to update the game data.

The almighty components

Components are the building blocks that will compose our app--it's the central concept of the Vue apps. They are small parts of the view, and they should be relatively small, reusable, and as self-sufficient as possible--structuring an app with components will then help maintain and evolve it, especially if it becomes large. In fact, this is becoming the standard method for creating huge web apps in an efficient and manageable way.

In concrete terms, your app will be a giant tree of smaller components:

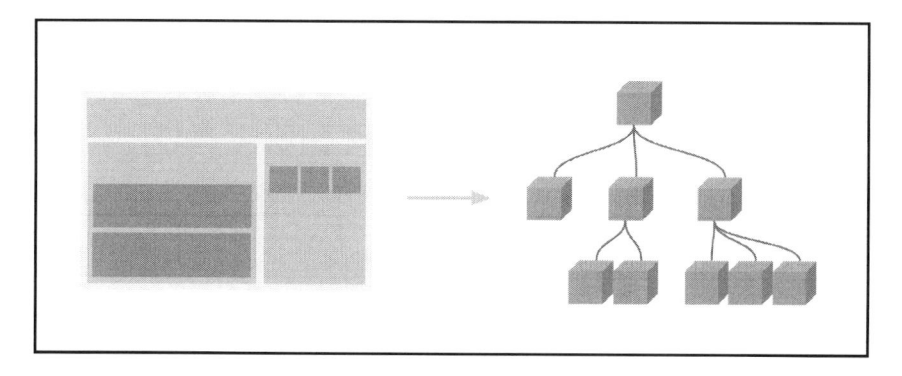

For example, your app could have a form component, which could contain several input components and button components. Each one would be a very specific part of the UI, and they would be reusable all across the app. Being quite small in scope, they would be easy to understand and reason about, and thus easier to maintain (issue fixing) or to evolve.

Building the user interface

The first components we will create are part of the UI layer. There will be a top bar with the players' names and a turn counter, the cards with their name and description, the hand with the current player cards, and the three overlays.

Our first component - the top bar

The top bar, our first component, will be placed at the top of the page and will display the names of the two players and a turn counter in the middle. It will also show an arrow facing the name of the player currently taking their turn.

It will look like this:

Adding some gameplay data to the state

Before creating the component, we need some new data properties:

- `turn`: The number of the current turn; starts at 1
- `players`: The array of player objects
- `currentPlayerIndex`: The index of the current player in the `players` array

Add them in the state in the `state.js` file:

```
// The consolidated state of our app
var state = {
  // World
  worldRatio: getWorldRatio(),
  // Game
  turn: 1,
  players: [
    {
      name: 'Anne of Cleves',
    },
    {
      name: 'William the Bald',
    },
  ],
  currentPlayerIndex: Math.round(Math.random()),
}
```

Chapter 3

> `Math.round(Math.random())` will use 0 or 1 randomly to choose who goes first.

We will use these properties to display the player names and the turn counter in the top bar.

Defining and using the components

We will write our UI components in a new file:

1. Create a `components` folder and a new `ui.js` file inside it. Include it in the main `index.html` page, just before the main script:

    ```
    <!-- Scripts -->
    <script src="utils.js"></script>
    <script src="cards.js"></script>
    <script src="state.js"></script>
    <script src="components/ui.js"></script>
    <script src="main.js"></script>
    ```

    In this file, we will register our components, so it's important that the main Vue instance is created afterward, and not before. Else, we would get errors of components not being found.

    To register a component, we can use the global `Vue.component()` function. It takes two arguments; the name under which we register the component, and its definition object, which is using the exact same options as the Vue instance that we already know.

2. Let's create the `top-bar` component in the `ui.js` file:

    ```
    Vue.component('top-bar', {
      template: `<div class="top-bar">
        Top bar
      </div>`,
    })
    ```

[69]

Now, we can use the `top-bar` component in our templates, just like any other HTML tags, for instance, `<top-bar>`.

3. In the main template, add a new `top-bar` tag:

```
new Vue({
  // ...
  template: `<div id="#app">
    <top-bar/>
  </div>`,
})
```

This template will create a new `top-bar` component and render it inside the `#app` element, using the definition object we just defined. If you open the devtools, you should see two entries:

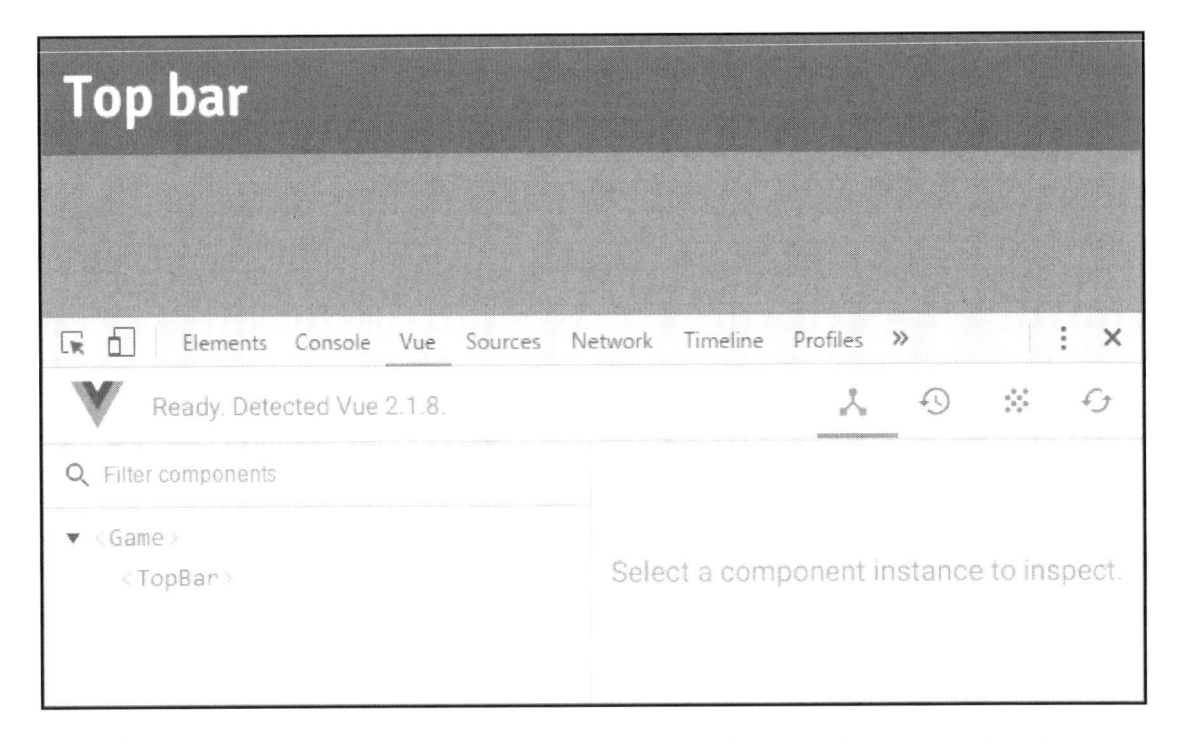

Each one is a Vue instance--Vue actually created a second instance using the definition we provided for the top-bar component.

Parent-to-child communication with Props

As we saw in the The almighty components section, our component-based app will have a tree of components, and we need them to communicate with each other. For now, we will only focus on descending, parent-to-child communication. This is accomplished with "props".

Our `top-bar` component needs to know who the players are, which one is currently playing, and what the current turn number is. So, we will need three props--`players`, `currentPlayerIndex`, and `turn`.

To add props to a component definition, use the `props` option. For now, we will simply list the names of our props. However, you should know that there is a more detailed notation with an object instead, which we will cover in the next chapters.

1. Let's add the props to our component:

   ```
   Vue.component('top-bar', {
     // ...
     props: ['players', 'currentPlayerIndex', 'turn'],
   })
   ```

   In the parent component, which is the root application, we can set the props value the exact same way we would for HTML attributes.

2. Go ahead and use the `v-bind` shorthand to wire the props value with the app data in the main template:

   ```
   <top-bar :turn="turn" :current-player-index="currentPlayerIndex"
   :players="players" />
   ```

   > **TIP**: Note that since HTML is case-insensitive and by convention, it is recommended to use the kebab-case (with dashes) names of our props, and the camel-case names in the JavaScript code.

   Now, we can use the props in our `top-bar` component just like data properties. For example, you could write something like this:

   ```
   Vue.component('top-bar', {
     // ...
     created () {
       console.log(this.players)
     },
   })
   ```

Project 2 - Castle Duel Browser Game

This would print the `players` array sent by the parent component (our app) in the browser console.

Props in our template

We will now use the props we created in the template of the `top-bar` component.

1. Change the `top-bar` template to display the player's name with the `players` prop:

```
template: `<div class="top-bar">
  <div class="player p0">{{ players[0].name }}</div>
  <div class="player p1">{{ players[1].name }}</div>
</div>`,
```

As you can see in the preceding code, we are also using the props like we did with properties in templates. You should see the player names displayed in the app.

2. Continue with the turn counter between `players` using the `turn` prop:

```
template: `<div class="top-bar">
  <div class="player p0">{{ players[0].name }}</div>
  <div class="turn-counter">
  <div class="turn">Turn {{ turn }}</div>
  </div>
  <div class="player p1">{{ players[1].name }}</div>
</div>`,
```

In addition to the label, we also want to display a big arrow facing the current player to make it more obvious.

3. Add the arrow image inside the `.turn-counter` element, and add a dynamic class using the `currentPlayerIndex` prop with the `v-bind` shorthand we used in `Chapter 2`, *Markdown Notebook*:

```
template: `<div class="top-bar" :class="'player-' + currentPlayerIndex">
  <div class="player p0">{{ players[0].name }}</div>
  <div class="turn-counter">
    <img class="arrow" src="svg/turn.svg" />
    <div class="turn">Turn {{ turn }}</div>
  </div>
  <div class="player p1">{{ players[1].name }}</div>
</div>`,
```

[72]

Now, the app should display the fully featured top bar, with the two players, names and the turn counter between them. You can test the Vue-automated reactivity by typing these commands into the browser console:

```
state.currentPlayerIndex = 1
state.currentPlayerIndex = 0
```

You should see the arrow turning around to face the correct player name, which gets emphasized:

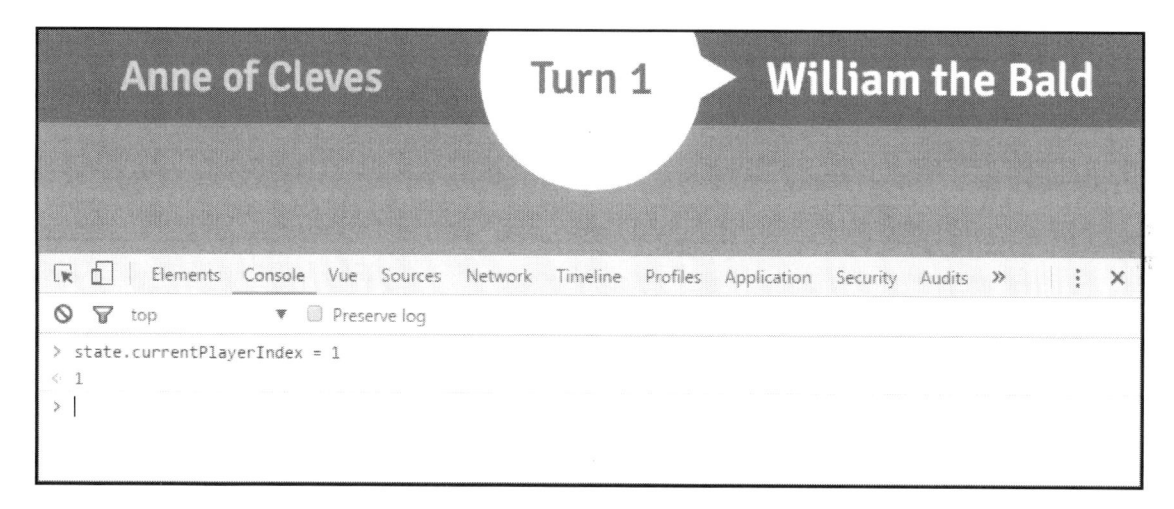

Displaying a card

All the cards are described in the card definition objects, declared in the `cards.js` file. You can open it, but you shouldn't have to modify its content. Each card definition has the following fields:

- `id`: Unique for each card
- `type`: Changes the color background to help distinguish the cards from each other
- `title`: The displayed name of the card
- `description`: An HTML text explaining what the card does
- `note`: An optional flavor text, in HTML too
- `play`: The function we will call when the card is played

Project 2 - Castle Duel Browser Game

We need a new component to display any card, either in the player hand or in the overlay, that describes what the opponent played last turn. It will look like this:

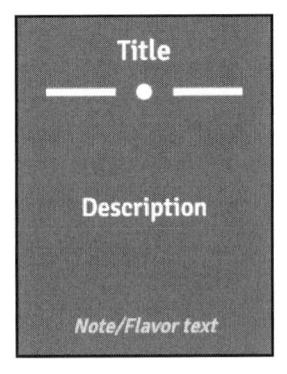

1. In the `components/ui.js` file, create a new `card` component:

   ```
   Vue.component('card', {
     // Definition here
   })
   ```

2. This component will receive a `def` prop that will be the card definition object we described above. Declare it with the `props` option as we did for the `top-bar` component:

   ```
   Vue.component('card', {
     props: ['def'],
   })
   ```

3. Now, we can add the template. Start with the main `div` element, with the `card` class:

   ```
   Vue.component('card', {
     template: `<div class="card">
     </div>`,
     props: ['def'],
   })
   ```

4. To change the background color depending on the card type, add a dynamic CSS class that uses the `type` property of the card object:

   ```
   <div class="card" :class="'type-' + def.type">
   ```

Chapter 3

For example, if the card has the `'attack'` type, the element will get the `type-attack` class. Then, it will have a red background.

5. Now, add the title of the card with the corresponding class:

```
<div class="card" :class="'type-' + def.type">
  <div class="title">{{ def.title }}</div>
</div>
```

6. Add the separator image, which will display some lines between the card title and the description:

```
<div class="title">{{ def.title }}</div>
<img class="separator" src="svg/card-separator.svg" />
```

After the image, append the description element.

> Note that since the `description` property of the card object is an HTML-formatted text, we need to use the special `v-html` directive introduced in the `Chapter 2`, *Markdown Notebook*.

7. Use the `v-html` directive to display the description:

```
<div class="description"><div v-html="def.description"></div></div>
```

> You may have noted that we added a nested `div` element, which will contain the description text. This is to center the text vertically using CSS flexbox.

8. Finally, add the card note (which is also in an HTML-formatted text). Note that some cards don't have note, so we have to use the `v-if` directive here:

```
<div class="note" v-if="def.note"><div v-html="def.note"></div></div>
```

The card component should now look like this:

```
Vue.component('card', {
  props: ['def'],
  template: `<div class="card" :class="'type-' + def.type">
    <div class="title">{{ def.title }}</div>
    <img class="separator" src="svg/card-separator.svg" />
    <div class="description"><div v-
```

[75]

```
        html="def.description"></div></div>
    <div class="note" v-if="def.note"><div v-
html="def.note"></div></div>
  </div>`,
})
```

Now, we can try our new card component in the main application component.

9. Edit the main template as follows and add a `card` component just after the top bar:

```
template: `<div id="#app">
  <top-bar :turn="turn" :current-player-
    index="currentPlayerIndex" :players="players" />
  <card :def="testCard" />
</div>`,
```

10. We also need to define a temporary computed property:

```
computed: {
  testCard () {
    return cards.archers
  },
},
```

Now, you should see a red attack card with a title, description, and flavor text:

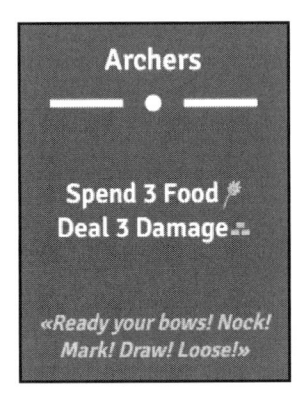

Archers

Spend 3 Food
Deal 3 Damage

«Ready your bows! Nock!
Mark! Draw! Loose!»

Listening to native events on components

Let's try adding a click event handler on our card:

```
<card :def="testCard" @click="handlePlay" />
```

With a dumb method in the main component:

```
methods: {
  handlePlay () {
    console.log('You played a card!')
  }
}
```

If you test this in the browser, you may be surprised that it doesn't work as expected. Nothing is output to the console...

This is because Vue has its own event system for components, called "custom events", that we will learn about in a moment. This system is separate from the browser events, so here Vue expects a custom `'click'` event, and not the browser one. Thus, the `handler` method is not called.

To get around this, you should use the `.native` modifier on the `v-on` directive, as follows:

```
<card :def="testCard" @click.native="handlePlay" />
```

Now, the `handlePlay` method is called when you click on the card, as expected.

Child-to-parent communication with custom events

Previously, we used props to communicate from a parent component to its children. Now, we would like to do the opposite and communicate from one child component to its parent. For our card component, we would like to tell the parent component that the card is being played by the player when they click on it. We can't use props here, but we can use custom events. In our components, we can emit events that can be caught by the parent component with the `$emit` special method. It takes one mandatory argument, which is the event type:

```
this.$emit('play')
```

We can listen to the custom events inside the same Vue instance with the `$on` special method:

```
this.$on('play', () => {
  console.log('Caught a play event!')
})
```

The `$emit` method also sends a `'play'` event to the parent component. We can listen to it in the parent component template with the `v-on` directive just like we did before:

```
<card v-on:play="handlePlay" />
```

You can also use the `v-bind` shorthand:

```
<card @play="handlePlay" />
```

We can also add as many arguments as we like that will get passed to the handler methods:

```
this.$emit('play', 'orange', 42)
```

Here, we emitted a `'play'` event with the following two arguments-- `'orange'` and `42`.

In the handle, we can get them via the arguments, as follows:

```
handlePlay (color, number) {
  console.log('handle play event', 'color=', color, 'number=', number)
}
```

The `color` argument will have the `'orange'` value and the `number` argument will have the `42` value.

> Like we saw in the preceding section, custom events are completely separate from the browser event system. The special methods--`$on` and `$emit`--are not aliases to the standard `addEventListener` and `dispatchEvent`. That explains why we need the `.native` modifier on components to listen to browser events such as `'click'`.

Back to our card component, we just need to emit a very simple event to tell the parent component that the card is being played:

1. First, add the method that will emit the event:

```
methods: {
  play () {
    this.$emit('play')
  },
},
```

2. We would like to call this method when the user clicks on the card. Just listen to a browser click event on the main card `div` element:

```
<div class="card" :class="'type-' + def.type" @click="play">
```

3. We are done with the card component. To test this, listen to the `'play'` custom event in the main component template:

```
<card :def="testCard" @play="handlePlay" />
```

Now, the `handlePlay` method will be called whenever the `'play'` event is emitted.

> **TIP**
>
> We could just have listened to a native click event instead, but it's in most cases a good idea to use custom events to communicate between components. For example, we could also emit the `'play'` event when the user uses another method, such as using the keyboard to select the card and pressing *Enter*; we won't implement that method in this book though.

The hand

Our next component will be the current player hand, holding the five cards they have. It will be animated with a 3D transition and will also be responsible for the card animations (when the card is drawn, and when it is played).

1. In the `components/ui.js` file, add a component registration with the `'hand'` ID and a basic template, with two `div` elements:

```
Vue.component('hand', {
  template: `<div class="hand">
    <div class="wrapper">
      <!-- Cards -->
    </div>
  </div>`,
})
```

> The wrapper element will help us position and animate the cards.

Each card in the hand will be represented by an object. For now, it will have the following properties:

- `id`: The card definition unique identifier
- `def`: The card definition object

Project 2 - Castle Duel Browser Game

> **TIP**: As a reminder, all the card definitions are declared in the `cards.js` file.

2. Our hand component will receive these card objects representing the player hand via a new array prop called `cards`:

```
Vue.component('hand', {
  // ...
  props: ['cards'],
})
```

3. We can now add the card components with the `v-for` directive:

```
<div class="wrapper">
  <card v-for="card of cards" :def="card.def" />
</div>
```

4. To test our hand component, we will create in the app state a temporary property called `testHand` (in the `state.js` file):

```
var state = {
  // ...
  testHand: [],
}
```

5. Add a `createTestHand` method in the main component (in the `main.js` file):

```
methods: {
  createTestHand () {
    const cards = []
    // Get the possible ids
    const ids = Object.keys(cards)

    // Draw 5 cards
    for (let i = 0; i < 5; i++) {
      cards.push(testDrawCard())
    }

    return cards
  },
},
```

Chapter 3

6. To test the hand, we also need this temporary `testDrawCard` method that simulates a random card draw:

   ```
   methods: {
     // ...
     testDrawCard () {
       // Choose a card at random with the ids
       const ids = Object.keys(cards)
       const randomId = ids[Math.floor(Math.random() * ids.length)]
       // Return a new card with this definition
       return {
         // Unique id for the card
         uid: cardUid++,
         // Id of the definition
         id: randomId,
         // Definition object
         def: cards[randomId],
       }
     }
   }
   ```

7. Use the `created` lifecycle hook to initialize the hand:

   ```
   created () {
     this.testHand = this.createTestHand()
   },
   ```

   > `cardUid` is a unique identifier on cards drawn by the players that will be useful to identify each of the cards in the hand, because many cards can share the exact same card definition, and we will need a way to differentiate them.

8. In the main template, add the hand component:

   ```
   template: `<div id="#app">
     <top-bar :turn="turn" :current-player-
       index="currentPlayerIndex" :players="players" />
     <hand :cards="testHand" />
   </div>`,
   ```

Project 2 - Castle Duel Browser Game

The result in your browser should look like this:

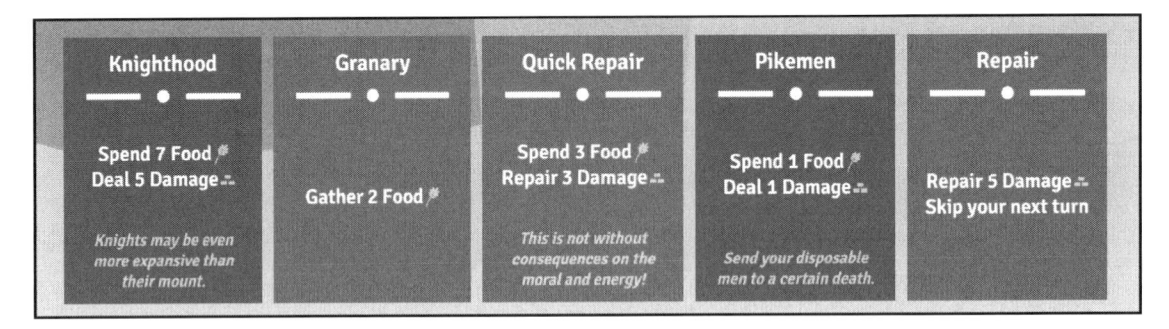

Animating the hand with transitions

During a game, the hand will be hidden when any overlay is shown. To make the app prettier, we will animate the hand when it is added or removed from the DOM. To do that, we will use CSS transitions together with a powerful Vue tool--the special <transition> component. It will help us work with CSS transitions when adding or removing elements with the v-if or v-show directives.

1. First, add a new `activeOverlay` data property to the app state in the `state.js` file:

   ```
   // The consolidated state of our app
   var state = {
     // UI
     activeOverlay: null,
     // ...
   }
   ```

2. In the main template, we will show the hand component only if `activeOverlay` is not defined, thanks to the `v-if` directive:

   ```
   <hand :cards="testHand" v-if="!activeOverlay" />
   ```

3. Now, if you change `state.activeOverlay` to any truthy value in the browser console, the hand will disappear:

   ```
   state.activeOverlay = 'player-turn'
   ```

[82]

4. Also, if you set it back to `null`, the hand will be shown again:

   ```
   state.activeOverlay = null
   ```

5. To apply a transition when a component is added or removed by a `v-if` or `v-show` directive, surround it with a transition component like this:

   ```
   <transition>
     <hand v-if="!activeOverlay" />
   </transition>
   ```

   Note that this also works on HTML elements:

   ```
   <transition>
     <h1 v-if="showTitle">Title</h1>
   </transition>
   ```

   > **TIP**: The `<transition>` special component will not appear in the DOM, like the `<template>` tag we used in Chapter 2, *Markdown Notebook*.

   When the element is added to the DOM (the enter phase), the transition component will automatically apply the following CSS classes to the element:

   - `v-enter-active`: Apply the class while the enter transition is active. This class is added before the element is inserted to the DOM, and it is removed when the animation finishes. You should add some `transition` CSS properties in this class and define their duration.
   - `v-enter`: The starting state of the element. This class is added before the element is inserted, and it is removed one frame after the element is inserted. For example, you could set the opacity to `0` in this class.
   - `v-enter-to`: The target state of the element. This class is added one frame after the element is inserted, at the same time `v-enter` is removed. It is removed when the animation finishes.

[83]

When the element is being removed from the DOM (the leave phase), they are replaced by the following:

- `v-leave-active`: Applied while the leave transition is active. This class is added when the leaving transition triggers, and it is removed after the element is removed from the DOM. You should add some `transition` CSS properties in this class and define their duration.
- `v-leave`: The starting state of the element when being removed. This class is also added when the leaving transition triggers and is removed one frame after.
- `v-leave-to`: The target state of the element. This class is added one frame after the leaving transition triggers, at the same time `v-leave` is removed. It is removed when the element is removed from the DOM.

> During the leave phase, the element is not immediately removed from the DOM. It will be removed when the transition finishes to allow the user to see the animation.

Here is a schema that summarizes the two enter and leave phases, with the corresponding CSS classes:

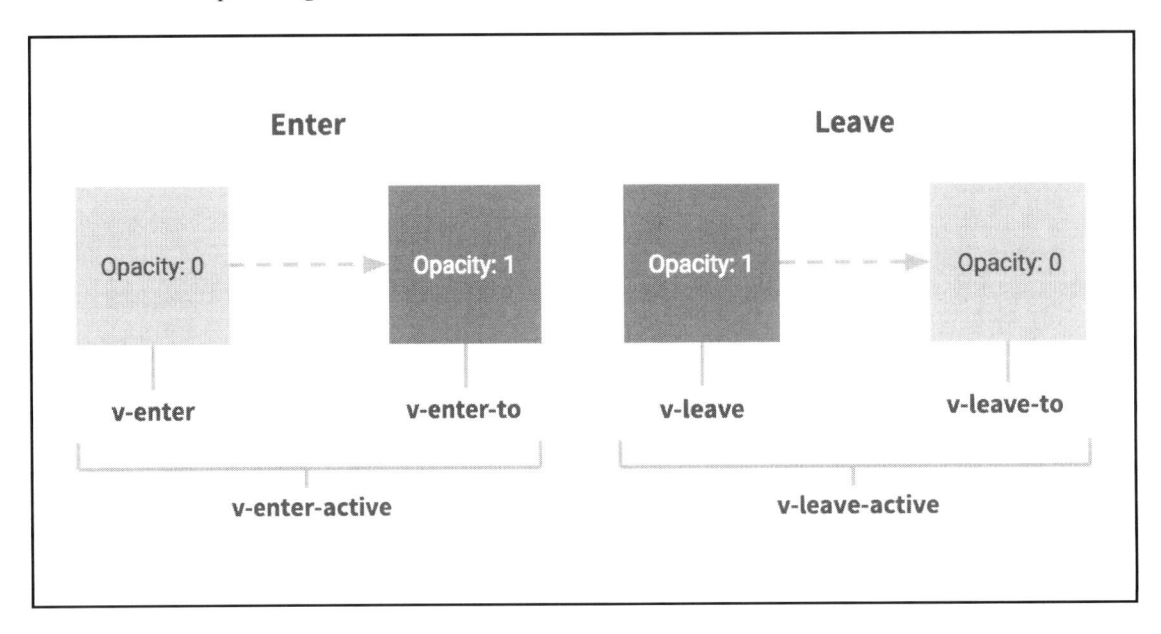

> The transition component will automatically detect the duration of the CSS transitions applied on the element.

6. We need to write some CSS to make our animation. Create a new `transitions.css` file and include it in the web page:

   ```
   <link rel="stylesheet" href="transitions.css" />
   ```

   Let's try a basic fading animation first. We want to apply a CSS transition on the opacity CSS property for 1 second.

7. To do that, use both the `v-enter-active` and `v-leave-active` classes since it will be the same animation:

   ```
   .hand.v-enter-active,
   .hand.v-leave-active {
     transition: opacity 1s;
   }
   ```

   When the hand is either being added or removed from the DOM, we want it to have an opacity of 0 (so it will be fully transparent).

8. Use both the `v-enter` and `v-leave-to` classes to apply this full transparency:

   ```
   .hand.v-enter,
   .hand.v-leave-to {
     opacity: 0;
   }
   ```

9. Back to the main template, surround the hand component with a transition special component:

   ```
   <transition>
     <hand v-if="!activeOverlay" :cards="testHand" />
   </transition>
   ```

   Now, when you hide or show the hand, it will fade in and out.

10. Since we may have to reuse this animation, we should give it a name:

```
<transition name="fade">
  <hand v-if="!activeOverlay" :cards="testHand" />
</transition>
```

We have to change our CSS classes, because Vue will now use `fade-enter-active` instead of `v-enter-active`.

11. In the `transition.css` file, modify the CSS selector to match this change:

```
.fade-enter-active,
.fade-leave-active {
  transition: opacity 1s;
}

.fade-enter,
.fade-leave-to {
  opacity: 0;
}
```

Now, we can reuse this animation on any element with `<transition name="fade">`.

A prettier animation

We will now make a more complex but better animation, with some 3D effects. In addition to the hand, we will animate the `.wrapper` element (for a 3D flip) and the `.card` elements. The cards will start being piled up and will progressively expand to their expected position in the hand. At the end, it will animate as if the player is picking up the cards from a table.

1. Start by creating new transition CSS classes with the `'hand'` name instead of `'fade'`:

```
.hand-enter-active,
.hand-leave-active {
  transition: opacity .5s;
}

.hand-enter,
.hand-leave-to {
  opacity: 0;
}
```

2. Change the transition name in the main template too:

```
<transition name="hand">
  <hand v-if="!activeOverlay" :cards="testHand" />
</transition>
```

3. Let's animate the wrapper element. Use the CSS transform property to apply a 3D transformation to the element:

```
.hand-enter-active .wrapper,
.hand-leave-active .wrapper {
  transition: transform .8s cubic-bezier(.08,.74,.34,1);
  transform-origin: bottom center;
}

.hand-enter .wrapper,
.hand-leave-to .wrapper {
  transform: rotateX(90deg);
}
```

The right rotating axis is the horizontal one, which is x. This will animate the cards just as if they were being picked up by the player. Note that there is a cubic-bezier easing function defined to make the animation smoother.

4. Finally, animate the cards themselves by setting a negative horizontal margin so that they will seem to be piled up:

```
.hand-enter-active .card,
.hand-leave-active .card {
  transition: margin .8s cubic-bezier(.08,.74,.34,1);
}

.hand-enter .card,
.hand-leave-to .card {
  margin: 0 -100px;
}
```

Now, if you hide and show the hand with the browser console like we did before, it will have a nice animation.

Project 2 - Castle Duel Browser Game

Playing a card

Now, we need to handle the `'play'` event in the hand component we emit in the cards when the user clicks on them, and emit a new `'card-play'` event to the main component with an additional argument--the played card in question.

1. First, create a new method called `handlePlay`. It takes a `card` argument and emits the new event to the parent component:

```
methods: {
  handlePlay (card) {
    this.$emit('card-play', card)
  },
},
```

2. Then, add a listener to our cards for the `'play'` event:

```
<card v-for="card of cards" :def="card.def"
@play="handlePlay(card) />
```

> **TIP**: As you can see here, we directly use the iterator variable `card` of the `v-for` loop. That way, we don't need the card component to emit its `card` item since we already know what it is.

To test the card play, we will only remove it from the hand for now.

3. Create a new temporary method called `testPlayCard` in the main component in the `main.js` file:

```
methods: {
  // ...
  testPlayCard (card) {
    // Remove the card from player hand
    const index = this.testHand.indexOf(card)
    this.testHand.splice(index, 1)
  }
},
```

4. Add the event listener for the `'card-play'` event on the `hand` component in the main template:

```
<hand v-if="!activeOverlay" :cards="testHand" @card-play="testPlayCard" />
```

Chapter 3

If you click on a card, it should now emit a `'play'` event to the hand component, which will then emit a `'card-play'` event to the main component. It will, in turn, remove the card from the hand, making it disappear. To help you debug this sort of use case, the devtools have an **Events** tab:

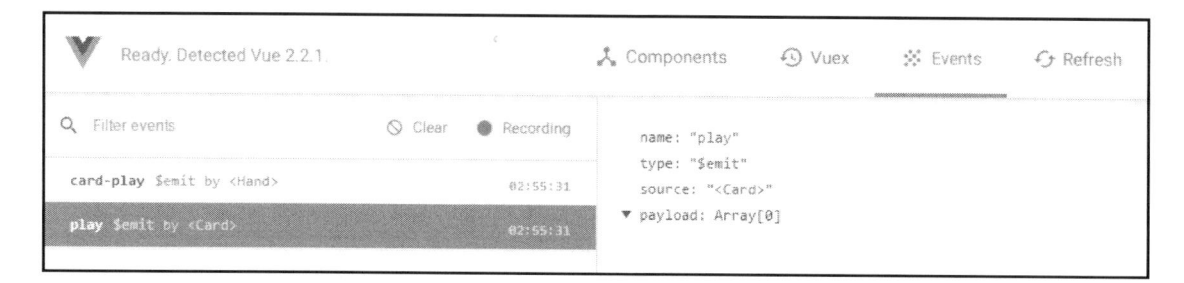

Animating the card list

There are three missing animations for our hand--when a card is either added or removed from the player hand, and when it is moved. When the turn begins, the player will draw a card. It means that we will add a card to the hand cards list, and it will slide from the right into the hand. When a card is played, we want it to go up and grow bigger.

To animate a list of elements, we will need another special component--`<transition-group>`. It animates the children when they are added, removed, and moved. In a template, it looks like this:

```
<transition-group>
  <div v-for="item of items" />
</transition-group>
```

Unlike the `<transition>` element, the transition group will appear in the DOM as a `<span>` element by default. You can change the HTML element with the `tag` prop:

```
<transition-group tag="ul">
  <li v-for="item of items" />
</transition-group>
```

In the template of our `hand` component, enclose the card components with a transition group, specify the name of the transition that we will call `"card"`, and add the `"cards"` CSS class:

```
<transition-group name="card" tag="div" class="cards">
  <card v-for="card of cards" :def="card.def" @play="handlePlay(card) />
</transition-group>
```

Before we can continue, there is one important thing missing--the children of the transition group must be identified by a unique key.

The key special attribute

When Vue is updating a list of DOM elements in a `v-for` loop, it tries to minimize the number of operations applied to the DOM, such as adding or removing elements. This is a very efficient way of updating the DOM in most cases and can improve the performance.

In order to do this, it reuses elements as much as it can and patches the DOM only where it is needed to have the desired result. It means repeated elements will be patched in place and won't be moved if an item is added or removed from the list. However, this also means that they won't animate if we apply transitions on them.

The following is a schema of how this works:

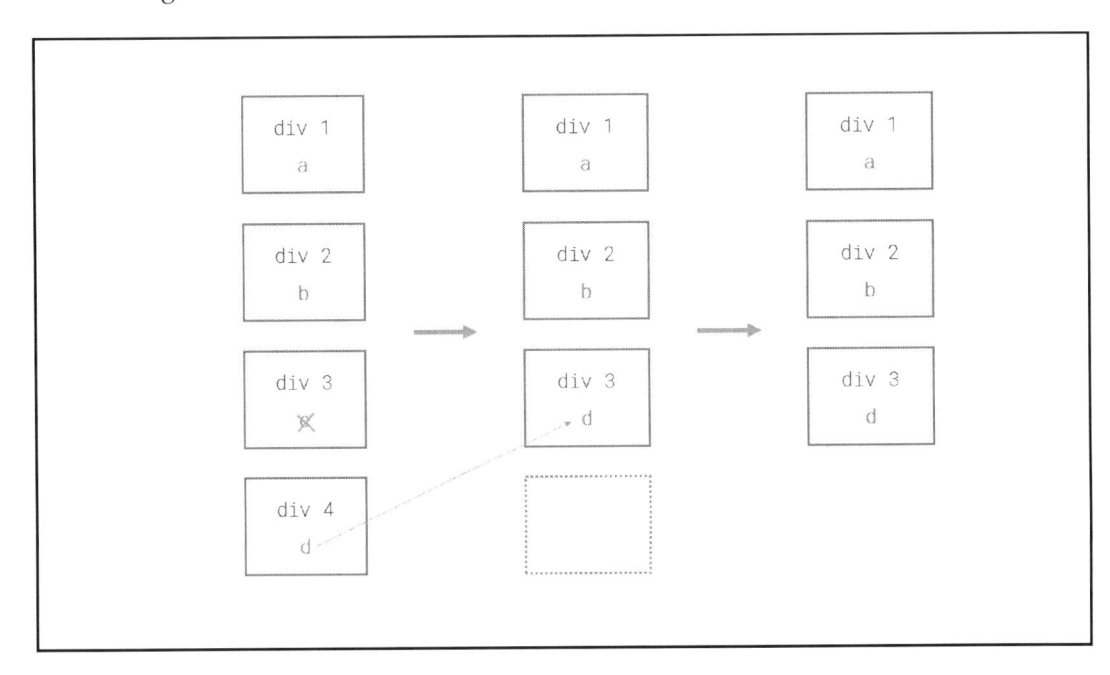

In this schema, we remove the third item in the list, which is c. However, the third `div` element will not be destroyed--it will be reused with the fourth item in the list, which is d. Actually, this is the fourth `div` element that is destroyed.

Fortunately, we can tell Vue how each element is identified so that it can reuse and reorder them. To do that, we will need to specify a unique identifier with the `key` special attribute. For example, each of our items could have a unique ID that we would use as the key:

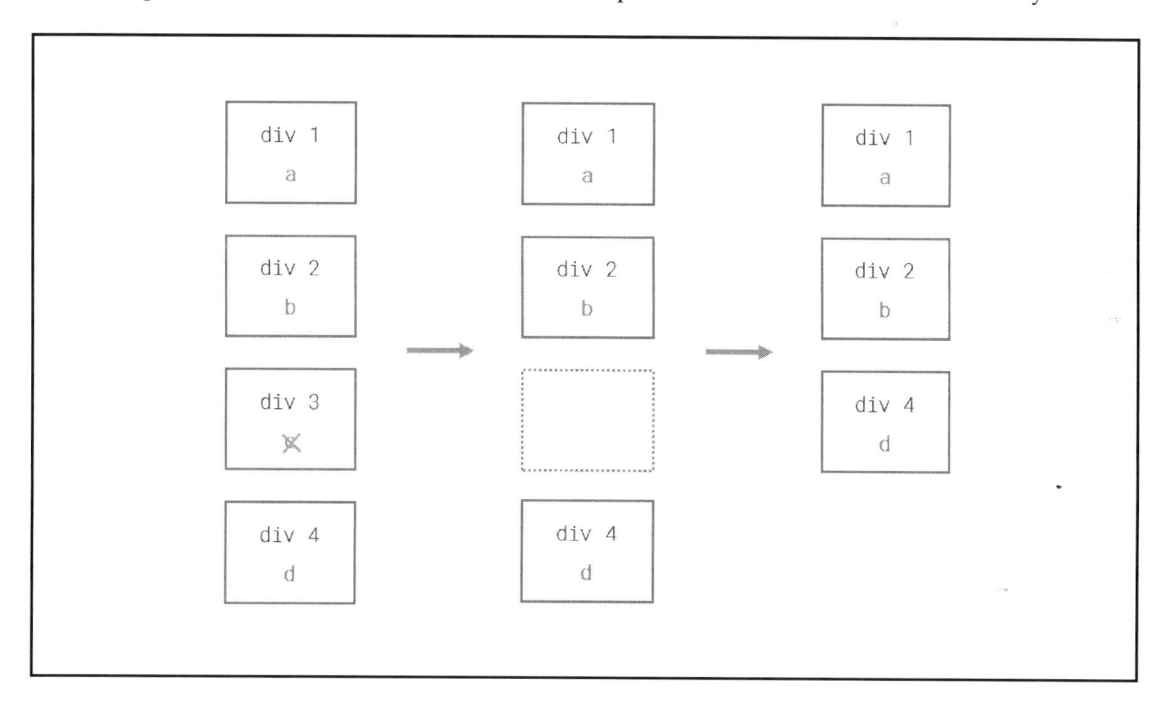

Here, we specify keys so that Vue knows the third `div` element should be destroyed and the fourth div element moved.

> **TIP**: The key special attribute works like a standard attribute, so we need to use the `v-bind` directive if we want to assign a dynamic value to it.

Back to our cards, we can use the unique identifier on the cards as the key:

```
<card v-for="card of cards" :def="card.def" :key="card.uid"
@play="handlePlay(card) />
```

Project 2 - Castle Duel Browser Game

Now, if we add, move, or delete a card item in the JavaScript, it will be reflected with the right order in the DOM.

The CSS transitions

Like before, we have the following six CSS classes at our disposal, prefixed with the name of our group transition, `'card'`: `card-enter-active`, `card-enter`, `card-enter-to`, `card-leave-active`, `card-leave`, and `card-leave-to`. They will be applied to the direct children of the group transition, that is, our cards components.

1. The group transition has an additional class applied to moving items--`v-move`. Vue will use the CSS `transform` property on the items to make them move, so we just need to apply a CSS transition on it with at least a duration:

   ```
   .card-move {
     transition: transform .3s;
   }
   ```

   Now, when you click on a card to play it, it should disappear and the remaining cards will move to their new position. You can also add cards to the hand.

2. Select the main component in the Vue devtools and execute this into the browser console:

   ```
   state.testHand.push($vm.testDrawCard())
   ```

   > **TIP**: Selecting a component in the devtools exposes it in the browser console as `$vm`.

   Like we did for the hand, we will also add animations for the cards when they enter the hand, and when they are played (and thus leave the hand).

3. Since we need to transition multiple CSS properties on the card with the same timings all the time (except during the leave transition), we will change the `.card-move` rule we just wrote into this:

   ```
   .card {
     /* Used for enter, move and mouse over animations */
     transition: all .3s;
   }
   ```

[92]

4. For the enter animation, specify the state of the card for the start of the transition:

   ```
   .card-enter {
     opacity: 0;
     /* Slide from the right */
     transform: scale(.8) translateX(100px);
   }
   ```

5. The leave animation requires a few more rules since the play card animation is more complex, and involves zooming the card upward:

   ```
   .card-leave-active {
     /* We need different timings for the leave transition */
     transition: all 1s, opacity .5s .5s;
     /* Keep it in the same horizontal position */
     position: absolute !important;
     /* Make it painted over the other cards */
     z-index: 10;
     /* Unclickable during the transition */
     pointer-events: none;
   }

   .card-leave-to {
     opacity: 0;
     /* Zoom the card upwards */
     transform: translateX(-106px) translateY(-300px) scale(1.5);
   }
   ```

   This is enough to make your cards all properly animated. You can try playing and adding cards to the hand again to see the result.

The overlays

The last UI elements we need are the overlays. The following are three of them:

- The 'new turn' overlay shows the name of the current player when it is their turn. Clicking on the 'new turn' player switches to the 'last play' overlay.
- The 'last play' overlay shows the player what their opponent did just before. It displays either of the following:
  - The card played by the opponent during the preceding turn
  - A reminder that their turn was skipped

- The 'game over' overlay shows whenever a player or both players lose. It displays the names of the players with the phrase "is victorious" or "is defeated". Clicking on the 'game over' overlay reloads the game.

All of these overlays have two things in common--they do something when the user clicks on them, and they have a similar layout design. So, we should be smart here and structure our components to reuse code as much as we can where it makes sense. The idea here is to create a generic overlay component, which will take care of the click event and the layout and three specific overlay-content components for each one of the overlays we need.

Before starting, add a new `activeOverlay` property to the app state in the `state.js` file:

```
// The consolidated state of our app
var state = {
  // UI
  activeOverlay: null,
  // ...
}
```

This will hold the name of the currently displayed overlay or will be `null` if no overlay is shown.

Content distribution with slots

It would be very convenient if we could put contents inside the overlay component in the main template, like this:

```
<overlay>
  <overlay-content-player-turn />
</overlay>
```

We would encapsulate additional layout and logic inside the `overlay` component while still being able to put any content inside. This is done through a special element--the `<slot>`.

1. Let's create our `overlay` component with two `div` elements:

   ```
   Vue.component('overlay', {
     template: `<div class="overlay">
       <div class="content">
         <!-- Our slot will be there -->
       </div>
     </div>`,
   })
   ```

2. Add a click event listener on the `.overlay` div, which calls the `handleClick` method:

   ```
   <div class="overlay" @click="handleClick">
   ```

3. Then, add the mentioned method where we emit a custom `'close'` event:

   ```
   methods: {
     handleClick () {
       this.$emit('close')
     },
   },
   ```

   This event will be helpful to know when to switch from one overlay to the next at the start of the turn.

4. Now, put a `<slot>` element inside the `.content` div:

   ```
   template: `<div class="overlay" @click="handleClick">
     <div class="content">
       <slot />
     </div>
   </div>`,
   ```

   Now, if we put something between the `overlay` tags when using our component, it will be included in the DOM and replace the `<slot>` tag. For example, we could do this:

```
<overlay>
  Hello world!
</overlay>
```

Also, it will render like this in the page:

```
<div class="overlay">
  <div class="content">
    Hello world!
  </div>
</div>
```

> **TIP:** It works with anything, so you can also put HTML or Vue components, and it will still work the same way!

5. The component is ready to be used in the main template, so add it at the end:

```
<overlay>
   Hello world!
</overlay>
```

Each of the three overlay contents will be a separate component:

- `overlay-content-player-turn` shows the beginning of the turn
- `overlay-content-last-play` displays the last card played by the opponent
- `overlay-content-game-over` shows when the game is over

Before diving into these, we need a bit more data about the two players in our state.

6. Go back to the `state.js` file and add the following properties for each player:

```
// Starting stats
food: 10,
health: 10,
// Is skipping is next turn
skipTurn: false,
// Skiped turn last time
skippedTurn: false,
hand: [],
lastPlayedCardId: null,
dead: false,
```

You should now have two items in the `players` array with the same properties, expect for the player names.

The 'player turn' overlay

The first overlay will display two different messages to the current player, depending on whether it is skipping their turn or not. The player prop will receive the current player so that we can access its data. We will use a `v-if` directive paired with a `v-else` directive and the `skipTurn` property we just added to the players:

```
Vue.component('overlay-content-player-turn', {
    template: `<div>
        <div class="big" v-if="player.skipTurn">{{ player.name }},<br>your turn is skipped!</div>
        <div class="big" v-else>{{ player.name }},<br>your turn has come!</div>
```

```
      <div>Tap to continue</div>
    </div>`,
    props: ['player'],
})
```

The 'last play' overlay

This one is a bit more complex. We need a new function to get the last played card by a player. In the `utils.js` file, add the new `getLastPlayedCard` function:

```
function getLastPlayedCard (player) {
  return cards[player.lastPlayedCardId]
}
```

We can now use this function in a `lastPlayedCard` computed property by passing the `opponent` prop:

```
Vue.component('overlay-content-last-play', {
  template: `<div>
    <div v-if="opponent.skippedTurn">{{ opponent.name }} turn was skipped!</div>
    <template v-else>
      <div>{{ opponent.name }} just played:</div>
      <card :def="lastPlayedCard" />
    </template>
  </div>`,
  props: ['opponent'],
  computed: {
    lastPlayedCard () {
      return getLastPlayedCard(this.opponent)
    },
  },
})
```

Note that we are directly reusing the `card` component we made earlier to display the card.

The 'game over' overlay

For this one, we will create another component called `player-result` that will show whether a player is victorious or defeated. We will display the name of the player passed with a prop. We will compute the result for this player with a computed property, which we will also use as a dynamic CSS class:

```
Vue.component('player-result', {
```

Project 2 - Castle Duel Browser Game

```
    template: `<div class="player-result" :class="result">
      <span class="name">{{ player.name }}</span> is
      <span class="result">{{ result }}</span>
    </div>`,
    props: ['player'],
    computed: {
      result () {
        return this.player.dead ? 'defeated' : 'victorious'
      },
    },
})
```

Now, we can create the game over overlay by looping over the `players` props and using the `player-result` component:

```
Vue.component('overlay-content-game-over', {
  template: `<div>
    <div class="big">Game Over</div>
    <player-result v-for="player in players" :player="player" />
  </div>`,
  props: ['players'],
})
```

Dynamic component

Now, it is time to put all of these into our overlay component and use the `activeOverlay` property we defined earlier.

1. Add the components and display them with the corresponding value of `activeOverlay` in the main template:

```
<overlay v-if="activeOverlay">
  <overlay-content-player-turn
    v-if="activeOverlay === 'player-turn'" />
  <overlay-content-last-play
    v-else-if="activeOverlay === 'last-play'" />
  <overlay-content-game-over
    v-else-if="activeOverlay === 'game-over'" />
</overlay>
```

> **TIP:** We will remove the overlay completely if the `activeOverlay` property is equal to `null`.

[98]

Before adding the props, we will need to modify the app state in the `state.js` file with a few getters.

2. The first one will return the `player` object from the `currentPlayerIndex` property:

```
get currentPlayer () {
  return state.players[state.currentPlayerIndex]
},
```

3. The second one will return the opposing `player` index:

```
get currentOpponentId () {
  return state.currentPlayerIndex === 0 ? 1 : 0
},
```

4. Finally, the third one will return the corresponding player object:

```
get currentOpponent () {
  return state.players[state.currentOpponentId]
},
```

5. Now, we can add the props to the overlay contents:

```
<overlay v-if="activeOverlay">
  <overlay-content-player-turn
    v-if="activeOverlay === 'player-turn'"
    :player="currentPlayer" />
  <overlay-content-last-play
    v-else-if="activeOverlay === 'last-play'"
    :opponent="currentOpponent" />
  <overlay-content-game-over
    v-else-if="activeOverlay === 'game-over'"
    :players="players" />
</overlay>
```

You can test the overlays by setting the `activeOverlay` property in the browser console:

```
state.activeOverlay = 'player-turn'
state.activeOverlay = 'last-play'
state.activeOverlay = 'game-over'
state.activeOverlay = null
```

Project 2 - Castle Duel Browser Game

> **TIP:** If you want to test the `last-play` overlay, you need to specify a valid value to the player `lastPlayedCardId` property, such as `'catapult'` or `'farm'`.

Our code is starting to be messy, with three conditionals. Thankfully, there is a special component that can turn itself into any component--it is the `component` component. You just have to set its `is` prop to a component name, a component definition object, or even an HTML tag, and it will morph into it:

```
<component is="h1">Title</component>
<component is="overlay-content-player-turn" />
```

It's a prop like any other, so we can use the `v-bind` directive to dynamically change the very nature of the component with a JavaScript expression. What if we used our `activeOverlay` property to do just that? Are our overlay content components conveniently named with the same `'over-content-'` prefix? Take a look:

```
<component :is="'overlay-content-' + activeOverlay" />
```

That's it. Now, by changing the value of the `activeOverlay` property, we will change the component displayed inside the overlay.

6. After adding back the props, the overlay should look like this in the main template:

```
<overlay v-if="activeOverlay">
  <component :is="'overlay-content-' + activeOverlay"
    :player="currentPlayer" :opponent="currentOpponent"
    :players="players" />
</overlay>
```

> **TIP:** Don't worry, unused props won't interfere with the different overlays workings.

[100]

The overlay animation

Like we did with the hand, we will use a transition to animate the overlay.

1. Add a transition called "zoom" around the overlay component:

   ```
   <transition name="zoom">
     <overlay v-if="activeOverlay">
       <component :is="'overlay-content-' + activeOverlay"
         :player="currentPlayer" :opponent="currentOpponent"
         :players="players" />
     </overlay>
   </transition>
   ```

2. Add the following CSS rules in the transition.css file:

   ```
   .zoom-enter-active,
   .zoom-leave-active {
     transition: opacity .3s, transform .3s;
   }

   .zoom-enter,
   .zoom-leave-to {
     opacity: 0;
     transform: scale(.7);
   }
   ```

   This is a simple animation that will zoom out the overlay while fading it out.

Key attribute

For now, if you try the animation in the browser, it should only work in two cases:

- When you don't have any overlay displayed, and you set one
- When you have an overlay shown and you set `activeOverlay` to `null` to hide it

If you switch between the overlays, the animation will not work. This is because of the way Vue updates the DOM; as we saw earlier in the *The key special attribute* section, it will reuse DOM elements as much as possible to optimize performance. In that case, we will need to use the key special attribute to give Vue a hint that we would like to treat the different overlays as separate elements. So, when we transition from one overlay to the other, both will be present in the DOM, and the animations can be played.

Let's add the key to our overlay component so that Vue will treat it as multiple separate elements when we change the `activeOverlay` value:

```
<transition name="zoom">
  <overlay v-if="activeOverlay" :key="activeOverlay">
    <component :is="'overlay-content-' + activeOverlay"
  :player="currentPlayer" :opponent="currentOpponent" :players="players" />
  </overlay>
</transition>
```

Now, if we set `activeOverlay` to `'player-turn'`, the overlay will have a key of `'player-turn'`. Then, if we set `activeOverlay` to `'last-play'`, an entirely new overlay will be created with a key of `'last-play'`, and we can animate the transition between the two. You can try this in the browser by setting different values to `state.activeOverlay`.

The overlay background

At this point, there is something missing--the overlay background. We can't include it inside the overlay component because it would be zoomed during the animation--this would be quite awkward. Instead, we will use the simple `fade` animation we have created already.

In the main template, add a new `div` element with the `overlay-background` class just before the `zoom` transition and the `overlay` component:

```
<transition name="fade">
  <div class="overlay-background" v-if="activeOverlay" />
</transition>
```

With the `v-if` directive, it will only be displayed when any overlay is displayed.

Game world and scenery

We are mostly done with the UI elements, so we can now go into the game scenery components. We will have some new components to do--the player castles, a health and food bubble for each one, and some animated clouds in the background for good measure.

Create a new `world.js` file in the `components` folder, and include it in the page:

```
<!-- ... -->
<script src="components/ui.js"></script>
<script src="components/world.js"></script>
<script src="main.js"></script>
```

We will start with the castles.

The castles

This one is actually pretty simple since it consists of only two images and a castle-banners component that will take care of the health and food display:

1. In the `world.js` file, create a new castle component with two images that accepts a `players` and an `index` prop:

   ```
   Vue.component('castle', {
     template: `<div class="castle" :class="'player-' + index">
       <img class="building" :src="'svg/castle' + index + '.svg'" />
       <img class="ground" :src="'svg/ground' + index + '.svg'" />
       <!-- Later, we will add a castle-banners component here -->
     </div>`,
     props: ['player', 'index'],
   })
   ```

   > For this component, there is a castle and a ground image for each player; that means four images in total. For example, for the player at index 0, there are `castle0.svg` and the `ground0.svg` images.

2. In the main template, just below the `top-bar` component, create a new `div` element with the `world` CSS class, loop over the players to display the two castles, and add another `div` element with the `land` class:

   ```
   <div class="world">
     <castle v-for="(player, index) in players" :player="player"
       :index="index" />
     <div class="land" />
   </div>
   ```

Project 2 - Castle Duel Browser Game

In the browser, you should see one castle for each player, as follows:

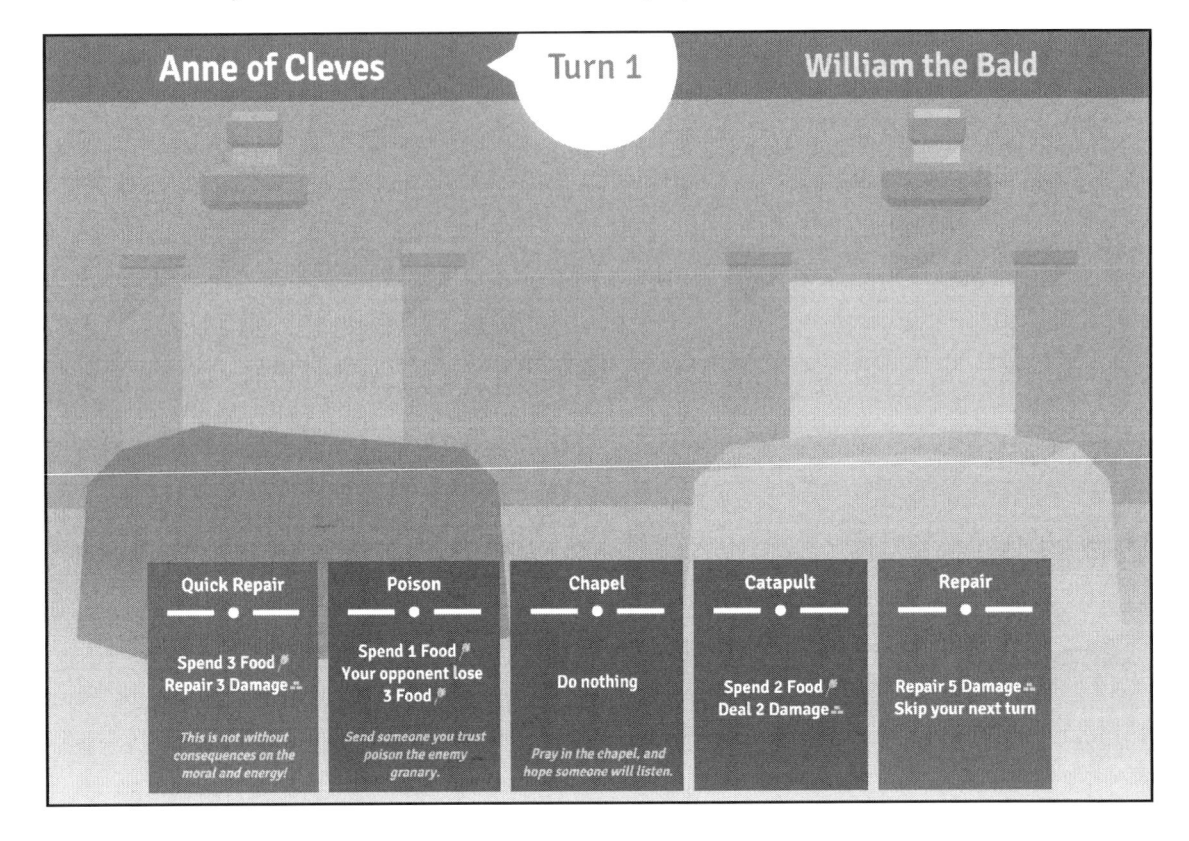

Castle banners

The castle banners will display the health and food for the castle. There will be two components inside the `castle-banners` component:

- A vertical banner whose height changes, depending of the amount of the stat
- A bubble with the actual number displayed

It will look like this:

1. First, create a new `castle-banners` component with only the stat icons and a `player` prop:

   ```
   Vue.component('castle-banners', {
     template: `<div class="banners">
       <!-- Food -->
       <img class="food-icon" src="svg/food-icon.svg" />
       <!-- Bubble here -->
       <!-- Banner bar here -->

       <!-- Health -->
       <img class="health-icon" src="svg/health-icon.svg" />
       <!-- Bubble here -->
       <!-- Banner bar here -->
     </div>`,
     props: ['player'],
   })
   ```

2. We also need two computed properties that calculate the health and food ratios:

```
computed: {
  foodRatio () {
    return this.player.food / maxFood
  },
  healthRatio () {
    return this.player.health / maxHealth
  },
}
```

> The `maxFood` and `maxHealth` variables are defined at the beginning of the `state.js` file.

3. In the `castle` component, add the new `castle-banners` component:

```
template: `<div class="castle" :class="'player-' + index">
  <img class="building" :src="'svg/castle' + index + '.svg'" />
  <img class="ground" :src="'svg/ground' + index + '.svg'" />
  <castle-banners :player="player" />
</div>`,
```

Food and health bubbles

This component contains an image and a text that displays the current amount for either the food or health of the castle. Its position will change depending on this amount--it will go up as the amount diminishes and will go down when it replenishes.

We will need three props for this component:

- `type` is either food or health; it will used for the CSS class and for the image path
- `value` is the amount displayed in the bubble
- `ratio` is the amount divided by the maximum amount

We also need a computed property to calculate the vertical position of the bubble with the `ratio` prop. The position will range from 40 pixels to 260 pixels. So, the position value will be given by this expression:

```
(this.ratio * 220 + 40) * state.worldRatio + 'px'
```

Chapter 3

> Remember to multiply every position or size with the `worldRatio` value, so the game takes into account the window size (it gets bigger if the window is bigger, or vice versa).

1. Let's write our new `bubble` component:

```
Vue.component('bubble', {
  template: `<div class="stat-bubble" :class="type + '-bubble'"
    :style="bubbleStyle">
    <img :src="'svg/' + type + '-bubble.svg'" />
    <div class="counter">{{ value }}</div>
  </div>`,
  props: ['type', 'value', 'ratio'],
  computed: {
    bubbleStyle () {
      return {
        top: (this.ratio * 220 + 40) * state.worldRatio + 'px',
      }
    },
  },
})
```

It has a root `div` element with the `stat-bubble` CSS class, a dynamic class (either `'food-bubble'` or `'health-bubble'`, depending on the `type` prop value) plus a dynamic CSS style we set with the `bubbleStyle` computed property.

It contains an SVG image, which is not the same for food and health, and a `div` element with the `counter` class that displays the amount.

2. Add a food and an health bubble to the `castle-banners` component:

```
template: `<div class="banners">
  <!-- Food -->
  <img class="food-icon" src="svg/food-icon.svg" />
  <bubble type="food" :value="player.food" :ratio="foodRatio" />
  <!-- Banner bar here -->

  <!-- Health -->
  <img class="health-icon" src="svg/health-icon.svg" />
  <bubble type="health" :value="player.health"
    :ratio="healthRatio" />
  <!-- Banner bar here -->
</div>`,
```

[107]

Banner bars

The other component we need is a vertical banner hanging up on one of the castle's towers. Its length will change depending on the amount of food or health. This time, we will create a dynamic SVG template so that we can modify the height of the banner.

1. First, create the component with two props (the color and the ratio) and the `height` computed property:

```
Vue.component('banner-bar', {
  props: ['color', 'ratio'],
  computed: {
    height () {
      return 220 * this.ratio + 40
    },
  },
})
```

For now, we defined our templates in two different ways--we either used the HTML of our page or we set a string into the `template` option of our components. We will use another method of writing component templates--a special script tag in the HTML. It works by writing the template inside this script tag with a unique ID and referencing this ID when defining the component.

2. Open the `banner-template.svg` file, which contains the SVG markup of the banner image we will use as a dynamic template. Copy the content of the file.

3. In the `index.html` file, after the `<div id="app">` element, add a `script` tag with the `text/x-template` type and the `banner` ID, and paste the `svg` content inside:

```
<script type="text/x-template" id="banner">
  <svg viewBox="0 0 20 260">
    <path :d="`m 0,0 20,0 0,${height} -10,-10 -10,10 z`"
    :style="`fill:${color};stroke:none;`" />
  </svg>
</script>
```

> **TIP**: As you can see, this is a standard template with all the syntax and directives available to use. Here, we use the `v-bind` directive shorthand twice. Note that you can use SVG markup inside all of your Vue templates.

Chapter 3

4. Now, back in our component definition, add the `template` option with the ID of our script tag template preceded by a hashtag:

```
Vue.component('banner-bar', {
  template: '#banner',
  // ...
})
```

Done! The component will now look up for a scrip tag template with the `banner` ID in the page and will use it as its template.

5. In the `castle-banners` component, add the two remaining `banner-bar` components with the corresponding colors and ratios:

```
template: `<div class="banners">
  <!-- Food -->
  <img class="food-icon" src="svg/food-icon.svg" />
  <bubble type="food" :value="player.food" :ratio="foodRatio" />
  <banner-bar class="food-bar" color="#288339" :ratio="foodRatio" />

  <!-- Health -->
  <img class="health-icon" src="svg/health-icon.svg" />
  <bubble type="health" :value="player.health" :ratio="healthRatio" />
  <banner-bar class="health-bar" color="#9b2e2e" :ratio="healthRatio" />
</div>`,
```

You should now see the banners that hang up on the castles and shrink if you change the food and health values.

Animating a value

These banners would be prettier if we could animate them when they shrink or grow. We can't rely on CSS transitions since we need to dynamically change the SVG path, so we need another way--we will animate the value of the `height` property used in the template.

1. First, let's rename our template computed property to `targetHeight`:

```
computed: {
  targetHeight () {
    return 220 * this.ratio + 40
  },
},
```

[109]

This `targetHeight` property will be calculated only once whenever the ratio changes.

2. Add a new `height` data property that we will be able to animate each time `targetHeight` changes:

```
data () {
  return {
    height: 0,
  }
},
```

3. Initialize the value of `height` with the value of `targetHeight` when the component has been created. Do this in the `created` hook:

```
created () {
  this.height = this.targetHeight
},
```

To animate the height value, we will use the popular **TWEEN.js** library, which is already included in the `index.html` file. This library works by creating a new `Tween` object that takes the starting values, an easing function, and the ending values. It provide callbacks such as `onUpdate` that we will use to update the `height` property from the animation.

4. We would like to start the animation whenever the `targetHeight` property changes, so add a watcher with the following animation code:

```
watch: {
  targetHeight (newValue, oldValue) {
    const vm = this
    new TWEEN.Tween({ value: oldValue })
      .easing(TWEEN.Easing.Cubic.InOut)
      .to({ value: newValue }, 500)
      .onUpdate(function () {
        vm.height = this.value.toFixed(0)
      })
      .start()
  },
},
```

> **TIP**
>
> The `this` context in the `onUpdate` callback is the `Tween` object and not the Vue component instance. That's why we need a good old temporary variable to hold the component instance `this` (here, that is the `vm` variable).

5. We need one last thing to make our animation work. In the `main.js` file, request the paint frames from the browser to make the `TWEEN.js` library tick, thanks to the browser's `requestAnimationFrame` function:

```
// Tween.js
requestAnimationFrame(animate);

function animate(time) {
  requestAnimationFrame(animate);
  TWEEN.update(time);
}
```

> **TIP**: If the tab is in the background, the `requestAnimationFrame` function will wait for the tab to become visible again. This means the animations won't play if the user doesn't see the page, saving the computer resources and battery. Note that it is also the case for CSS transitions and animations.

Now when you change the food or the health of a player, the banners will progressively shrink or grow.

The animated clouds

To add some life to the game world, we will create a few clouds that will slide in the sky. Their position and animation duration will be random and they will go from the left to the right of the window.

1. In the `world.js file`, add the minimum and maximum durations for the cloud animation:

```
const cloudAnimationDurations = {
  min: 10000, // 10 sec
  max: 50000, // 50 sec
}
```

2. Then, create the cloud component with an image and a `type` prop:

```
Vue.component('cloud', {
  template: `<div class="cloud" :class="'cloud-' + type" >
    <img :src="'svg/cloud' + type + '.svg'" />
  </div>`,
  props: ['type'],
})
```

> **TIP**
> There will be five different clouds, so the `type` prop will range from 1 to 5.

3. We will need to change the `z-index` and `transform` CSS properties of the component with a reactive `style` data property:

```
data () {
  return {
    style: {
      transform: 'none',
      zIndex: 0,
    },
  }
},
```

4. Apply these style properties with the `v-bind` directive:

```
<div class="cloud" :class="'cloud-' + type" :style="style">
```

5. Let's create a method to set the position of the cloud component using the `transform` CSS property:

```
methods: {
  setPosition (left, top) {
    // Use transform for better performance
    this.style.transform = `translate(${left}px, ${top}px)`
  },
}
```

Chapter 3

6. We need to initialize the horizontal position of the cloud when the image is loaded, so that it's outside of the viewport. Create a new `initPosition` that uses the `setPosition` method:

```
methods: {
  // ...
  initPosition () {
    // Element width
    const width = this.$el.clientWidth
    this.setPosition(-width, 0)
  },
}
```

7. Add an event listener on the image with the `v-on` directive shorthand that listens to the `load` event and calls the `initPosition` method:

```
<img :src="'svg/cloud' + type + '.svg'" @load="initPosition" />
```

The animation

Now, let's move on to the animation itself. Like we did for the castle banners, we will use the `TWEEN.js` library:

1. First, create a new `startAnimation` method that calculates a random animation duration and accepts a delay parameter:

```
methods: {
  // ...

  startAnimation (delay = 0) {
    const vm = this
    // Element width
    const width = this.$el.clientWidth

    // Random animation duration
    const { min, max } = cloudAnimationDurations
    const animationDuration = Math.random() * (max - min) + min

    // Bing faster clouds forward
    this.style.zIndex = Math.round(max - animationDuration)
    // Animation will be there
  },
}
```

[113]

Project 2 - Castle Duel Browser Game

> **TIP:** The faster a cloud is, the lower its animation duration will be. Faster clouds will be displayed before slower clouds, thanks to the `z-index` CSS property.

2. Inside the `startAnimation` method, calculate a random vertical position for the cloud and then create a `Tween` object. It will animate the horizontal position with a delay and set the position of the cloud each time it updates. When it completes, we will start another animation with a random delay:

```
// Random position
const top = Math.random() * (window.innerHeight * 0.3)

new TWEEN.Tween({ value: -width })
  .to({ value: window.innerWidth }, animationDuration)
  .delay(delay)
  .onUpdate(function () {
    vm.setPosition(this.value, top)
  })
  .onComplete(() => {
    // With a random delay
    this.startAnimation(Math.random() * 10000)
  })
  .start()
```

3. In the `mounted` hook of the component, call the `startAnimation` method to begin the initial animation (with a random delay):

```
mounted () {
  // We start the animation with a negative delay
  // So it begins midway
  this.startAnimation(-Math.random() *
cloudAnimationDurations.min)
},
```

Our cloud component is ready.

4. Add some clouds to the main template in the `world` element:

```
<div class="clouds">
  <cloud v-for="index in 10" :type="(index - 1) % 5 + 1" />
</div>
```

> **TIP**
> Be careful to pass a value to the `type` prop ranging from 1 to 5. Here, we use the `%` operator to return the division remainder for 5.

Here is what it should look like:

Gameplay

All of our components are done! We only need to add some gameplay logic for the app to be playable. When the game begins, each players draws their initial hand of cards.

Then, each player's turn follows these steps:

1. The `player-turn` overlay is displayed so that the player knows it's their turn.
2. The `last-play` overlay shows them what the other player played during the last run.
3. The player plays a card by clicking on it.
4. The card is removed from their hand and its effects applied.
5. We wait a bit so that the player can see these effects in action.
6. Then, the turn ends, and we switch the current player to the other one.

Drawing cards

Before drawing the cards, we will need to add two properties to the app state in the state.js file:

```
var state = {
  // ...
  drawPile: pile,
  discardPile: {},
}
```

The `drawPile` property is the pile of cards that can be drawn by the players. It is initialized with the `pile` object defined in the `cards.js` file. Each key is the ID of a card definition, and the value is the amount of cards of this type in the pile.

The `discardPile` property is the equivalent of the `drawPile` property, but it serves a different purpose--all the cards played by the player will be removed from their hand and put into the discard pile. At some point, if the draw pile is empty, it will be refilled with the discard pile (which will be emptied).

The initial hand

At the beginning of the game, each player draws some cards.

1. In the `utils.js` file, there is a function that draws the hand of a player:

   ```
   drawInitialHand(player)
   ```

2. In the `main.js` file, add a new `beginGame` function that calls the `drawInitialHand` function for each player:

   ```
   function beginGame () {
     state.players.forEach(drawInitialHand)
   }
   ```

3. Call this inside the `mounted` hook of our main component in the `main.js` file, when the app is ready:

   ```
   mounted () {
     beginGame()
   },
   ```

The hand

To display the cards in the current player hand, we need a new getter in the app state:

1. Add the `currentHand` getter to the `state` object in the `state.js` file:

   ```
   get currentHand () {
     return state.currentPlayer.hand
   },
   ```

2. We can now remove the `testHand` property and replace it with `currentHand` in the main template:

   ```
   <hand v-if="!activeOverlay" :cards="currentHand" @card-play="testPlayCard" />
   ```

3. You can also remove the `createTestHand` method and this `created` hook we wrote on the main component for testing purposes:

   ```
   created () {
     this.testHand = this.createTestHand()
   },
   ```

Playing a card

Playing the card is split into the following three steps:

1. We remove the card from the player's hand and add it to the pile. This triggers the card animation.
2. We wait for the card animation to finish.
3. We apply the effect of the card.

No cheating allowed

When playing, cheating shouldn't be allowed. When writing the gameplay logic, we should keep this in mind:

1. Let's start by adding a new `canPlay` property to the app state in the `state.js` file:

   ```
   var state = {
     // ...
     canPlay: false,
   }
   ```

   This will prevent the player from playing a card, if it has been already played during their turn--we have a lot of animation and waiting going on, so we don't want them to cheat.

   We will use it both when a player plays a card to check whether they played one already, and also in the CSS to disable mouse events on the hand cards.

2. So, add a `cssClass` computed property in the main component that will add the `can-play` CSS class if the `canPlay` property is true:

   ```
   computed: {
     cssClass () {
       return {
         'can-play': this.canPlay,
       }
     },
   },
   ```

3. And add a dynamic CSS class on the root `div` element in the main template:

   ```
   <div id="#app" :class="cssClass">
   ```

Removing the card from the hand

When the card is played, it should be removed from the current player hand; follow these steps to do so:

1. Create a new `playCard` function in the `main.js` file that takes a card as an argument, checks whether the player can play a card, and then removes the card from their hand to put it into the discard pile with the `addCardToPile` function (defined in the `utils.js` file):

   ```
   function playCard (card) {
     if (state.canPlay) {
       state.canPlay = false
       currentPlayingCard = card

       // Remove the card from player hand
       const index = state.currentPlayer.hand.indexOf(card)
       state.currentPlayer.hand.splice(index, 1)

       // Add the card to the discard pile
       addCardToPile(state.discardPile, card.id)
     }
   }
   ```

   > **TIP**
   > We store the card the player played in the `currentPlayingCard` variable, because we need to apply its effect later.

2. In the main component, replace the `testPlayCard` method with a new `handlePlayCard` one that calls the `playCard` function:

   ```
   methods: {
     handlePlayCard (card) {
       playCard(card)
     },
   },
   ```

3. Don't forget to change the event listener on the `hand` component in the main template:

   ```
   <hand v-if="!activeOverlay" :cards="currentHand" @card-play="handlePlayCard" />
   ```

[119]

Waiting for the card transition to end

When the card is played, which means removed from the hand card list, it triggers a leaving animation. We would like to wait for it to finish before continuing. Fortunately, the `transition` and `transition-group` components emit events.

The one we need here is the `'after-leave'` event, but there are other events corresponding to each phase of the transitions--`'before-enter'`, `'enter'`, `'after-enter'`, and so on.

1. In the hand component, add an event listener of the type `'after-leave'`:

    ```
    <transition-group name="card" tag="div" class="cards" @after-leave="handleLeaveTransitionEnd">
    ```

2. Create the corresponding method that emits a `'card-leave-end'` event to the main template:

    ```
    methods: {
      // ...
      handleLeaveTransitionEnd () {
        this.$emit('card-leave-end')
      },
    },
    ```

3. In the main template, add a new event listener of the `'card-leave-end'` type on the hand component:

    ```
    <hand v-if="!activeOverlay" :cards="currentHand" @card-play="handlePlayCard" @card-leave-end="handleCardLeaveEnd" />
    ```

4. Create the corresponding method:

    ```
    methods: {
      // ...

      handleCardLeaveEnd () {
        console.log('card leave end')
      },
    }
    ```

We will write its logic a bit later.

Applying the card effect

After the animation is played, the card effects will be applied to the players. For example, it could increase the current player's food or decrease the opponent's health.

1. In the `main.js` file, add the `applyCard` function that uses the `applyCardEffect` defined in the `utils.js` file:

   ```
   function applyCard () {
     const card = currentPlayingCard

     applyCardEffect(card)
   }
   ```

   Then, we will wait for some time so that the player can see the effects being applied and understand what is going on. Then, we will check whether at least one player is dead to end the game (thanks to the `checkPlayerLost` function defined in `utils.js`) or continue to the next turn.

2. In the `applyCard` function, add the following corresponding logic:

   ```
   // Wait a bit for the player to see what's going on
   setTimeout(() => {
     // Check if the players are dead
     state.players.forEach(checkPlayerLost)

     if (isOnePlayerDead()) {
       endGame()
     } else {
       nextTurn()
     }
   }, 700)
   ```

3. For now, add the empty `nextTurn` and `endGame` functions just after the `applyCard` one:

   ```
   function nextTurn () {
     // TODO
   }

   function endGame () {
     // TODO
   }
   ```

Project 2 - Castle Duel Browser Game

4. We can now change the `handleCardLeaveEnd` method in the main component to call the `applyCard` function we just created:

```
methods: {
  // ...

  handleCardLeaveEnd () {
    applyCard()
  },
}
```

The next turn

The `nextTurn` function is quite simple--we will increment the turn counter by one, change the current player, and display the player-turn overlay.

Add the corresponding code into the `nextTurn` function:

```
function nextTurn () {
  state.turn ++
  state.currentPlayerIndex = state.currentOpponentId
  state.activeOverlay = 'player-turn'
}
```

New turn

We also need some logic when a turn begins after the overlays:

1. First is the `newTurn` function that hides any active overlay; it either skips the turn of the current player because of a card or starts the turn:

```
function newTurn () {
  state.activeOverlay = null
  if (state.currentPlayer.skipTurn) {
    skipTurn()
  } else {
    startTurn()
  }
}
```

[122]

A player will have their turn skipped if its `skipTurn` property is true--this property will be set by some of the cards. They also have a `skippedTurn` property, which we will need to show the next player that their opponent has skipped their last turn in the `last-play` overlay.

2. Create the `skipTurn` function that sets `skippedTurn` to `true` and the `skipTurn` property to `false` and go directly to the next turn:

```
function skipTurn () {
  state.currentPlayer.skippedTurn = true
  state.currentPlayer.skipTurn = false
  nextTurn()
}
```

3. Create the `startTurn` function, which reset the `skippedTurn` property of the player and makes them draw a card if it's their second turn (so that they always have five cards at the beginning of their turn):

```
function startTurn () {
  state.currentPlayer.skippedTurn = false
  // If both player already had a first turn
  if (state.turn > 2) {
    // Draw new card
    setTimeout(() => {
      state.currentPlayer.hand.push(drawCard())
      state.canPlay = true
    }, 800)
  } else {
    state.canPlay = true
  }
}
```

It is at this moment that we can allow the player to play a card using the `canPlay` property.

Overlay close actions

Now, we will need to handle the action triggered when the user clicks on each overlay. We will create a map, with the key being the type of overlay and the value a function called when the action is triggered.

1. Add it in the `main.js` file:

   ```
   var overlayCloseHandlers = {
     'player-turn' () {
       if (state.turn > 1) {
         state.activeOverlay = 'last-play'
       } else {
         newTurn()
       }
     },
     'last-play' () {
       newTurn()
     },
     'game-over' () {
       // Reload the game
       document.location.reload()
     },
   }
   ```

   > **TIP**: For the player-turn overlay, we only switch to the `last-play` overlay if it's the second or more turn, since at the start of the very first turn, the opponent does not play any card.

2. In the main component, add the `handleOverlayClose` method that calls the action function corresponding to the currently active overlay with the `activeOverlay` property:

   ```
   methods: {
     // ...
     handleOverlayClose () {
       overlayCloseHandlers[this.activeOverlay]()
     },
   },
   ```

[124]

3. On the overlay component, add an event listener of the `'close'` type that will be triggered when the user clicks on the overlay:

   ```
   <overlay v-if="activeOverlay" :key="activeOverlay"
   @close="handleOverlayClose">
   ```

Game Over!

Finally, set the `activeOverlay` property to `'game-over'` inside the `endGame` function:

```
function endGame () {
  state.activeOverlay = 'game-over'
}
```

This will display the `game-over` overlay if at least one player is dead.

Summary

Our card game is finished. We saw a lot of new features provided by Vue that enable us to create rich and interactive experiences easily. However, the one most important thing we introduced and used in this chapter is the component-based approach to web application development. This helps us develop larger applications by splitting our frontend logic into small, isolated, and reusable components. We covered how to make components communicate with each other, from parent to children with props and from child to parent with custom events. We also added animations and transitions (with the `<transition>` and `<transition-group>` special components) to the game to make it more alive. We even manipulated SVG inside our templates and dynamically displayed a component with the special `<component>` component.

In the next chapter, we will set up a more advanced application with Vue component files, among other features that will help us build even larger applications.

4
Advanced Project Setup

After this chapter, we will begin building more complex applications, and we will need some additional tools and libraries. We will cover the following topics:

- Setting up our development environment
- Using vue-cli to scaffold Vue applications
- Writing and using Single-File Components

Setting up our development environment

To create more complex Single-Page Applications, it is recommended to use a few tools to ease the development. In this section, we will install them to have a good development environment ready. You need to have both Node.js and npm installed on your computer. Ensure that you have at least Node 8.x, but the latest Node version is recommended.

Installing vue-cli, the official command-line tool

The first package we will need is vue-cli, which is a command-line tool that will help us create Vue applications:

1. Enter this command in the terminal, and it will install vue-cli and save it as a global package:

   ```
   npm install -g vue-cli
   ```

   > You may need to run this command as an administrator.

2. To test whether vue-cli is working, print its version with the following command:

   ```
   vue --version
   ```

Code editors

Any text editor will do, but I recommend using Visual Studio Code (https://code.visualstudio.com/) or Atom (https://atom.io/). For Visual Studio Code, you need the vetur extension from octref (https://github.com/vuejs/vetur) and for Atom, the language-vue extension from hedefalk (https://atom.io/packages/language-vue).

Recent versions of Jetbrains' WebStorm IDE support Vue out of the box.

You can also install the extensions that add support to the preprocessor languages such as Sass, Less, or Stylus.

Our first full-blown Vue application

The previous applications were both made in quite an old-school way, with `script` tags and simple JavaScript. In this section, we will discover new ways of creating Vue applications with some powerful features and tools. In this part, we will create a mini project to demonstrate the new tools we will use as we move on.

Scaffolding the project

The vue-cli tool enables us to create ready-to-use app skeletons to help us get started on a new project. It works with a project template system that can ask you some questions to customize the skeleton to your needs:

1. List the official project templates with the following command:

    vue list

    Here's the list displayed in the terminal:

    ```
    Available official templates:

    * browserify - A full-featured Browserify + vueify setup with hot-reload, linting & unit testing.
    * browserify-simple - A simple Browserify + vueify setup for quick prototyping.
    * simple - The simplest possible Vue setup in a single HTML file
    * webpack - A full-featured Webpack + vue-loader setup with hot reload, linting, testing & css extraction.
    * webpack-simple - A simple Webpack + vue-loader setup for quick prototyping.
    ```

    There are three main types of official templates:

    - **simple**: Uses no build tools
    - **webpack**: Uses the very popular webpack bundler (recommended)
    - **browserify**: Uses the browserify build tool

    > **TIP**: The recommended official template is the `webpack` template. It features all you need to create a full-scale SPA with Vue. For the purpose of this book, we will use `webpack-simple` and introduce features progressively.

    To create a new application project using one of these templates, use the `npm init` command:

    vue init <template> <dir>

    We will use the `webpack-simple` official template in a new `demo` folder:

2. Run the following command:

    vue init webpack-simple demo

Advanced Project Setup

This project template features a ready-to-use minimal webpack configuration. The command will ask a few questions.

3. Answer the questions of vue-cli like this:

   ```
   ? Project name demo
   ? Project description Trying out Vue.js!
   ? Author Your Name <your-mail@mail.com>
   ? License MIT
   ? Use sass? No
   ```

   Vue-cli should have now created a `demo` folder. It has a `package.json` file and other configuration files already filled for us. The `package.json` file is very important; it holds the main information about the project; for example, it lists all the packages that the project depends on.

4. Go to the newly created `demo` folder and install the default dependencies already declared in the `package.json` file added by the `webpack-simple` template (such as vue and webpack):

   cd demo
   npm install

   Our app is now set up!

   > From now on, we will fully use the ECMAScript 2015 syntax and the `import`/`export` keywords to use or expose modules (which means files that export JavaScript elements).

Creating the app

Any Vue app need a JavaScript entry file where the code will start:

1. Remove the content of the `src` folder.
2. Create a new JavaScript file called `main.js` with the following content:

   ```
   import Vue from 'vue'

   new Vue({
     el: '#app',
     render: h => h('div', 'hello world'),
   })
   ```

Chapter 4

First, we import the Vue core library into the file. Then, we create a new root Vue instance that will attach to the element of `id` app in the page.

> **TIP**
> A default `index.html` file is provided by vue-cli for the page with an empty `<div id="app"></div>` tag. You can edit it to change the page HTML to your liking.

Finally, we display a `div` element containing the `'hello world'` text, thanks to the `render` option we will introduce in the "Render functions" section.

Running our application

Run the `dev` npm script generated by vue-cli to start the app in development mode:

```
npm run dev
```

This will launch a web app on a web server port. The terminal should display that the compilation was successful and what URL to use to access the app:

```
Project is running at http://localhost:8080/
webpack output is served from /dist/
404s will fallback to /index.html
```

Open this URL in your browser to see the result:

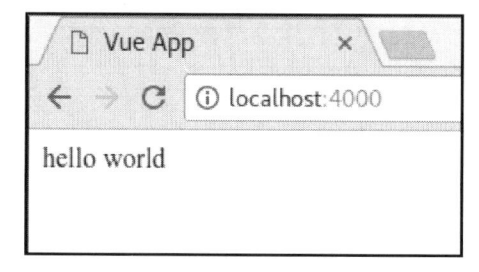

Vue App — localhost:4000

hello world

[131]

Render functions

Vue uses a virtual DOM implementation that consists of a tree of elements with JavaScript objects. It then applies the virtual DOM to the real browser DOM by computing the differences between the two. This helps avoid DOM operations as much as possible since they are usually the main performance bottleneck.

> Actually, when you use templates, Vue will compile them into render functions. If you need the full power and flexibility of JavaScript, you can directly write the render functions yourself, or write JSX, which will be discussed later.

A render function returns a small part of that tree, that is specific to its component. It uses the `createElement` method, which is passed as the first argument.

> By convention, `h` is an alias of `createElement`, which is very common and needed to write JSX. It comes from the name of this technique consisting of describing HTML with JavaScript--Hyperscript.

The `createElement` (or h) method takes up to three arguments:

1. The first one is the type of the element. It can be an HTML tag name (such as `'div'`), a component name registered in the application, or directly a component definition object.
2. The second argument is optional. It is the data object that defines attributes, props, event listeners, and the like.
3. The third argument is optional too. It is either a simple plain text, or an array of other elements created with `h`.

   Consider the following `render` function as an example:

   ```
   render (h) {
     return h('ul', { 'class': 'movies' }, [
       h('li', { 'class': 'movie' }, 'Star Wars'),
       h('li', { 'class': 'movie' }, 'Blade Runner'),
     ])
   }
   ```

It will output the following DOM in the browser:

```html
<ul class="movies">
  <li class="movie">Star Wars</li>
  <li class="movie">Blade Runner</li>
</ul>
```

We will cover render functions in further detail in `Chapter 6`, *Project 4 - Geolocated Blog*.

Configuring babel

Babel is a very popular tool that compiles JavaScript code so that we can use new features in older and current browsers (such as JSX or arrow functions). It is recommended to use babel in any serious JavaScript project.

By default, the `webpack-simple` template comes with a default babel configuration, which uses the `env` babel preset that supports all the stable JavaScript version from ES2015. It also includes another babel preset called `stage-3`, which supports the upcoming JavaScript features such as the `async/await` keywords and the object spread operator that are commonly used in the Vue community.

We will need to add a third preset specific to Vue, which will add support for JSX (we will need it in the 'JSX' section later in the chapter).

We also need to include the polyfills provided by babel so that new features such as `Promise` and generators work in the older browsers.

> A polyfill is code that checks whether a feature is available in the browser, and if not, it implements this feature so that it works like it is native.

Babel Vue preset

We will now install and use the `babel-preset-vue` in the Babel configuration of our app.

1. So first, we need to install this new preset in the dev dependencies:

   `npm i -D babel-preset-vue`

Advanced Project Setup

> **TIP**
> The main babel configuration is done in the `.babelrc` JSON file already present in the project root.
>
> This file may be hidden in your file explorer, depending on the system (its name starts with a dot). However, it should be visible in your code editor if it has a file tree view.

2. Open this `.babelrc` file and add the `vue` preset to the corresponding list:

```
{
  "presets": [
    ["env", { "modules": false }],
    "stage-3",
    "vue"
  ]
}
```

Polyfills

Let's also add the Babel polyfills to use new JavaScript features in older browsers.

1. Install the `babel-polyfill` package in your dev dependencies:

   npm i -D babel-polyfill

2. Import it at the beginning of the `src/main.js` file:

   ```
   import 'babel-polyfill'
   ```

This will enable all the necessary polyfills for the browser.

Updating the dependencies

After the project has been scaffolded, you may need to update the packages that it uses.

Updating manually

To check whether there are new versions available of the packages used in the project, run this command in the root folder:

`npm outdated`

If new versions are detected, a table is displayed:

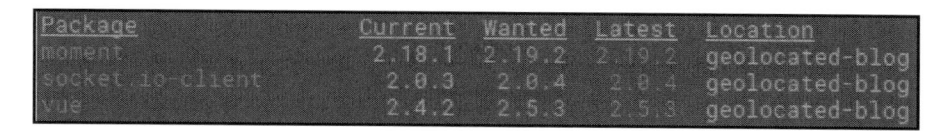

Package	Current	Wanted	Latest	Location
moment	2.18.1	2.19.2	2.19.2	geolocated-blog
socket.io-client	2.0.3	2.0.4	2.0.4	geolocated-blog
vue	2.4.2	2.5.3	2.5.3	geolocated-blog

The `Wanted` column is the version number compatible with the version range specified in the `package.json` file. To learn more about this, visit the npm documentation at https://docs.npmjs.com/getting-started/semantic-versioning.

To update a package manually, open the `package.json` file and locate the corresponding line. Change the version range and save the file. Then, run this command to apply the changes:

`npm install`

> **TIP**
> Don't forget to read the change logs of the packages you update! There might be breaking changes or improvement you will be happy to know about.

Updating automatically

To update the packages automatically, use this command in the root folder of the project:

`npm update`

> This command will only update the versions compatible with those specified in the `package.json` file. If you want to update packages to other versions, you need to do it manually.

Updating Vue

When you update the `vue` package containing the core library, you should also update the `vue-template-compiler` package. It is the package that compiles all your component templates when using webpack (or another build tool).

> Both of these packages must always be at the same version. For example, if you use `vue 2.5.3`, then `vue-template-compiler` should also be at version `2.5.3`.

Building for production

When it will be time to put your app into production on a real server, you will need to run this command to compile your project:

```
npm run build
```

By default, when using the `webpack-simple` template, it will output the JavaScript files into a `/dist` folder in the project. You will only need to upload this folder and the `index.html` file that is present in the root folder. You should have the following file tree on your server:

```
- index.html
- favicon.png
- [dist] - build.js
        L build.map.js
```

Single-File Components

In this section, we will introduce an important format widely used in the creation of real production Vue apps.

Vue has its own format call **Single-File Component** (**SFC**). This format was created by the Vue team, and the file extension is `.vue`. It allows you to write one component per file, with both the template, and the logic and styling of this component in one place. The main advantage here is that each component is clearly self-contained, more maintainable, and easily shared.

An SFC describes a Vue component with an HTML-like syntax. It can contain three types of root blocks:

- `<template>`, which describes the template of the component with the template syntax we already used
- `<script>`, which contains the JavaScript code of the component
- `<style>`, which contains the style used by the component

Here's an example of an SFC:

```
<template>
  <div>
    <p>{{ message }}</p>
    <input v-model="message"/>
  </div>
</template>

<script>
export default {
  data () {
    return {
      message: 'Hello world',
    }
  },
}
</script>

<style>
p {
  color: grey;
}
</style>
```

Let's try this component now!

1. Put the above component source in a new `Test.vue` file in the `src` folder.
2. Edit the `main.js` file and import the SFC using the `import` keyword:

   ```
   import Test from './Test.vue'
   ```

Advanced Project Setup

3. Remove the `render` option and instead, copy the definition of the `Test` component with the object spread operator:

```
new Vue({
  el: '#app',
  ...Test,
})
```

> **TIP**: In the preceding snippet, I demonstrated another way to add the root component to the app--using the JavaScript Spread operator--so the `...App` expression will copy the properties to the app definition object. The main advantage is that we won't have a useless top component in the dev tools anymore; it will be our direct root component now.

4. Go ahead and open the URL displayed in the terminal to see the result:

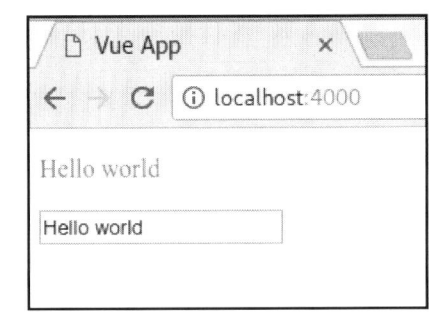

Template

The `<template>` tag contains the template of the component. Like earlier, it is HTML with the Vue special syntax (directives, text interpolation, shorthands, and so on).

Here's an example of a `<template>` tag in an SFC:

```
<template>
  <ul class="movies">
    <li v-for="movie of movies" class="movie">
      {{ movie.title }}
    </li>
  </ul>
</template>
```

In this example, the template of our component will consist of a `ul` element containing a list of `li` elements displaying the titles of the movies.

> If you don't put a `<template>` tag in your SFC, you will need to write a render function or your component won't be valid.

Using Pug

Pug (formerly Jade) is a language that compiles to HTML. We can use it inside our `<template>` tag with the `lang` attribute set to "pug":

```
<template lang="pug">
ul.movies
  li.movie Star Wars
  li.movie Blade Runner
</template>
```

To compile the Pug code in our SFC, we need to install these packages:

```
npm install --save-dev pug pug-loader
```

> Packages that are needed for the development are called development dependencies and should be installed with the `--save-dev` flag. The direct dependencies that the app requires to run (for example, a package to compile markdown to HTML) should be installed with the `--save` flag.

Script

The `<script>` tag contains the JavaScript code associated with the component. It should export the component definition object.

Here's an example of a `<script>` tag:

```
<script>
export default {
  data () {
    return {
      movies: [
        { title: 'Star Wars' },
        { title: 'Blade Runner' },
      ],
```

Advanced Project Setup

```
    }
  },
}
</script>
```

In this example, the component will have a `data` hook returning an initial state with a `movies` array.

> **TIP:** The `<script>` tag is optional if you don't need any options in the component options, which defaults to an empty object.

JSX

JSX is a special notation used inside the JavaScript code to express HTML markup. It makes the code responsible for describing the view closer to the pure HTML syntax, while still having the full power of JavaScript available.

Here's an example of a render function written with JSX:

```
<script>
export default {
  data () {
    return {
      movies: [
        { title: 'Star Wars' },
        { title: 'Blade Runner' },
      ],
    }
  },
  render (h) {
    const itemClass = 'movie'
    return <ul class='movies'>
      {this.movies.map(movie =>
        <li class={ itemClass }>{ movie.title }</li>
      )}
    </ul>
  },
}
</script>
```

[140]

> **TIP**: You can use any JavaScript expression inside single brackets.

As you can see in this example, we can use any JavaScript code to compose our view. We can even use the `map` method of the `movies` array to return some JSX for each item. We also used a variable to dynamically set the CSS class of the movie elements.

During the compilation, what really happened is that a special module called `babel-plugin-transform-vue-jsx` included in `babel-preset-vue` transformed the JSX code into pure JavaScript code. After compilation, the preceding render function will look like this:

```
render (h) {
  const itemClass = 'movie'
  return h('ul', { class: 'movies' },
    this.movies.map(movie =>
      h('li', { class: itemClass }, movie.title)
    )
  )
},
```

As you can see, JSX is a syntax that helps write render functions. The final JavaScript code will be quite close to what we could have written using `h` (or `createElement`) manually.

We will cover render functions in more detail in Chapter 6, *Project 4 - Geolocated Blog*.

Style

The Single-File Component can include multiple `<style>` tags to add CSS to the app that is related to this component.

Here's a very simple example of component style applying some CSS rules to the `.movies` class:

```
<style>
.movies {
  list-style: none;
  padding: 12px;
  background: rgba(0, 0, 0, .1);
  border-radius: 3px;
}
</style>
```

Scoped styles

We can scope the CSS contained inside a `<style>` tag to the current component with the scoped attribute. It means that this CSS will only be applied to the elements of this component's template.

For example, we can use generic class names such as movie and ensure that it won't conflict with the rest of the app:

```
<style scoped>
.movie:not(:last-child) {
  padding-bottom: 6px;
  margin-bottom: 6px;
  border-bottom: solid 1px rgba(0, 0, 0, .1);
}
</style>
```

The result will look like this:

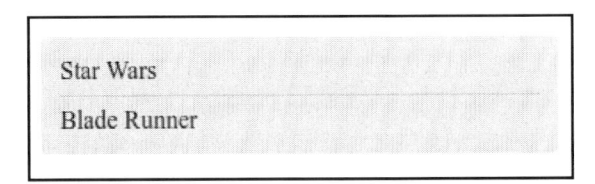

Star Wars

Blade Runner

This works, thanks to a special attribute applied to both the template and the CSS with PostCSS (a processing tool). For example, consider the following scoped styled component:

```
<template>
  <h1 class="title">Hello</h1>
</template>
```

```
<style scoped>
.title {
  color: blue;
}
</style>
```

It is equivalent to the following:

```
<template>
  <h1 class="title" data-v-02ad4e58>Hello</h1>
</template>

<style>
.title[data-v-02ad4e58] {
  color: blue;
}
</style>
```

As you can see, a unique attribute was added to all the template elements and to all the CSS selectors so that it will only match this component's template and will not conflict with other components.

> **TIP**
> Scoped styles don't eliminate the need for classes; due to the way browsers render CSS, there might be performance loss when selecting a plain element with an attribute. For example, `li { color: blue; }` will be many times slower than `.movie { color: blue; }` when scoped to the component.

Adding preprocessors

Nowadays, CSS is rarely used as is. It is common to write styles with a more powerful and feature-rich preprocessor language.

On the `<style>` tags, we can specify one of these languages to use with the `lang` attribute.

We will take this template as the base for our component:

```
<template>
  <article class="article">
    <h3 class="title">Title</h3>
  </article>
</template>
```

Advanced Project Setup

Sass

Sass is a well-known CSS preprocessor used by a lot of tech companies:

1. To enable Sass in your component, install the following packages:

   `npm install --save-dev node-sass sass-loader`

2. Then, in your component, add a `<style>` tag with the `lang` attribute set to `"sass"`:

   ```
   <style lang="sass" scoped>
   .article
     .title
       border-bottom: solid 3px rgba(red, .2)
   </style>
   ```

3. Now, test your component with the `vue build` command. You should have a result similar to this one:

> **TIP:** If you want to use the SCSS syntax variant of Sass, you need to use `lang="scss"`.

Less

Less has a simpler syntax than other CSS preprocessing languages:

1. To use Less, you need to install the following packages:

   `npm install --save-dev less less-loader`

2. Then, in your component, set the `lang` attribute to `"less"`:

```
<style lang="less" scoped>
.article {
  .title {
    border-bottom: solid 3px fade(red, 20%);
  }
}
</style>
```

Stylus

Stylus is more recent that Less and Sass, and is also quite popular:

1. Finally, for Stylus, you need these packages:

   ```
   npm install --save-dev stylus stylus-loader
   ```

2. On the `<style>` tag, set the `lang` attribute to `"stylus"`:

   ```
   <style lang="stylus" scoped>
   .article
     .title
       border-bottom solid 3px rgba(red, .2)
   </style>
   ```

Components inside components

Now that we know how to write Single-File Components, we want to use them inside other components to compose the interface of the app.

To use a component inside another component, we need to import it and expose it to the template:

1. First, create a new component. For example, here's a `Movie.vue` component:

   ```
   <template>
     <li class="movie">
       {{ movie.title }}
     </li>
   </template>

   <script>
   export default {
   ```

[145]

Advanced Project Setup

```
  props: ['movie'],
}
</script>

<style scoped>
.movie:not(:last-child) {
  padding-bottom: 6px;
  margin-bottom: 6px;
  border-bottom: solid 1px rgba(0, 0, 0, .1);
}
</style>
```

We will also need a `Movies.vue` component if you haven't created it already. It should look like this:

```
<template>
  <ul class="movies">
    <li v-for="movie of movies" class="movie">
      {{ movie.title }}
    </li>
  </ul>
</template>

<script>
export default {
  data () {
    return {
      movies: [
        { id: 0, title: 'Star Wars' },
        { id: 1, title: 'Blade Runner' },
      ],
    }
  },
}
</script>
```

2. Then, import the `Movie` SFC in the script of the `Movies` component:

```
<script>
import Movie from './Movie.vue'

export default {
  // ...
}
</script>
```

3. Set the `components` option to expose some components to the template, with an object (the key is the name that we will use in the template, and the value is the component definition):

   ```
   export default {
     components: {
       Movie,
       // Equivalent to `Movie: Movie,`
     },

     // ...
   }
   ```

4. We can now use the component with the `Movie` tag in the template:

   ```
   <template>
     <ul class="movies">
       <Movie v-for="movie of movies"
         :key="movie.id"
         :movie="movie" />
     </ul>
   </template>
   ```

   If you are using JSX, you don't need the `components` option, as you can use a component definition directly if it starts with a capital letter:

   ```
   import Movies from './Movies.vue'

   export default {
     render (h) {
       return <Movies/>
       // no need to register Movies via components option
     }
   }
   ```

Summary

In this chapter, we installed several tools that will allow us to write a real production-ready application using the recommended methods. Now, we can scaffold an entire project skeleton to start building great new apps. We can write components in various ways, but we can do so in a coherent and maintainable manner with the Single-File Components. We can use these components inside our application or inside other components to compose our user interface with multiple reusable components.

In the next chapter, we will create our third application with all we learned to this point, plus some new topics, such as routing!

5
Project 3 - Support Center

In this chapter, we will build a more complex application with a routing system (this means multiple virtual pages). This is going to be a support center for a fictional company called "My Shirt Shop". It will have two main parts:

- An FAQ page with a few questions and answers
- A support ticket management page where the user will be able to display and create new tickets

The application will have an authentication system that will allow users to create an account or log in.

We will first start creating some basic routes, then we will integrate this account system to finish with more advanced topics regarding routing. Through the chapter, we will reuse our code as much as possible and apply best practices.

General app structure

In this first part, we are going to create the project structure and learn more about routing and pages.

Setting up the project

For setting up the project, the following steps need to be followed:

1. First, generate a Vue project with the `vue init webpack-simple <folder>` command, like we did in Chapter 4, *Advanced Project Setup*:

   ```
   vue init webpack-simple support-center
   cd support-center
   npm install
   npm install --save babel-polyfill
   ```

2. Install the packages necessary to compile Stylus code (our style will be written using Stylus):

   - `stylus`
   - `stylus-loader`

   ```
   npm install --save-dev stylus stylus-loader
   ```

   > **TIP**: Don't forget to save the development tools packages in the development dependencies of your `package.json` file with the `--save-dev` flag.

3. Remove the content of the `src` folder where we will put all the sources of our app.
4. Then create a `main.js` file with the code needed to create a Vue app:

   ```
   import 'babel-polyfill'
   import Vue from 'vue'
   
   new Vue({
     el: '#app',
     render: h => h('div', 'Support center'),
   })
   ```

   You can now try to run the app with the `npm run dev` command!

5. Most the style for the app is already available. Download it (https://github.com/Akryum/packt-vue-project-guide/tree/master/chapter5-download) and extract the Stylus files into a `style` folder inside the `src` directory. Extract the `assets` folder too.

Routing and pages

Our app will be organized in six main pages:

- The home page
- The public FAQ page
- The login page
- The tickets page
- A page to send a new ticket
- A page showing one ticket details and conversation

A route is a path representing a state of the application, usually in the form of pages. Each route is associated with a URL pattern that will trigger the route when the address matches. Then, the corresponding page will be presented to the user.

Vue plugins

To enable routing in our app, we need an official Vue plugin called `vue-router`. A Vue plugin is some JavaScript code designed to add more features to the Vue library. You can find many plugins on the npm registry, and I recommend the awesome-vue GitHub repository (`https://github.com/vuejs/awesome-vue`) that lists them by category:

1. Download the `vue-router` package from npm with the following command in the project directory:

   ```
   npm install --save vue-router
   ```

   We will put all the routing-related code in a new `router.js` file next to the `main.js` file, which you need to create. Then, we need to install the plugin we want to use (which is `vue-router` in our case) with the global `Vue.use()` method.

2. Create the `router.js` file and import both the `Vue` library and the `VueRouter` plugin from their corresponding packages:

   ```
   import Vue from 'vue'
   import VueRouter from 'vue-router'
   ```

Project 3 - Support Center

3. Then install the plugin into Vue:

   Vue.use(VueRouter)

   The `vue-router` plugin is now ready to be used!

Our first routes with vue–router

In this section, we will go through the steps required to set up routing in our Vue application.

Layouts with router–view

Before adding routes, we need to setup a layout for the app where the route components will be rendered.

1. Let's create a component called `AppLayout.vue` in a new `components` folder inside the `src` directory.
2. Write the template of the component--a `<div>` element containing a `<header>` with an image and some text. Then, add a `<router-view />` component after the header:

```
<template>
  <div class="app-layout">
    <header class="header">
      <div><img class="img"
        src="../assets/logo.svg"/></div>
      <div>My shirt shop</div>
    </header>

    <!-- Menu will be here -->
    <router-view />
  </div>
</template>
```

[152]

The `<router-view />` component is a special component provided by the `vue-router` plugin that will render the component of the current matching route. It is not a real component since it doesn't have its own template, and it will not appear in the DOM.

3. After the template, add a `style` tag importing the main Stylus file from the `styles` folder you downloaded earlier in the *Setting up the project* section. Don't forget to specify that we are using `stylus` with the `lang` attribute:

```
<style lang="stylus">
@import '../style/main';
</style>
```

4. Since we can have as many `style` tags as we need in a SFC, add another one, but scoped this time. We will specify the size of the `header` logo in this second style section:

```
<style lang="stylus" scoped>
.header {
  .img {
    width: 64px;
    height: 64px;
  }
}
</style>
```

> To improve the performance, it is recommended to use classes inside scoped styles.

Our layout component is ready to be included in our app!

5. In the `main.js` file, import it and render it on the `root` Vue instance:

```
import AppLayout from './components/AppLayout.vue'

new Vue({
  el: '#app',
  render: h => h(AppLayout),
})
```

Project 3 - Support Center

We can't start the app yet, since we are not finished with routing!

> If you look at the console of your browser, you might see an error message complaining about the `<router-view />` component being missing. This is because we don't have the imported `router.js` file where we installed the `vue-router` plugin into Vue, so the code isn't included in our app yet.

Creating routes

Let's create a few dumb pages for test routing:

1. In the `components` folder, create a `Home.vue` component containing a very simple template with a `<main>` element, a title, and some text:

   ```
   <template>
     <main class="home">
       <h1>Welcome to our support center</h1>
       <p>
         We are here to help! Please read the <a>F.A.Q</a> first,
         and if you don't find the answer to your question, <a>send
         us a ticket!</a>
       </p>
     </main>
   </template>
   ```

2. Then, create an `FAQ.vue` component next to `Home.vue`. It should also contain a `<main>` element, inside of which you can add a simple title:

   ```
   <template>
     <main class="faq">
       <h1>Frenquently Asked Questions</h1>
     </main>
   </template>
   ```

We now have what we need to create a few routes.

3. In the `router.js` file, import the two components we just created:

   ```
   import Home from './components/Home.vue'
   import FAQ from './components/FAQ.vue'
   ```

4. Then, create a `routes` array:

   ```
   const routes = [
     // Routes will be here
   ]
   ```

   A route is an object containing a path, a name, and a component to render:

   ```
   { path: '/some/path', name: 'my-route', component: ... }
   ```

   The path is the pattern that the current URL should match for the route to be activated. The component will be rendered in the special `<router-view />` component.

   > **TIP**: The route name is optional, but I strongly recommend using it. It allows you to specify the names of the routes instead of the path, so that you can move and change your routes around without ending up with broken links.

5. With that in mind, we can now add our two routes in the `routes` array:

   ```
   const routes = [
     { path: '/', name: 'home', component: Home },
     { path: '/faq', name: 'faq', component: FAQ },
   ]
   ```

Let's review what it will do:

- When the browser URL is `http://localhost:4000/`, the `Home.vue` component will be rendered
- When the URL is `http://localhost:4000/faq/`, the `FAQ.vue` component will be displayed

The router object

With our routes ready, we need to create a `router` object that will take care of managing the routing for us. We will use the `VueRouter` constructor from the `vue-router` package. It takes one `options` parameter and for now, we are going to use the `routes` parameter:

1. After the `routes` array in the `router.js` file, create a new `router` object and specify the `routes` parameter:

   ```
   const router = new VueRouter({
     routes,
   })
   ```

   > The plugin we installed is also the router constructor, so we are using the same `VueRouter` variable. `VueRouter` is in fact a valid Vue plugin because it has an `install` method. We will create our own plugin in this chapter!

2. Export the `router` object as the default exported value of the module:

   ```
   export default router
   ```

3. Now back to our `main.js` file, we need to provide the `router` object to the Vue application. Import the `router` we just created:

   ```
   import router from './router'
   ```

4. Then add it as a definition option to the root Vue instance:

   ```
   new Vue({
     el: '#app',
     render: h => h(AppLayout),
     // Provide the router to the app
     router,
   })
   ```

That is all we need to have routing working! You can now try to change the URL in your browser to either `http://localhost:4000/#/` or `http://localhost:4000/#/faq` and get a different page each time:

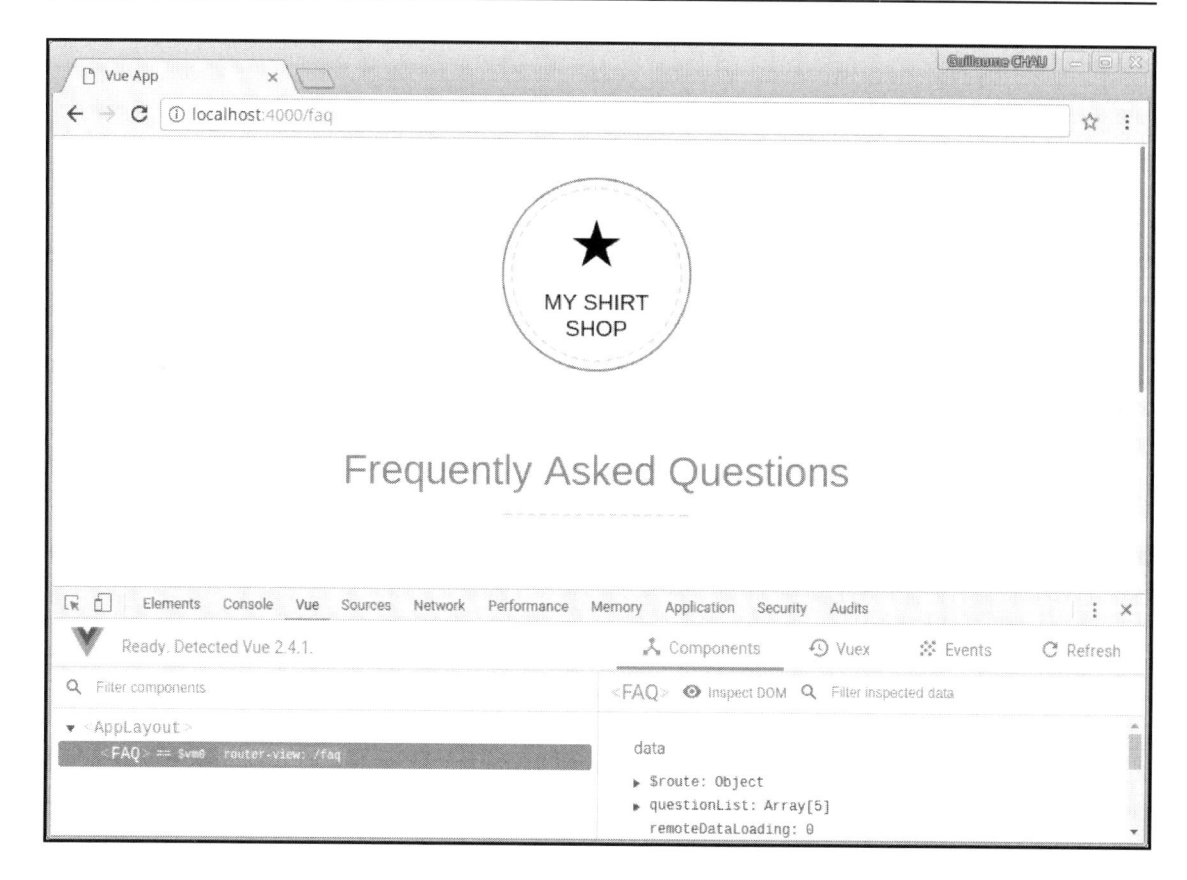

> **TIP:** Don't forget the sharp # character in the URL; it is needed to fake the route changes while not changing the real web page. This is the default router mode called `hash`, and it works with any browser and server.

Router modes

We can change the router mode with the `mode` parameter in the constructor options. It can either be `'hash'` (default), `'history'`, or `'abstract'`.

The `hash` mode is the default we are already using. It is the "safest" choice since it is compatible with any browser and server. It consists of using the "hash" part of the URL (which means the part after the sharp character) and change it or react to changes to it. The big advantage is that changing the hash part will not change the real web page where our app is running (which would be very unfortunate). The obvious drawback is that it forces us to separate the URL in two with the not so pretty sharp symbol.

Project 3 - Support Center

Thanks to the HTML5 `history.pushState` API, we can get rid of this sharp character and get a real URL for our app! We need to change the mode to `'history'` in the constructor:

```
const router = new VueRouter({
  routes,
  mode: 'history',
})
```

Now we can use pretty URLs such as `http://localhost:4000/faq` in our Single-Page App! There are two problems though:

- The browser needs to support this HTML5 API, which means it won't work on Internet Explorer 9 or less (all other major browsers have supported it for quite some time).
- The server has to be configured to send the home page instead of throwing a 404 error when accessing a route such as `/faq`, since it doesn't really exist (you don't have a file called `faq.html`). This also means we will have to implement the 404 page ourselves.

Thankfully, the webpack server used by `vue build` is configured to support this by default. So you can go ahead and try the new `http://localhost:4000/faq` URL!

There is a third mode called `abstract` that can be used in any JavaScript environment (including Node.js). If there is no browser API available, the router will be forced to use this mode.

Creating a navigation menu

Instead of manually typing the URL, it would be great to have a proper navigation `menu` in our app! Let's create a new `NavMenu.vue` file in our `components` folder:

```
<template>
  <nav class="menu">
    <!-- Links here -->
  </nav>
</template>
```

Next, we will add it in the layout. Import the new component in the `AppLayout` one:

```
<script>
import NavMenu from './NavMenu.vue'
export default {
  components: {
    NavMenu,
  },
}
</script>
```

Then add it to the `AppLayout` template:

```
<header class="header">
  <div><img class="img" src="../assets/logo.svg"/></div>
  <div>My shirt shop</div>
</header>

<NavMenu />
```

Router links

The `vue-router` plugin provides us with another handy special component--`<router-link>`. It is a component that will change to a specified route when clicked thanks to its `to` prop. By default, it will be a `<a>` HTML element, but this can be customized with the `tag` prop.

For example, a link to the FAQ page would be:

```
<router-link to="/faq">FAQ</router-link>
```

The `to` prop can also get an object with the name property instead of the path:

```
<router-link :to="{ name: 'faq' }">FAQ</router-link>
```

This will dynamically generate the correct path for the route. I recommend you to use this second method as opposed to only specifying the path--that way, if you change the paths of your routes, your navigation links will still work.

> **TIP**: When using the object notation, don't forget to bind the `to` prop with `v-bind` or the `:` shorthand, or else the `router-link` component will get a string and won't understand it's an object.

Now we can add the links to our `NavMenu` component:

```
<template>
  <nav class="menu">
    <router-link :to="{ name: 'home' }">Home</router-link>
    <router-link :to="{ name: 'faq' }">FAQ</router-link>
  </nav>
</template>
```

You should now have a working menu in the app:

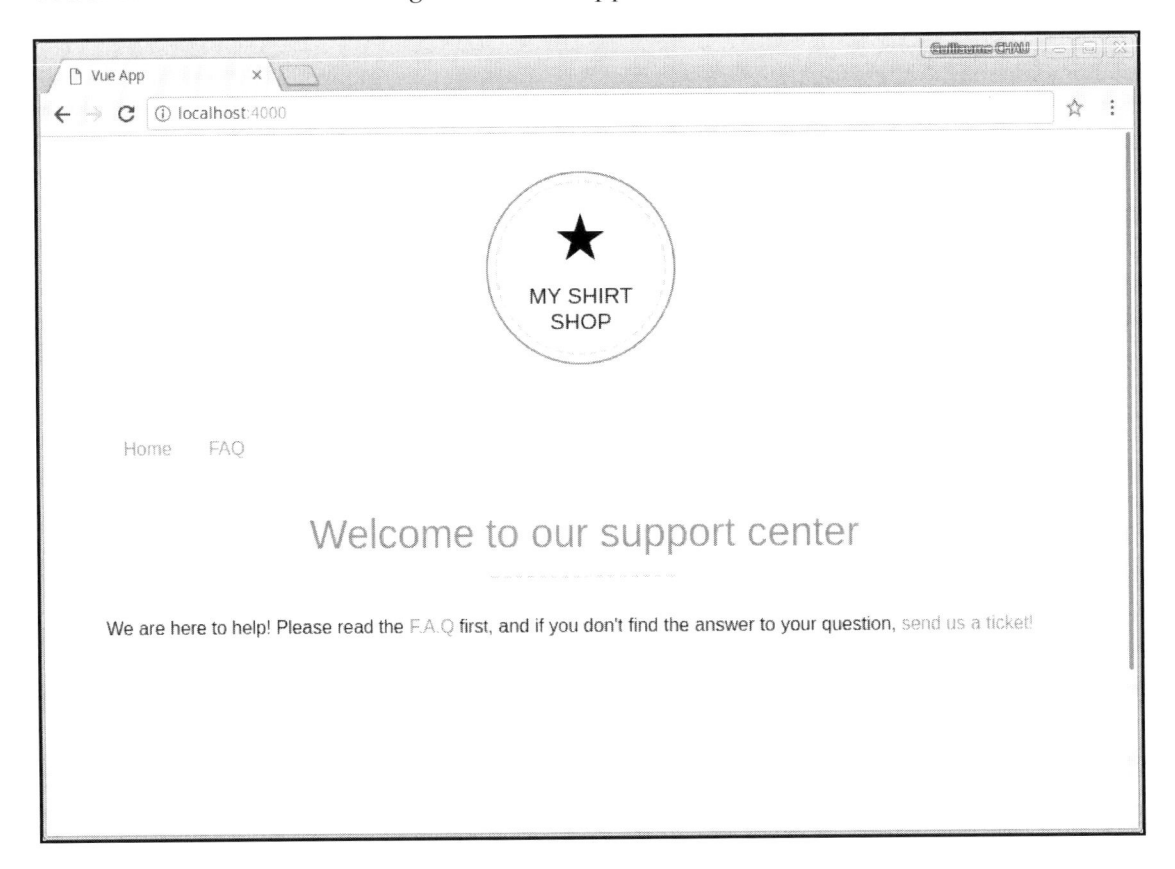

Active class

A router link gets the active class when the route it is associated with is currently active. By default, the component gets the `router-link-active` CSS class, so you can change its visuals accordingly:

1. In our `NavMenu.vue` component, declare some scoped style to add a bottom border to the active link using Stylus:

   ```
   <style lang="stylus" scoped>
   @import '../style/imports';

   .router-link-active {
     border-bottom-color: $primary-color;
   }
   </style>
   ```

   > We include the `$primary-color` variable with the `@import '../style/imports';` statement, which imports the `imports.styl` file containing the Stylus variables.

   If you try the app now, you will find that something weird is happening with our menu. If you go to the **Home** page, it is working as expected:

   But when you go to the **FAQ** page, both the **Home** and the **FAQ** links are highlighted:

This is because by default, the active class matching behavior is inclusive! This means `<router-link to="/faq">` will get the active class if the path is `/faq` or starts with `/faq/`. But it also means `<router-link to="/">` will get the class if the current path starts with `/`, which are all possible paths! That's why our Home link will always get the class.

To prevent this from happening, there is the `exact` prop, which is a Boolean. If it is set to `true`, the link will only get the active class if the current path is matching exactly.

2. Add the `exact` prop to the **Home** link:

   ```
   <router-link :to="{ name: 'home' }" exact>Home</router-link>
   ```

   Now, only the **FAQ** link should be highlighted:

FAQ - Consuming an API

In this section, we will create the FAQ page, which will get data from the server. It will display a loading animation and then the list of questions and answers.

Server setup

This is our first app that will communicate with a server. You will get a server with a ready-to-use API.

You can download the server files (https://github.com/Akryum/packt-vue-project-guide/tree/master/chapter5-download). Extract them into another folder than our app and run the following commands to install the dependencies and launch the server:

```
cd server_folder
npm install
npm start
```

You should now have the server running on port 3000. When this is done, we can continue building our app with a real backend this time!

Using fetch

In the `FAQ.vue` Single File Component, we will use the standard `fetch` API of the web browser to retrieve the questions from our server. The request will be a very simple `GET` request to `http://localhost:3000/questions` with no authentication. Each question object will have `title` and `content` fields:

1. Open `FAQ.vue` and start by adding the `questions` data property in the component script, which will hold the array of questions retrieved from the server. We also need an `error` property to display a message when something goes wrong during the network request:

   ```
   <script>
   export default {
     data () {
       return {
         questions: [],
         error: null,
       }
     },
   }
   </script>
   ```

2. Now we can add the questions and answers to the template with a `v-for` loop, and the following error message:

   ```
   <template>
     <main class="faq">
       <h1>Frequently Asked Questions</h1>

       <div class="error" v-if="error">
         Can't load the questions
       </div>

       <section class="list">
         <article v-for="question of questions">
           <h2 v-html="question.title"></h2>
           <p v-html="question.content"></p>
   ```

Project 3 - Support Center

```
        </article>
      </section>
  </main>
</template>
```

We are ready to fetch! The fetch API is promised-based and quite simple to use. Here is an example of `fetch` usage:

```
fetch(url).then(response => {
  if (response.ok) {
    // Returns a new promise
    return response.json()
  } else {
    return Promise.reject('error')
  }
}).then(result => {
  // Success
  console.log('JSON:', result)
}).catch(e => {
  // Failure
  console.error(e)
})
```

We first call `fetch` with the first parameter being the URL of the request. It returns a promise with a `response` object, which holds information about the request result. If it was successful, we use `response.json()`, which returns a new promise with the JSON parsed result object.

The request will be made inside the component as soon as it is created when the route is matched, which means that you should use the `created` life cycle hook in the component definition:

```
data () {
  // ...
},
created () {
  // fetch here
},
```

If everything goes well, we will set the questions property with the JSON parsed result. Or else we will display an error message.

3. Start by calling `fetch` with the right URL:

   ```
   created () {
     fetch('http://localhost:3000/questions')
   },
   ```

4. Add the first `then` callback with the `response` object:

   ```
   fetch('http://localhost:3000/questions').then(response => {
     if (response.ok) {
       return response.json()
     } else {
       return Promise.reject('error')
     }
   })
   ```

5. We need another `then` callback since `response.json()` returns a new promise:

   ```
   // ...
   }).then(result => {
     // Result is the JSON parsed object from the server
     this.questions = result
   })
   ```

6. Finally, we catch all possible errors to display the error message:

   ```
   // ...
   }).catch(e => {
     this.error = e
   })
   ```

   Here is a summary of our `created` hook:

   ```
   created () {
     fetch('http://localhost:3000/questions').then(response => {
       if (response.ok) {
         return response.json()
       } else {
         return Promise.reject('error')
       }
     }).then(result => {
       this.questions = result
     }).catch(e => {
       this.error = e
     })
   },
   ```

We can rewrite this code using the `async` and `await` JavaScript keywords to make it look like sequential code:

```
async created () {
  try {
    const response = await fetch('http://localhost:3000/questions')
    if (response.ok) {
      this.questions = await response.json()
    } else {
      throw new Error('error')
    }
  } catch (e) {
    this.error = e
  }
},
```

You can now try the page, which should display a list of questions and answers:

Frequently Asked Questions

Why won't my discount code work?

Inventore iste reprehenderit aut reiciendis repellendus. Quas cumque aliquam accusantium et itaque quisquam voluptatem. Commodi quo quia occaecati dicta ratione qui at tempore. At saepe est et saepe accusamus voluptates.

How do i return an item?

Voluptate cupiditate officia quia accusantium. Fugiat ut praesentium quia ut et labore reiciendis fugit. Voluptas eos maiores itaque aut. Sequi harum dolor neque sunt rerum iste ducimus. Quas sapiente cumque voluptatem repudiandae ipsum. Natus quis aut aut fugiat. Nisi non sed reprehenderit mollitia commodi et qui error. Velit autem omnis et repellendus facere libero praesentium. Sit aut possimus eligendi consectetur beatae. Iste et officia delectus modi ratione inventore enim voluptatem.

To see if our error management is working, you can go to the console where the server is running, and stop it (for example, with the *Ctrl+C* keyboard shortcut). Then, you can reload the app and the following error message should be displayed:

> **Frequently Asked Questions**
>
> ❗ Can't load the questions

Loading animation

There is one last thing missing--we should show a loading animation to inform the user that an operation is in progress instead of an empty screen. To this effect, the server is faking a 1.5 s delay on the `/questions` request so we can easily see the loading animation.

Since we are going to display loading animations inside multiple components, we are going to create a new global component:

1. In the `components` folder, create a new `Loading.vue` file with the following template:

   ```
   <template>
     <div class="loading">
       <div></div>
     </div>
   </template>
   ```

2. Create a new `global-components.js` file next to the `main.js` file in the `main` folder. In this file, we are going to register the `Loading` component globally with the `Vue.component()` method:

   ```
   import Vue from 'vue'
   import Loading from './components/Loading.vue'

   Vue.component('Loading', Loading)
   ```

Project 3 - Support Center

> This is the file where we will register all the global components used across all the application.

3. Then, in the `main.js` file, import the `global-components.js` module:

   ```
   import './global-components'
   ```

4. Back to our `FAQ.vue` component, we need a new `loading` Boolean data property to toggle the display of the animation:

   ```
   data () {
     return {
       questions: [],
       error: null,
       loading: false,
     }
   },
   ```

5. In the template, add the loading animation:

   ```
   <Loading v-if="loading" />
   ```

6. Finally, change the `created` hook a bit by setting `loading` to `true` at the beginning, and `false` when everything is done:

   ```
   async created () {
     this.loading = true
     try {
       const response = await
    fetch('http://localhost:3000/questions')
       // ...
     } catch (e) {
       this.error = e
     }
     this.loading = false
   }
   ```

[168]

You can now reload the page and briefly see the loading animation before the questions appear:

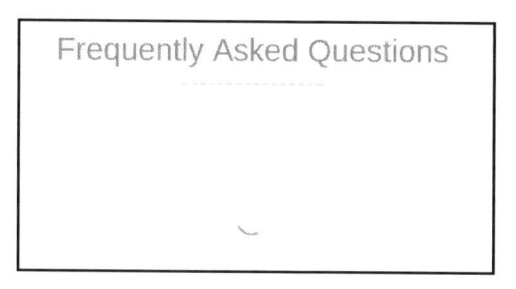

Frequently Asked Questions

Extending Vue with our own plugin

Since we will use fetch in multiple components for our application and we want to reuse code as much as possible, it would be nice to have a method on all of our components that makes a request to the server with a predefined URL.

This a nice use case for a custom Vue plugin! Don't worry, writing a plugin is actually pretty simple.

Creating a plugin

To create a plugin, there is only one rule--a plugin should be an object with an `install` method, which takes the Vue constructor as the first argument, and an optional `options` argument. This method will then add new features to the framework by modifying the constructor:

1. Create a new `plugins` folder in the `src` folder.
2. Inside the `plugins` folder, create a `fetch.js` file where we will write our plugin. In this case, our plugin will add a new `$fetch` special method on all of our components. We will do that by changing the prototype of Vue.
3. Let's try creating a very simple plugin, by exporting an object with an `install` method:

   ```
   export default {
     install (Vue) {
       console.log('Installed!')
     }
   }
   ```

Project 3 - Support Center

That's it! We have created a Vue plugin! Now, we need to install it into our application.

4. In the `main.js` file, import the plugin and then call the `Vue.use()` method just like we did for `vue-router`:

```
import VueFetch from './plugins/fetch'
Vue.use(VueFetch)
```

You should now see the `'Installed!'` message in your browser console.

Plugin options

We can configure the plugin with an `options` parameter:

1. Edit the `install` method to add this parameter after `Vue`:

```
export default {
  install (Vue, options) {
    console.log('Installed!', options)
  },
}
```

We can now add a configuration object to the `Vue.use()` method in the `main.js` file.

2. Let's add a `baseUrl` property to the configuration:

```
Vue.use(VueFetch, {
  baseUrl: 'http://localhost:3000/',
})
```

You should now see the `options` object in the browser console.

3. Store `baseUrl` into a variable so we can use it later:

```
let baseUrl

export default {
  install (Vue, options) {
    console.log('Installed!', options)

    baseUrl = options.baseUrl
  },
}
```

[170]

Fetch method

Now, we are going to write the `$fetch` method. We will take most of the code we used in the `created` hook of the FAQ component:

1. Implement the `$fetch` method using `fetch`:

    ```
    export async function $fetch (url) {
      const response = await fetch(`${baseUrl}${url}`)
      if (response.ok) {
        const data = await response.json()
        return data
      } else {
        const error = new Error('error')
        throw error
      }
    }
    ```

    We export it so we can use it in our plain JavaScript code too. The `url` parameter is now just the path of the query without the domain, which is now in our `baseUrl` variable--this allows us to change it easily without having to refactor each component. We also take care of the JSON parsing, since all the data from the server will be encoded in JSON.

2. To make it available in all components, simply add it to the prototype of Vue (which is the constructor used to create components):

    ```
    export default {
      install (Vue, options) {
        // Plugin options
        baseUrl = options.baseUrl

        Vue.prototype.$fetch = $fetch
      },
    }
    ```

3. Then, refactor the FAQ component to use our new special `$fetch` method in the `created` hook:

    ```
    this.loading = true
    try {
      this.questions = await this.$fetch('questions')
    } catch (e) {
      this.error = e
    }
    this.loading = false
    ```

Project 3 - Support Center

Our code in the component is now shorter, easier to read, and more scalable since we can change the base URL easily.

Reusing code with mixins

We have seen how to create plugins, but there is another way to improve our code--what if we could reuse component definitions such as computed properties, methods, or watchers across multiple components? This is what mixins are for!

A mixin is a component definition object that can be applied to other definition objects (including other mixins). It is very simple to write, because it looks exactly the same as a regular component definition!

Our objective here is to have a RemoteData mixin that will allow any component to make requests to the server in order to fetch data. Let's add a new mixins folder in the src directory, and create a new RemoteData.js file:

1. We will start simple by exporting a definition with a data property:

    ```
    export default {
      data () {
        return {
          remoteDataLoading: 0,
        }
      },
    }
    ```

    > This remoteDataLoading property will be used to count the number of requests that are currently loading, to help us display a loading animation.

2. Now, to use this mixin in our FAQ component, we need to import it and add it in the mixins array:

    ```
    <script>
    import RemoteData from '../mixins/RemoteData'

    export default {
      mixins: [
        RemoteData,
      ],
    ```

```
    // ...
  }
</script>
```

If you inspect the component, you should now see an additional `remoteDataLoading` property displayed:

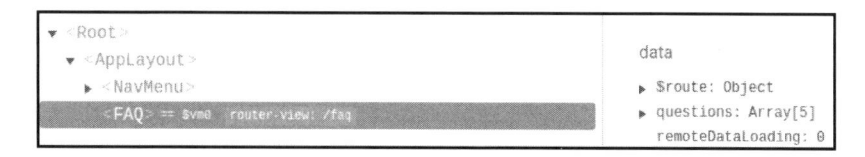

```
▼ <Root>                                    data
  ▼ <AppLayout>                               ▶ $route: Object
    ▶ <NavMenu>                               ▶ questions: Array[5]
      <FAQ> == $vm0  router-view: /faq          remoteDataLoading: 0
```

So what happened? The mixin got applied and merged into the component definition of `FAQ.vue`, which means that the data hook was called twice--first from the mixin, then from the FAQ definition and a new property was added!

> **TIP**: Vue will automatically merge the standard options such as hooks, data, computed, methods, and watch, but if you have, for example, a property of a method with the same name, the last one applied will override the previous ones.

3. Let's try overriding the new property in our component with another value:

```
data () {
  return {
    questions: [],
    error: null,
    loading: false,
    remoteDataLoading: 42,
  }
},
```

As you can see in the component inspector, the final component definition has a higher priority than the mixin. Also, you may have noticed that the `mixins` option is an array, thus we can apply multiple mixins to the definition, which will be merged in order. For example, consider we have two mixins and want to apply them to a component definition. Here is what will happen:

   1. The definition object contains the options of mixin 1.
   2. The options of mixin 2 are merged into the definition object (existing property/method names are overriden).
   3. In the same way, the options of the component are merged into the final definition object.

You can now remove the duplicate `remoteDataLoading: 42,` from the FAQ component definition.

> **TIP**: Hooks such as `data`, `created`, `mounted`... are each called individually in the order they were applied to the final definition. This also means that the final component definition hooks will be called last.

Fetching remote data

We have a problem--each component using our `RemoteData` mixin will have different data properties to fetch. Therefore, we need to pass parameters to our mixin. Since a mixin is essentially a definition object, why not use a function that can take parameters and then return a definition object? That's what we will do in our case!

1. Wrap the object we have defined inside a function with a `resources` parameter:

   ```
   export default function (resources) {
     return {
       data () {
         return {
           remoteDataLoading: 0,
         }
       },
     }
   }
   ```

   The `resources` parameter will be an object with each key being the name of the data property we want to add, and the value being the path of the request that needs to be made to the server.

2. So we need to change the way we use the mixin in our `FAQ.vue` component to a function call:

   ```
   mixins: [
     RemoteData({
       questionList: 'questions',
     }),
   ],
   ```

   Here, we are going to fetch the `http://localhost:3000/questions` URL (with the special `$fetch` method we created earlier) and put the result in the `questionList` property.

Now onto our `RemoteData` mixin!

3. First things first, we need to initialize each data property to a `null` value, so Vue can set up reactivity on them:

```
data () {
  let initData = {
    remoteDataLoading: 0,
  }

  // Initialize data properties
  for (const key in resources) {
    initData[key] = null
  }

  return initData
},
```

> **TIP**
> This step is important--if you don't initialize the data, it won't be made reactive by Vue, so the component will not be updated when the properties change.

You can try the app and see in the component inspector that a new `questionList` data property has been added to the FAQ component:

```
data
  ▶ $route: Object
  ▶ questionList: Array[5]
```

4. Then, we will create a new `fetchResource` method that fetches one resource and update the corresponding data property:

```
methods: {
  async fetchResource (key, url) {
    try {
      this.$data[key] = await this.$fetch(url)
    } catch (e) {
      console.error(e)
    }
  },
},
```

[175]

Our component now has access to this new method and can use it directly.

5. To make our mixin smarter, we will automatically call it inside the `created` hook (which will be merged):

```
created () {
  for (const key in resources) {
    let url = resources[key]
    this.fetchResource(key, url)
  }
},
```

You can now verify that the `questionList` data property gets updated with a new request made to the server:

```
▼ questionList: Array[5]
  ▶ 0: Object
  ▶ 1: Object
  ▶ 2: Object
  ▶ 3: Object
  ▶ 4: Object
```

6. Then, you can remove the old code with the `questions` property in the `FAQ.vue` component and change the template to use the new property:

```
<article v-for="question of questionList">
```

Loading management

The next thing we want to do is provide a way to know if the loading animation should be displayed. Since we could potentially have multiple requests, we are going to use a numeric counter instead of a Boolean--`remoteDataLoading` that we already declared in the `data` hook. Each time a request is made, we increment the counter, and when it is complete we decrement the counter. This means if it is equal to zero no request is currently pending, and if it is greater or equal to one we should display a loading animation:

1. Add the two statements incrementing and decrementing the `remoteDataLoading` counter in the `fetchResource` method:

```
async fetchResource (key, url) {
  this.$data.remoteDataLoading++
  try {
```

```
      this.$data[key] = await this.$fetch(url)
    } catch (e) {
      console.error(e)
    }
    this.$data.remoteDataLoading--
  },
```

2. To make our life easier when using the mixin, let's add a computed property called remoteDataBusy that will be true when we need to display the loading animation:

```
computed: {
  remoteDataBusy () {
    return this.$data.remoteDataLoading !== 0
  },
},
```

3. Back to our FAQ component, we can now remove the loading property, change the v-if expression for the Loading component, and use the remoteDataLoading computed property:

```
<Loading v-if="remoteDataBusy" />
```

You can try refreshing the page to see the loading animation displayed before the data is retrieved.

Error management

Finally, we could manage the errors that could occur for any resource request:

1. We will store the errors for each resource in a new remoteErrors object, which needs to be initialized:

```
// Initialize data properties
initData.remoteErrors = {}
for (const key in resources) {
  initData[key] = null
  initData.remoteErrors[key] = null
}
```

The key of the remoteErrors object will be the same as the resource, and the value will be the error or null if there is no error.

Next, we need to modify the `fetchResource` method:

- Before the request, reset the error by setting it to `null`
- If there is an error in the catch block, put it into the `remoteErrors` object at the right key

2. The `fetchResource` method should now look as follows:

```
async fetchResource (key, url) {
  this.$data.remoteDataLoading++
  // Reset error
  this.$data.remoteErrors[key] = null
  try {
    this.$data[key] = await this.$fetch(url)
  } catch (e) {
    console.error(e)
    // Put error
    this.$data.remoteErrors[key] = e
  }
  this.$data.remoteDataLoading--
},
```

We could now display specific error messages for each resource, but we will simply display a generic error message in this project. Let's add another computed property called `hasRemoteErrors`, which will return true if there is at least one error.

3. Using the JavaScript `Object.keys()` method, we can iterate on the keys of the `remoteErrors` object and check if some values are not `null` (which means that they are truthy):

```
computed: {
  // ...

  hasRemoteErrors () {
    return Object.keys(this.$data.remoteErrors).some(
      key => this.$data.remoteErrors[key]
    )
  },
},
```

[178]

4. We can now change the FAQ component template again by replacing the `error` property with the new one:

   ```
   <div class="error" v-if="hasRemoteErrors">
   ```

   Like we did before, you can shut down the server to see the error message displayed.

   We have now finished the FAQ component, whose script should now look as follows:

   ```
   <script>
   import RemoteData from '../mixins/RemoteData'

   export default {
     mixins: [
       RemoteData({
         questionList: 'questions',
       }),
     ],
   }
   </script>
   ```

As you can see, it is very concise now!

Support tickets

In this last part, we will create an authenticated section of our app, where the user will be able to add and view support tickets. All the necessary requests are available on the server you already downloaded and if you are curious about how this has been done in the node with `passport.js`, you can take a look at the sources!

User authentication

In this first section, we will take care of the user system of our app. We will have both login and sign up components, to be able to create new users.

Storing the user in a centralized state

We will store the user data inside a state object like we did in Chapter 3, *Project 2 - Castle Duel Browser Game*, so we can access it in any component of the app:

1. Create a new `state.js` file next to `main.js`, which exports the state object:

   ```
   export default {
     user: null,
   }
   ```

   The `user` property will be null when no user is logged in, or else it will contain the user data.

2. Then, in the `main.js` file, import the state:

   ```
   import state from './state'
   ```

3. Then, use it as the data of the root instance so Vue makes it reactive:

   ```
   new Vue({
     el: '#app',
     data: state,
     router,
     render: h => h(AppLayout),
   })
   ```

Another plugin

We could then import the state in component files when we need it, but it would be more convenient to be able to access it with a special getter called `$state` on the Vue prototype like we did for the `fetch` plugin. We will pass the state object to the plugin options, and the getter will return it.

1. In the `plugins` folder, create a `state.js` file that exports the new plugin:

   ```
   export default {
     install (Vue, state) {
       Object.defineProperty(Vue.prototype, '$state', {
         get: () => state,
       })
     }
   }
   ```

Here we are using the JavaScript `Object.defineProperty()` method to set up a getter on the Vue prototype, so every component will inherit it!

One last thing--we need to install the state plugin!

2. In the `main.js` file, import the new plugin:

   ```
   import VueState from './plugins/state'
   ```

3. Then install it with the state object as the options parameter:

   Vue.use(VueState, state)

   We can now use `$state` in our components to access the global state! Here is an example:

   ```
   console.log(this.$state)
   ```

This should output the state object with the `user` property.

Login forms

In this section, we will first create new components to help us build forms faster, and then we will add the sign up and the login forms to the application with a `Login.vue` component. In later sections, we will create another form to submit new support tickets.

Smart form

This generic component will take care of the very general structure of our form components, and will automatically call an `operation` function, display a loading animation and the eventual error messages thrown by the operation. Most of the time, the operation will be a `POST` request made to the server.

The template is essentially a form with a title, a default slot where the inputs will be rendered, an `actions` slot for the buttons, a loading animation, and a place for the error messages. This will be generic enough for the two forms we need in the application:

1. Create a new `SmartForm.vue` component in the `components` folder:

   ```
   <template>
     <form @submit.prevent="submit">
       <section class="content">
         <h2>{{ title }}</h2>
   ```

Project 3 - Support Center

```
      <!-- Main content -->
      <slot />
      <div class="actions">
        <!-- Action buttons -->
        <slot name="actions" />
      </div>

      <div class="error" v-if="error">{{ error }}</div>
    </section>

    <transition name="fade">
      <!-- Expanding over the form -->
      <Loading v-if="busy" class="overlay" />
    </transition>
  </form>
</template>
```

> **TIP:** On the `<form>` element, we set up an event listener on the `'submit'` event, which prevents the default behavior of the browser (reloading the page) with the `prevent` modifier.

For now, the `SmartForm` component will have three props:

- `title`: This is displayed in the `<h2>` element.
- `operation`: The asynchronous function called when the form is submitted. It should return a promise.
- `valid`: A Boolean to prevent calling the operation if the form is not valid.

2. Add them to the `script` part of the component:

```
<script>
export default {
  props: {
    title: {
      type: String,
      required: true,
    },
    operation: {
      type: Function,
      required: true,
    },
    valid: {
      type: Boolean,
      required: true,
    },
```

```
    },
  }
</script>
```

As you can see, we are now using a different way of declaring the props--by using an object, we can specify more details of the prop. For example, with `required: true`, Vue will warn us if we forget a prop. We can also put a type that Vue will check too. This syntax is recommended since it helps both understanding the props of the component and avoiding errors.

We also need two data properties:

- `busy`: A Boolean to toggle the display of the loading animation
- `error`: This is the error message or `null` if there aren't any

3. Add them with the `data` hook:

```
data () {
  return {
    error: null,
    busy: false,
  }
},
```

4. Finally, we need to write the `submit` method called when the form is submitted:

```
methods: {
  async submit () {
    if (this.valid && !this.busy) {
      this.error = null
      this.busy = true
      try {
        await this.operation()
      } catch (e) {
        this.error = e.message
      }
      this.busy = false
    }
  },
},
```

If the form isn't valid or is still busy, we don't call the operation. Or else we reset the `error` property and then call the `operation` prop, with the `await` keyword since it should be an asynchronous function that returns a promise. If we catch an error, we set the message to the `error` property so it is displayed.

5. Now that our generic form is ready, we can register it in the `global-components.js` file:

```
import SmartForm from './components/SmartForm.vue'
Vue.component('SmartForm', SmartForm)
```

Form input component

In our forms, we will have many inputs with the same markup and functionalities. This is the perfect occasion to make another generic and reusable component. It will have a small template with mainly an `<input>` element and will be able to show the user that it is invalid with a red border:

1. Start by creating a new `FormInput.vue` component with the following props:
    - `name` is the HTML name of the input, needed for the browser autocompletion to work.
    - `type` will be `'text'` by default, but we will need to set `'password'` eventually.
    - `value` is the current value of the input.
    - `placeholder` is the label displayed inside the input.
    - `invalid` is a Boolean to toggle the invalid display (the red border). It will default to `false`.

    The script should look like this with the prop object notation:

```
<script>
export default {
  props: {
    name: {
      type: String,
    },
    type: {
      type: String,
      default: 'text',
    },
    value: {
      required: true,
    },
    placeholder: {
      type: String,
    },
    invalid: {
      type: Boolean,
```

```
      default: false,
    },
  },
}
</script>
```

2. For the invalid display, we will add a computed property to dynamically change the CSS classes of the input:

```
computed: {
  inputClass () {
    return {
      'invalid': this.invalid,
    }
  },
},
```

3. Now we can write our template. It will have a `<div>` element containing the `<input>`:

```
<template>
  <div class="row">
    <input
      class="input"
      :class="inputClass"
      :name="name"
      :type="type"
      :value.prop="value"
      :placeholder="placeholder"
    />
  </div>
</template>
```

> **TIP**
> We use the `prop` modifier on the `v-bind:value` directive to tell Vue to set the DOM node `value` property directly instead of setting the HTML attribute. This is a good practise when dealing with properties such as `value` for input HTML elements.

4. To begin testing it, we can register the component in the `global-components.js` file:

```
import FormInput from './components/FormInput.vue'
Vue.component('FormInput', FormInput)
```

Project 3 - Support Center

5. Create a new `Login.vue` component using the `FormInput` component:

```
<template>
  <main class="login">
    <h1>Please login to continue</h1>
    <form>
      <FormInput
        name="username"
        :value="username"
        placeholder="Username" />
    </form>
  </main>
</template>

<script>
export default {
  data () {
    return {
      username: '',
    }
  },
}
</script>
```

6. Don't forget the corresponding route in the `router.js` file:

```
import Login from './components/Login.vue'

const routes [
  // ...
  { path: '/login', name: 'login', component: Login },
]
```

You can test the component by opening the app with the `/login` path in the URL:

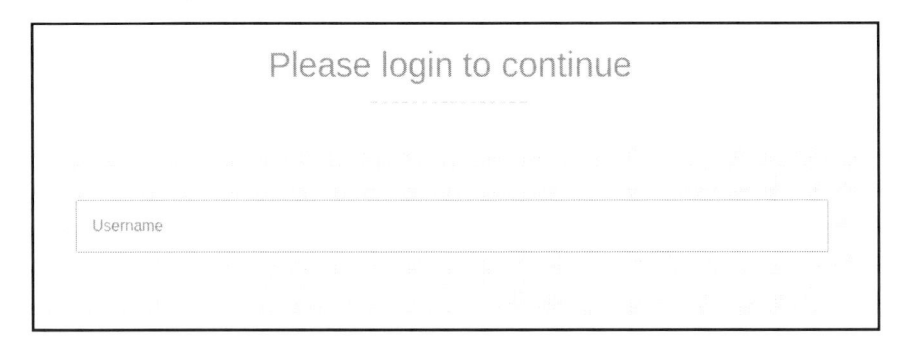

Please login to continue

Username

For now, the `FormInput` component is read-only because we don't do any thing when the user types something into the field.

7. Let's add a method to take care of that:

```
methods: {
  update (event) {
    console.log(event.currentTarget.value)
  },
},
```

8. Then we can listen to the `input` event on the text field:

```
@input="update"
```

Now if you type into the text field, the content should be printed to the console.

9. In the `update` method, we are going to emit an event to send the new value to the parent component. By default, the `v-model` directive listens to the `input` event, with the new value being the first parameter:

```
methods: {
  update (event) {
    this.$emit('input', event.currentTarget.value)
  },
},
```

To understand how things work, we are not going to use `v-model` yet.

10. We can now listen to this `input` event and update the `username` prop:

```
<FormInput
  name="username"
  :value="username"
  @input="val => username = val"
  placeholder="Username" />
```

Project 3 - Support Center

The value of the `username` prop should be updated on the `Login` component:

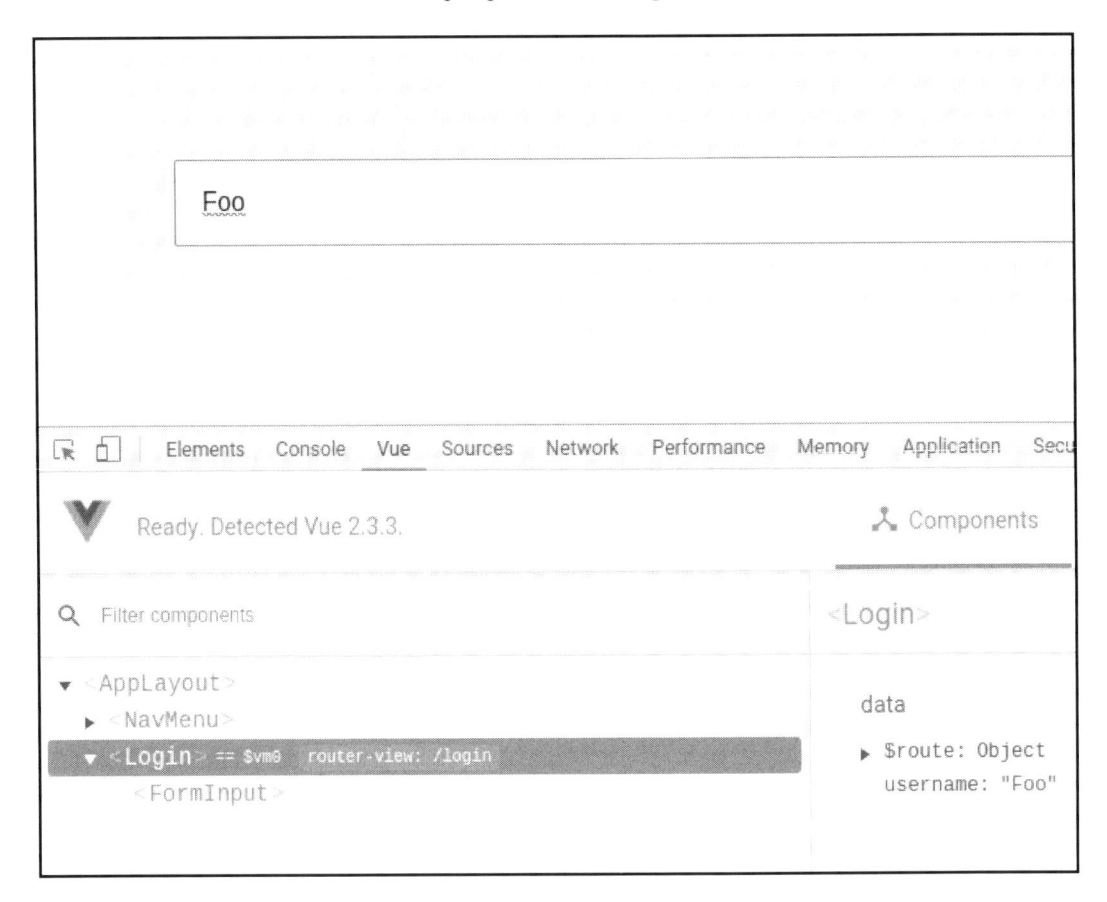

11. Using the `v-model` directive, we can simplify this code:

    ```
    <FormInput
      name="username"
      v-model="username"
      placeholder="Username" />
    ```

    It will use the `value` prop and listen to the `input` event for us!

Customizing v-model

By default, `v-model` uses the `value` prop and the `input` event as we just saw, but we can customize that:

1. Inside the `FormInput` component, add the `model` option:

   ```
   model: {
    prop: 'text',
    event: 'update',
   },
   ```

2. We then need to change the name of our `value` prop to `text`:

   ```
   props: {
     // ...
     text: {
        required: true,
     },
   },
   ```

3. And in the template:

   ```
   <input
    ...
    :value="text"
    ... />
   ```

4. Plus the `input` event should be renamed to `update`:

   ```
   this.$emit('update', event.currentTarget.value)
   ```

   The component should still work in the `Login` component, since we told `v-model` to use the `text` prop and `update` event!

Our input component is now ready! For this project, we have kept this component simple, but you can add more features into it if you want to, such as icons, error messages, floating label, and so on.

Login component

We can now continue building the `Login` component, which will take care of signing in and signing up the user.

Project 3 - Support Center

There are several data properties we need for the state of this component:

- `mode`: This can either be `'login'` or `'signup'`. We will change the layout a bit depending on this.
- `username`: Used in both modes.
- `password`: Also used in both modes.
- `password2`: Used to verify the password when signing up.
- `email`: Used in sign up mode.

1. Our `data` hook should now look like this:

```
data () {
  return {
    mode: 'login',
    username: '',
    password: '',
    password2: '',
    email: '',
  }
},
```

2. We can then add a `title` computed property to change the form title depending on the mode:

```
computed: {
  title () {
    switch (this.mode) {
      case 'login': return 'Login'
      case 'signup': return 'Create a new account'
    }
  },
},
```

We will also add some basic input validation. First, we would like to highlight the retype `password` field when it's not equal to the first password.

3. Let's add another computed property for that:

```
retypePasswordError () {
  return this.password2 && this.password !== this.password2
},
```

Then, we will also check that no field is empty since they are all mandatory.

4. This time, we will break it up into two computed properties, since we don't want to check the sign up specific fields when in `login` mode:

   ```
   signupValid () {
     return this.password2 && this.email &&
     !this.retypePasswordError
   },
   valid () {
     return this.username && this.password &&
     (this.mode !== 'signup' || this.signupValid)
   },
   ```

5. Next, add the methods we will use to either `login` or `sign up` the user (we will implement them later in the *Sign up operation* and *Login operation* sections):

   ```
   methods: {
     async operation () {
       await this[this.mode]()
     },
     async login () {
       // TODO
     },
     async signup () {
       // TODO
     },
   }
   ```

6. We can now move onto the template. Start by adding a `SmartForm` component:

   ```
   <template>
     <main class="login">
       <h1>Please login to continue</h1>
       <SmartForm
         class="form"
         :title="title"
         :operation="operation"
         :valid="valid">
         <!-- TODO -->
       </SmartForm>
     </main>
   </template>
   ```

[191]

Project 3 - Support Center

7. Then we can add the `input` fields:

```
<FormInput
  name="username"
  v-model="username"
  placeholder="Username" />
<FormInput
  name="password"
  type="password"
  v-model="password"
  placeholder="Password" />
<template v-if="mode === 'signup'">
  <FormInput
    name="verify-password"
    type="password"
    v-model="password2"
    placeholder="Retype Password"
    :invalid="retypePasswordError" />
  <FormInput
    name="email"
    type="email"
    v-model="email"
    placeholder="Email" />
</template>
```

> **TIP**: Don't forget the name attributes--it will allow the browser to auto-complete the fields.

8. Below the `input` fields, we need two different buttons for each mode. For the login mode, we need a `sign up` and `login` button. For the `sign up` mode, we need a **Back** button and a **Create account** button:

```
<template slot="actions">
  <template v-if="mode === 'login'">
    <button
      type="button"
      class="secondary"
      @click="mode = 'signup'">
      Sign up
    </button>
    <button
      type="submit"
      :disabled="!valid">
      Login
```

[192]

```
        </button>
      </template>
      <template v-else-if="mode === 'signup'">
        <button
          type="button"
          class="secondary"
          @click="mode = 'login'">
          Back to login
        </button>
        <button
          type="submit"
          :disabled="!valid">
          Create account
        </button>
      </template>
    </template>
```

Now you can test the component and switch between the `login` and `sign up` modes:

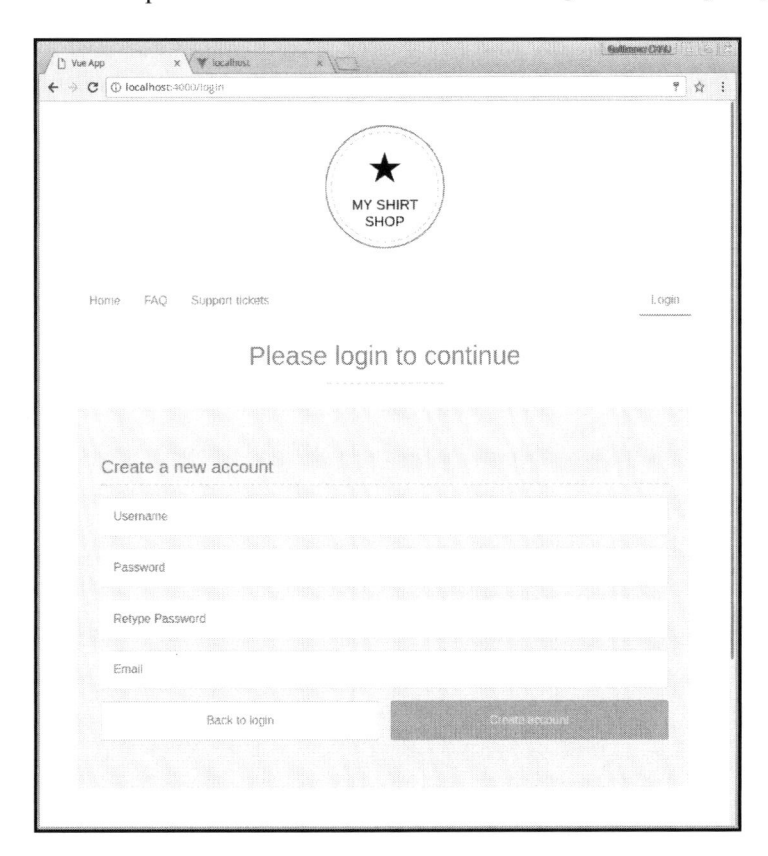

Style children of scoped elements

The form is currently taking all the space available. It would be better to shrink it a bit.

> **TIP**: For this section to work, you need the latest `vue-loader` package installed in your project.

Let's add some style to put a maximum width to the form:

```
<style lang="stylus" scoped>
.form {
  >>> .content {
    max-width: 400px;
  }
}
</style>
```

The `>>>` combinator allows us to target elements inside the components used in the template, while still scoping the rest of the CSS selector. In our example, the generated CSS will look as follows:

```
.form[data-v-0e596401] .content {
  max-width: 400px;
}
```

If we didn't use this combinator, we would have this CSS:

```
.form .content[data-v-0e596401] {
  max-width: 400px;
}
```

This wouldn't work since the `.content` element is inside the `SmartForm` component we are using in the template.

> **TIP**: If you are using SASS, you need to use the `/deep/` selector instead of the `>>>` combinator.

[194]

The form should look like this now:

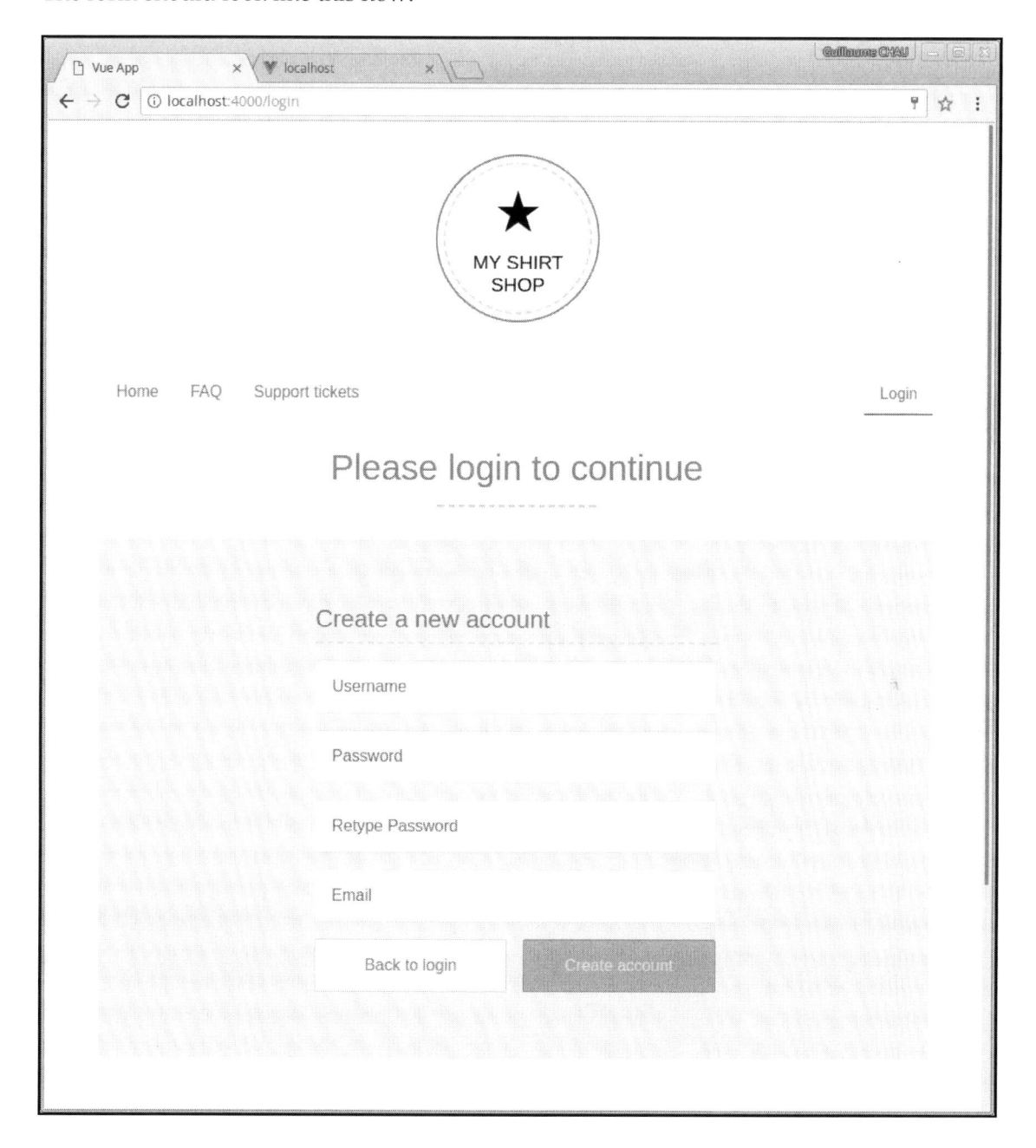

Improving our fetch plugin

Currently, our `$fetch` method can only make `GET` requests to the server. It was enough for loading the FAQ, but now we need to add more features to it:

1. In the `plugins/fetch.js` file, edit the signature of the function to accept a new `options` parameter:

   ```
   export async function $fetch (url, options) {
     // ...
   }
   ```

   The `options` argument is an optional object for the browser's `fetch` method that will allow us to change different parameters, such as the HTTP method used, the request body, and more.

2. At the beginning of the `$fetch` function, we would like to put some default values for this `options` parameter:

   ```
   const finalOptions = Object.assign({}, {
     headers: {
       'Content-Type': 'application/json',
     },
     credentials: 'include',
   }, options)
   ```

   The default options tell the server we will always send JSON in the request body, and tell the browser that we will also include the authorization token necessary to authenticate the user if they are logged in. Then, the provided `options` argument, if any, add its value to the `finalOptions` object (for example, the `method` property or the `body` property).

3. Next, we add the new options to the `fetch` browser method:

   ```
   const response = await fetch(`${baseUrl}${url}`, finalOptions)
   ```

4. Also, the server will always send errors as text, so we can catch them and display them to the user:

```
if (response.ok) {
  const data = await response.json()
  return data
} else {
  const message = await response.text()
  const error = new Error(message)
  error.response = response
  throw error
}
```

We are now ready to make our first POST request to the server in order to create for the user a new account and then log him in!

Sign up operation

We will start with the account creation, since we don't have any user yet. The path to call on the server is /signup, and it expects a POST request with a JSON object in the request body containing the username, password, and email of the new account:

Let's implement this using the $fetch method we just improved:

```
async signup () {
  await this.$fetch('signup', {
    method: 'POST',
    body: JSON.stringify({
      username: this.username,
      password: this.password,
      email: this.email,
    }),
  })
  this.mode = 'login'
},
```

> **TIP**
> We don't manage errors here, as it's the job of the SmartForm component we built earlier.

Project 3 - Support Center

That's it! You can now create a new account with a simple `password` you will have to remember for later. If the account creation succeeds, the form goes back to `login` mode.

> **TIP**: One thing we don't do here, but that could be improved, is to let the user know their account has been created and that they can now log in. You could add a message below the form, or even make a floating notification appear!

Login operation

The login method will be almost identical to the sign up. The differences are:

- We only send the `username` and `password` in the request body, to the `/login` path
- The response is the user object we need to set into the global state so every component can know if there is a connected user (using the plugin we made exposing the `$state` property)
- Then we redirect to the home page

It should look like this now:

```
async login () {
  this.$state.user = await this.$fetch('login', {
    method: 'POST',
    body: JSON.stringify({
      username: this.username,
      password: this.password,
    }),
  })
  this.$router.push({ name: 'home' })
},
```

You can now try to log in with the `username` and the `password` you used to create the account earlier. If the login is successful, you should be redirected to the home page thanks to the `router.push()` method.

The `user` object returned by this request contains the `username` field that will be displayed in the navigation menu.

User menu

Now it is time to add the user-related features to the navigation menu we made at the beginning in the `NavMenu.vue` file:

1. We want them to appear to the far right side of the menu, so we will add this element just after the router links we already wrote:

   ```
   <div class="spacer"></div>
   ```

   This will simply grow to take all the available space in the menu using the CSS flexbox properties, so that anything we put after will be pushed to the right.

   Thanks to the plugin we made earlier in the *Storing the user in a centralized State* section, we have access to the global state with the `$state` property. It contains the `user` object, which allows us to know if the user is logged in, and displays their `username` and a `logout` link.

2. Add the user menu in the `NavMenu.vue` component:

   ```
   <template v-if="$state.user">
     <a>{{ $state.user.username }}</a>
     <a @click="logout">Logout</a>
   </template>
   ```

3. If the user isn't connected, we just display a `login` link (add this below the `template` we just added):

   ```
   <router-link v-else :to="{name: 'login'}">Login</router-link>
   ```

The `logout` link needs a new `logout` method that we will create now.

Logout method

The logout method consists of a simple call to the `/logout` path on the server, which should return an object with the `status` property equal to `'ok'`:

```
<script>
export default {
  methods: {
    async logout () {
      const result = await this.$fetch('logout')
      if (result.status === 'ok') {
        this.$state.user = null
      }
    }
```

Project 3 - Support Center

```
    },
  },
}
</script>
```

If the user successfully logged out, we reset the `user` value in the global state.

Private routes with navigation guards

Now that we have an authentication system ready, we can have different types of routes:

- Public routes are always accessible
- Private routes are restricted to logged users
- Guest routes are accessible only to users that are not connected yet

We are going to create one of the routes components ahead of time to test our code:

1. Let's create the `TicketsLayout.vue` component that we will use later to display either of the user support tickets:

   ```
   <template>
     <main class="tickets-layout">
       <h1>Your Support tickets</h1>
       <!-- TODO -->
     </main>
   </template>
   ```

2. Then, add the corresponding route in the `router.js` file:

   ```
   import TicketsLayout from './components/TicketsLayout.vue'

   const routes = [
     // ...
     { path: '/tickets', name: 'tickets',
       component: TicketsLayout },
   ]
   ```

3. Finally, add the link to this new page in the navigation menu:

   ```
   <router-link :to="{ name: 'tickets' }">
     Support tickets</router-link>
   ```

[200]

Route meta properties

We can add the page access type information in the `meta` object on the impacted routes in the `router.js` file.

The route we just created should be private and only accessible to connected users:

- Add the `private` attribute to the `meta` object on the route:

    `{ path: '/tickets', /* ... */, `**`meta: { private: true }`**` },`

Now, if you go to the tickets page and inspect any component, you should see the `$route` object exposed by the `vue-router` plugin. It contains the `private` property in the `meta` object:

```
Ready. Detected Vue 2.4.1.                                      Components    Vuex

Filter components                                        <TicketsLayout>    Inspect DOM

▼ <Root>
  ▼ <AppLayout>                                          data
    ▶ <NavMenu>                                          ▼ $route: Object
    ▶ <TicketsLayout> == $vm0   router-view: /tickets        fullPath: "/tickets/"
                                                            ▼ meta: Object
                                                                private: true
                                                              name: "tickets"
                                                            ▶ params: Object (empty)
                                                              path: "/tickets/"
                                                            ▶ query: Object (empty)
```

> **TIP**
> You can put any additional information in the `meta` object of a route to extend the router capabilities.

Router navigation guards

Now that we know the tickets route is private, we would like to execute some logic before the route is resolved to check if the user is connected. That is where navigation guards come in handy--there are function hooks called when something happens regarding routes and they can change the behavior of the router.

The navigation guard we need is `beforeEach` and it is run each time before a route is resolved. It allows us to replace the target route with another one if necessary. It accepts a callback with three arguments:

- `to` is the route currently being targeted
- `from` is the previous route
- `next` is a function we have to call at some point for the resolution to proceed

> **TIP**
> If you forget to call `next` in your navigation guard, your app will be stuck. This is because you can do asynchronous operations before calling it, so the router doesn't make any assumption on its own.

1. Before exporting the router instance, add the `beforeEach` navigation guard:

   ```
   router.beforeEach((to, from, next) => {
     // TODO
     console.log('to', to.name)
     next()
   })
   ```

2. Now we need to determine if the route we target is a private route:

   ```
   if (to.meta.private) {
     // TODO Redirect to login
   }
   ```

3. To check if the user is connected, we need the global state--you can import it at the start of the file:

   ```
   import state from './state'
   ```

4. Change the condition to also check for the user state:

   ```
   if (to.meta.private && !state.user) {
     // TODO Redirect to login
   }
   ```

The next function can be called with a route argument, to redirect the navigation to another route.

5. So here, we can redirect to the login route just like we would do with the `router.push()` method:

```
if (to.meta.private && !state.user) {
  next({ name: 'login' })
  return
}
```

> **TIP**: Don't forget to return, or you will call `next` a second time at the end of the function!

We can now try to log out and click on the **support tickets** link. You should be immediately redirected to the login page instead.

> **TIP**: When redirecting with `next`, no additional entry is added to the browser history for each redirection. Only the final route has a history entry.

As you can see in the browser console, the navigation guard was called each time we try to resolve to a route:

```
to tickets
to login
```

That explains why the function is called `next`--the resolving process will continue until we don't redirect to another route.

> **TIP**: This means the navigation guard can be called multiple times, but this also means you should be careful of not creating an infinite "loop" of resolutions!

Redirecting to the wanted route

After the user is logged in, the app should redirect him to the page they initially wanted to browse:

1. Pass the current wanted URL as a parameter to the login route:

   ```
   next({
     name: 'login',
     params: {
       wantedRoute: to.fullPath,
     },
   })
   ```

   Now if you click on the **support tickets** link and get redirected to the login page, you should see the `wantedRoute` parameter in the `$route` object on any component:

   ```
   data
   ▼ $route: Object
       fullPath: "/login"
     ▶ meta: Object
       name: "login"
     ▼ params: Object
         wantedRoute: "/tickets"
       path: "/login"
     ▶ query: Object (empty)
   ```

2. In the `Login` component, we can change the redirection in the `login` method and use this parameter:

   ```
   this.$router.replace(this.$route.params.wantedRoute ||
     { name: 'home' })
   ```

   > The `router.replace()` method is very similar to the `router.push()` method, the difference being it replaces the current entry in the browser history with the new route instead of adding a new entry.

Now if you log in, you should be redirected to the support ticket page instead of the home page.

Initializing user authentication

When the page load and the application start, we need to check if the user is already connected. For this reason, the server has a `/user` path that returns the user object if they are logged in. We will put it in the global state just like if we logged in. Then, we will start the Vue app:

1. In the `main.js` file, import `$fetch` from our plugin:

    ```
    import VueFetch, { $fetch } from './plugins/fetch'
    ```

2. Then we need to create a new asynchronous function called `main`, inside of which we will request the user data and then start the app:

    ```
    async function main () {
      // Get user info
      try {
        state.user = await $fetch('user')
      } catch (e) {
        console.warn(e)
      }
      // Launch app
      new Vue({
        el: '#app',
        data: state,
        router,
        render: h => h(AppLayout),
      })
    }

    main()
    ```

Now if you log in and then you refresh the page, you should still be connected!

Guest routes

There is another case we don't manage yet--we don't want an already connected user to access the login route!

1. That's why we will mark it as a guest route:

    ```
    { path: '/login', name: 'login', component: Login,
      meta: { guest: true } },
    ```

Project 3 - Support Center

2. Inside the `beforeEach` navigation guard, we will check if the route is guest-only and if the user is already connected, then redirect to the home page:

```
router.beforeEach((to, from, next) => {
  // ...
  if (to.meta.guest && state.user) {
    next({ name: 'home' })
    return
  }
  next()
})
```

If you are logged in, you can try going to the login URL--you should be immediately redirected to the home page! You can only access this page if you are not logged in.

Displaying and adding tickets

In this section, we will add the ticket support content to the app. First we will display them and then build a form to let the user create new ones. We will have two components for this, nested in the `TicketsLayout` component we made earlier.

Don't worry! When you created your account, an example support ticket was automatically created for your user.

Tickets list

The tickets can be requested at `/tickets` on the server:

1. Create a new `Tickets.vue` component that will be pretty much like the FAQ component.
2. Use the `RemoteData` mixin to fetch the tickets:

```
<script>
import RemoteData from '../mixins/RemoteData'

export default {
  mixins: [
    RemoteData({
      tickets: 'tickets',
    }),
  ],
}
</script>
```

[206]

3. Then add the template with a loading animation, an empty message, and the list of the tickets:

```
<template>
  <div class="tickets">
    <Loading v-if="remoteDataBusy"/>

    <div class="empty" v-else-if="tickets.length === 0">
      You don't have any ticket yet.
    </div>

    <section v-else class="tickets-list">
      <div v-for="ticket of tickets" class="ticket-item">
        <span>{{ ticket.title }}</span>
        <span class="badge">{{ ticket.status }}</span>
        <span class="date">{{ ticket.date }}</span>
      </div>
    </section>
  </div>
</template>
```

We need a filter to display the ticket date!

4. Kill the client compilation and install `moment js` with the following command:

   npm install --save moment

5. Create a new `filters.js` file next to the `main.js` file, with a `date` filter:

```
import moment from 'moment'

export function date (value) {
  return moment(value).format('L')
}
```

6. Then in `main.js`, import the `filters` and register them with a handy loop:

```
import * as filters from './filters'
for (const key in filters) {
  Vue.filter(key, filters[key])
}
```

Project 3 - Support Center

7. We can now display the dates in a more human-friendly way in the `Tickets` component:

   ```
   <span class="date">{{ ticket.date | date }}</span>
   ```

You can then add this new component to the `TicketsLayout` component and get the list of tickets:

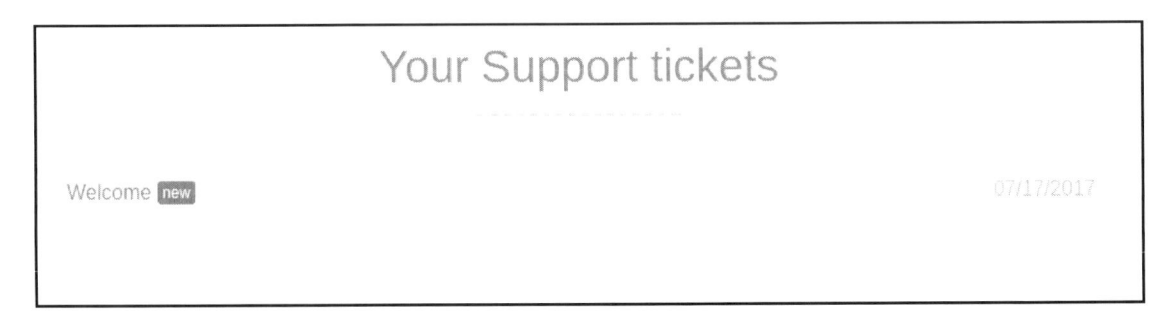

Don't forget to import `Tickets` and set it in the `components` option!

Session expiration

After some time, the user session might become no longer valid. This could happen because of timed expiration (for this server this is set to three hours), or simply because the server was restarted. Let's try to reproduce this kind of situation--we are going to restart the server and try to load the tickets again:

1. Make sure you are logged into the application.
2. Type `rs` and then press `Return` in the Terminal where the server is running to restart it.
3. Click on the **Home** button in the app.
4. Click on the **support ticket** button to go back to the tickets list page.

You should have a stuck loading animation and an error message in the console:

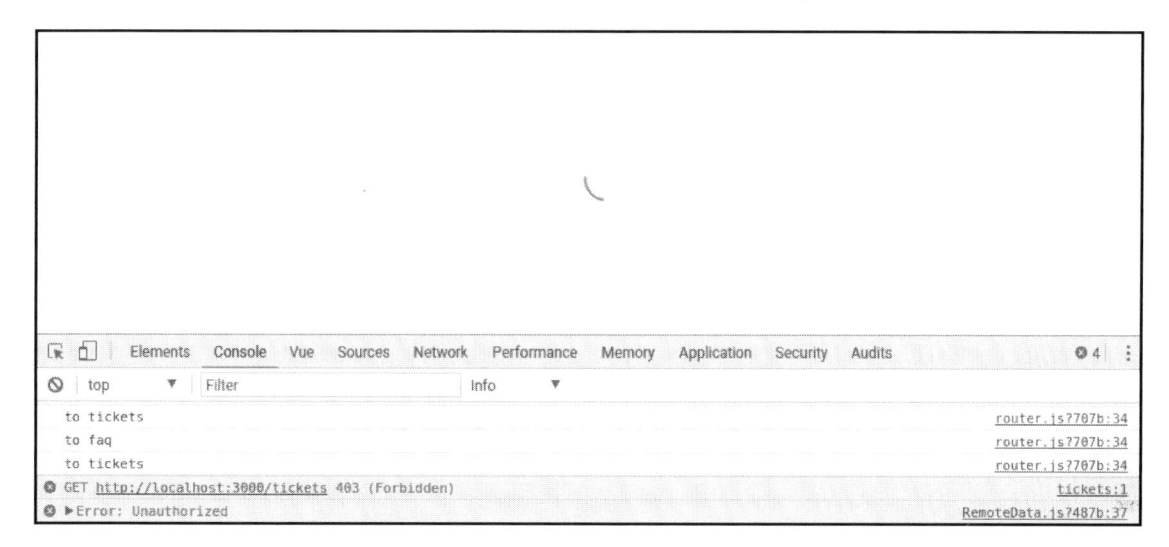

```
to tickets                                              router.js?707b:34
to faq                                                  router.js?707b:34
to tickets                                              router.js?707b:34
⊘ GET http://localhost:3000/tickets 403 (Forbidden)              tickets:1
⊘ ▶ Error: Unauthorized                              RemoteData.js?487b:37
```

The server has returned an unauthorized error--that's because we are no longer logged in!

To fix this, we need to log the user out and redirect them to the login page if we are in a private route.

The best place to put our code is the `$fetch` method used in all our components, located in the `plugins/fetch.js` file. The server will always return a 403 error when trying to access a path restricted to connected users.

1. Before modifying the method, we need to import both the state and the router:

   ```
   import state from '../state'
   import router from '../router'
   ```

2. Let's add a new case in the response processing:

   ```
   if (response.ok) {
     // ...
   } else if (response.status === 403) {
     // If the session is no longer valid
     // We logout
     state.user = null
     // If the route is private
     // We go to the login screen
     if (router.currentRoute.matched.some(r => r.meta.private)) {
       router.replace({ name: 'login', params: {
   ```

```
            wantedRoute: router.currentRoute.fullPath,
      }})
    }
  } else {
    // ...
  }
```

> **TIP**
> We use the `replace` method instead of `push` because we don't want to create a new navigation in the browser history. Imagine if the user clicks the back button, it will redirect again to the login page and the user will not be able to go back to the page before the private one.

You can now try again--when you restart the server and click on the **support tickets** link, you should be redirected to the login page and the navigation menu should not display your username anymore.

Nested routes

Since we also want to switch to a form in this page, it would be a good idea to structure our components with nested routes--each route can have child routes if they have at least a router view! So under the `/tickets` router, we will have two children for now:

- `''` will be the tickets list (full path will be `/tickets/`). It acts like the default route under `/tickets`.
- `'/new'` will be the form to send new tickets (full path will be `/tickets/new/`).

1. Create a new `NewTicket.vue` component with a temporary template:

    ```
    <template>
      <div class="new-ticket">
        <h1>New ticket</h1>
      </div>
    </template>
    ```

2. In the `routes.js` file, add the two new routes under the `/tickets` route inside the children attribute:

    ```
    import Tickets from './components/Tickets.vue'
    import NewTicket from './components/NewTicket.vue'

    const routes = [
      // ...
      { path: '/tickets', component: TicketsLayout,
        meta: { private: true }, children: [
    ```

```
        { path: '', name: 'tickets', component: Tickets },
        { path: 'new', name: 'new-ticket', component: NewTicket },
    ] },
]
```

> **TIP:** Since the first child route is an empty string, it will be the default when the parent route is resolved. This means you should move the name of the route (`'tickets'`) from the parent to it.

3. Finally, we can change the `TicketsLayout` component to use a router view along with a few buttons to switch between the child routes:

```
<template>
  <main class="tickets-layout">
    <h1>Your Support tickets</h1>
    <div class="actions">
      <router-link
        v-if="$route.name !== 'tickets'"
        tag="button"
        class="secondary"
        :to="{name: 'tickets'}">
        See all tickets
      </router-link>
      <router-link
        v-if="$route.name !== 'new-ticket'"
        tag="button"
        :to="{name: 'new-ticket'}">
        New ticket
      </router-link>
    </div>
    <router-view />
  </main>
</template>
```

> **TIP:** You can use the `tag` prop on router links to change the HTML tag used to render it.

As you can see, we hide each button depending on the current route name--we don't want to display the **Show tickets** button when we are already on the tickets page, and we don't want the **New ticket** button when we are already on the corresponding form!

You can now switch between the two child routes and see the URL change accordingly:

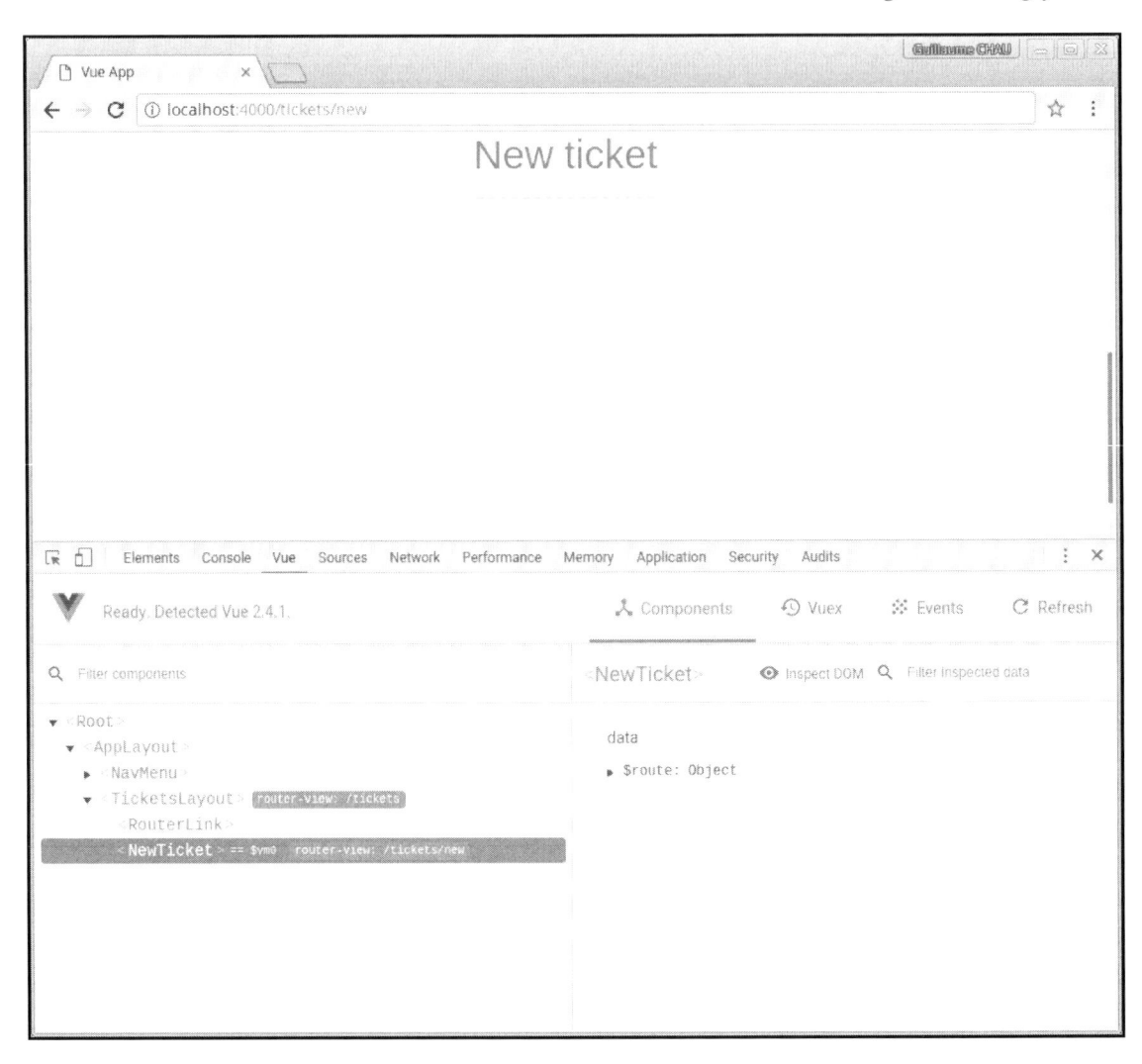

Fixing our navigation guard

If you log out and then go to the tickets page, you should be surprised to be able to access the page! This is because there is a flaw in the implementation of our `beforeEach` navigation guard--we poorly designed it without taking into account the fact we could have nested routes! The reason for this issue is that the `to` parameter is only the target route, which is the first child route of the `/tickets` route--it doesn't have the `private` meta attribute!

So instead of relying solely on the target route, we should also check all the matched nested route objects. Thankfully, every route object gives us access to the list of these route objects with the `matched` property. We can then use the `some` array method to verify if at least one route object has the desired meta attribute.

We can change the conditions code to this in the `beforeEach` navigation guard in the `router.js` file:

```
router.beforeEach((to, from, next) => {
  if (to.matched.some(r => r.meta.private) && !state.user) {
    // ...
  }
  if (to.matched.some(r => r.meta.guest) && state.user) {
    // ...
  }
  next()
})
```

Now our code works regardless of the number of nested routes!

> **TIP**: It is strongly recommended to use this approach with the `matched` property every time to avoid errors.

Sending a form

In this section, we are going to complete the `NewTicket` component that will allow the user to send a new support ticket. We need two fields to create a new ticket--`title` and `description`:

1. In the template of the `NewTicket.vue` component, we can already add a `SmartForm` component with the title `InputForm` component:

   ```
   <SmartForm
     title="New ticket"
     :operation="operation"
     :valid="valid">
     <FormInput
       name="title"
       v-model="title"
       placeholder="Short description (max 100 chars)"
       maxlength="100"
       required/>
   </SmartForm>
   ```

2. We can also add the two data properties, the `operation` method and some input validation with the `valid` computed property:

   ```
   <script>
   export default {
     data () {
       return {
         title: '',
         description: '',
       }
     },
     computed: {
       valid () {
         return !!this.title && !!this.description
       },
     },
     methods: {
       async operation () {
         // TODO
       },
     },
   }
   </script>
   ```

Form textarea

For the `description` field, we need a `<textarea>` element so the user can write a multiline text. Unfortunately, our `FormInput` component doesn't support this yet, so we need to modify it a bit. We will use the `type` prop of the component with the value `'textarea'` to change the `<input>` element to a `<textarea>` element:

1. Let's create a new computed property to determine which kind of HTML element we are going to render:

   ```
   computed: {
     // ...
     element () {
       return this.type === 'textarea' ? this.type : 'input'
     },
   },
   ```

   So when the value `'textarea'` is passed, we need to render a `<textarea>`. All the other types will make the component render an `<input>` element.

   We can now use the special `<component>` component, which can render either elements with the `is` prop, instead of the static `<input>` element.

2. The line in the template should now look like this:

   ```
   <component
     :is="element"
     class="input"
     :class="inputClass"
     :name="name"
     :type="type"
     :value.prop="text"
     @input="update"
     :placeholder="placeholder"
   />
   ```

3. We can now add the `description` textarea to the `NewTicket` form just after the `title` input:

   ```
   <FormInput
     type="textarea"
     name="description"
     v-model="description"
     placeholder="Describe your problem in details"/>
   ```

Binding attributes

Among other elements, `<textarea>` has some handy attributes we would like to use, such as the `rows` attribute. We could create a prop for each of them, but this could become tedious very quickly. Instead, we are going to use the handy `$attrs` special property of the Vue component, which gets all the non-prop attributes set on the component as an object with the keys being the names of the attributes.

This means that if you have let's say, one `text` prop on your component and that you write this in another component:

```
<FormInput :text="username" required>
```

Vue will treat `required` as an attribute, since it is not in the list of props exposed by the `FormInput` component. Then you can access it with `$attrs.required`!

The `v-bind` directive can get an object with the keys being the names of the props and attributes to set. This will be very useful!

1. We can write this on `<component>` in the `FormInput.vue` component:

   ```
   <component
     ...
     v-bind="$attrs" />
   ```

2. Now you can add the `rows` attribute on the `description` input in the `NewTicket.vue` component:

   ```
   <FormInput
     ...
     rows="4"/>
   ```

You should see in the rendered HTML that the attribute has been set on the `<textarea>` element inside the `FormInput` component:

```
<textarea data-v-ae2eb904="" type="textarea" placeholder="Describe your problem in details" rows="4" class="input"></textarea>
```

User actions

We will now implement the few actions the users will be able to do in the form:

1. In the `SmarForm` component, add these two buttons after the inputs:

   ```
   <template slot="actions">
     <router-link
       tag="button"
       :to="{name: 'tickets'}"
       class="secondary">
       Go back
     </router-link>
     <button
       type="submit"
       :disabled="!valid">
       Send ticket
     </button>
   </template>
   ```

2. Then implement the `operation` method, which will be similar to what we have done in the `Login` component. The server path we need to send the `POST` request to is `/tickets/new`:

   ```
   async operation () {
     const result = await this.$fetch('tickets/new', {
       method: 'POST',
       body: JSON.stringify({
         title: this.title,
         description: this.description,
       }),
     })
     this.title = this.description = ''
   },
   ```

You can now create new tickets!

Backup user input

To improve the user experience, we should automatically back up what the user has typed into the form in case something goes wrong--for example, the browser could crash or the user could accidentally refresh the page.

We are going to write a mixin that will automatically save some data properties into the browser local storage, and restore them when the component is created:

1. Create a new `PersistantData.js` file in the `mixins` folder.
2. Like the other mixin we did, it will have some parameters, so we need to export it as a function:

   ```
   export default function (id, fields) {
     // TODO
   }
   ```

   The `id` argument is the unique identifier to store the data for this specific component.

   First we are going to watch all the fields passed in the mixin.

3. For that, we will dynamically create the `watch` object, with each key being the field and the value being the handler function that will save the value into the local storage:

   ```
   return {
     watch: fields.reduce((obj, field) => {
       // Watch handler
       obj[field] = function (val) {
         localStorage.setItem(`${id}.${field}`, JSON.stringify(val))
       }
       return obj
     }, {}),
   }
   ```

4. Go back to the `NewTicket` component and add the mixin:

   ```
   import PersistantData from '../mixins/PersistantData'

   export default {
     mixins: [
       PersistantData('NewTicket', [
         'title',
         'description',
       ]),
     ],
     // ...
   }
   ```

   So, the mixin added watchers to the component with the reduce producing the equivalent of this:

   ```
   {
     watch: {
       title: function (val) {
         let field = 'title'
         localStorage.setItem(`${id}.${field}`, JSON.stringify(val))
       },
       description: function (val) {
         let field = 'description'
         localStorage.setItem(`${id}.${field}`, JSON.stringify(val))
       },
     },
   }
   ```

   > We are saving the property values as JSON since the local storage only supports strings.

Project 3 - Support Center

You can try typing into the fields, and then look at the browser dev tools to see that two new local storage items have been saved:

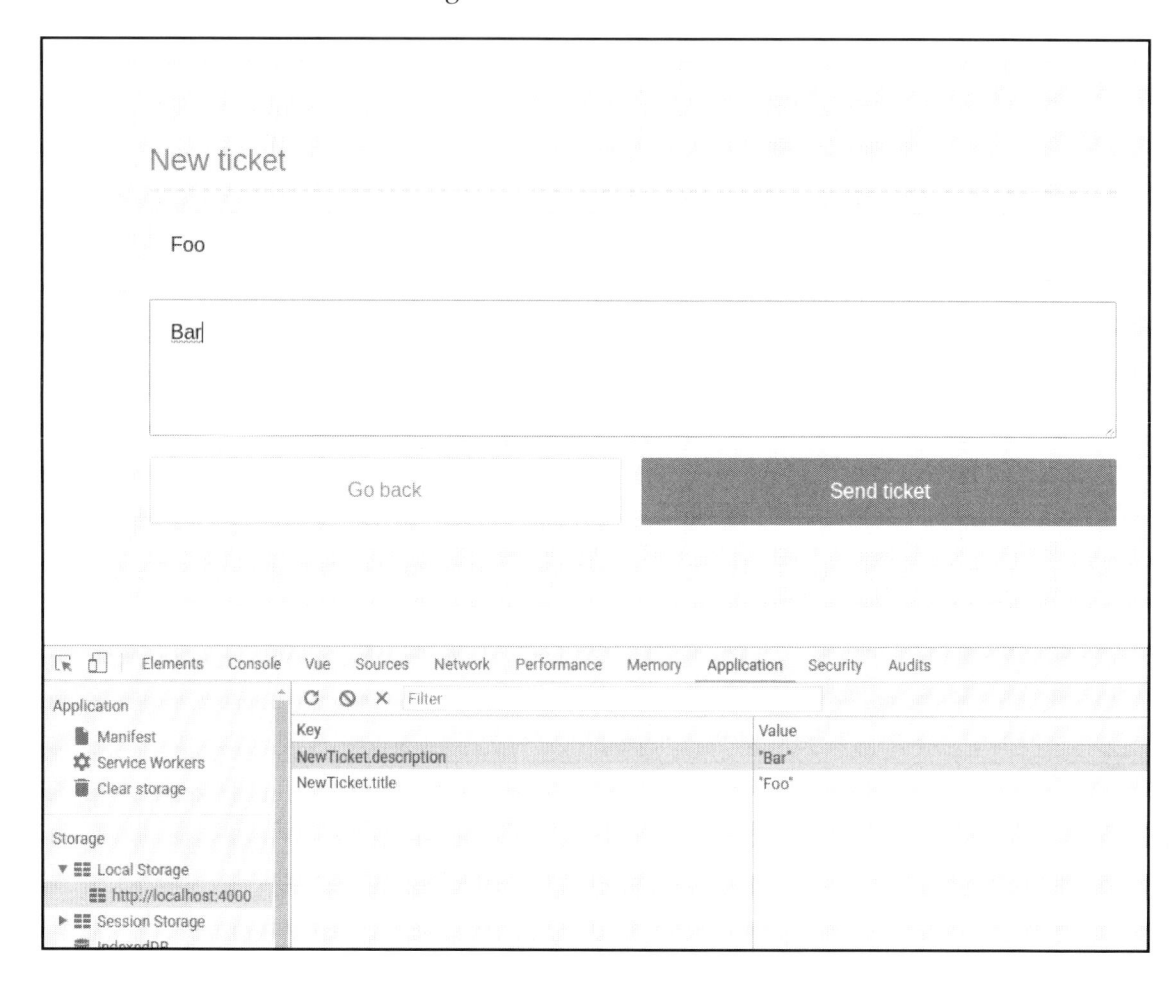

5. In the mixin, we can also save the fields when the component is destroyed:

```
methods: {
  saveAllPersistantData () {
    for (const field of fields) {
      localStorage.setItem(`${id}.${field}`,
      JSON.stringify(this.$data[field]))
    }
  },
},
beforeDestroy () {
  this.saveAllPersistantData()
},
```

6. Finally, we need to restore the values when the component is created:

```
created () {
  for (const field of fields) {
    const savedValue = localStorage.getItem(`${id}.${field}`)
    if (savedValue !== null) {
      this.$data[field] = JSON.parse(savedValue)
    }
  }
},
```

Now if you type something into the form, and then refresh the page, what you typed should be still in the form!

> With the session expiration management we added to $fetch, you will be redirected to the login page if you try to send your new ticket while you are no longer connected. Then, once you're logged in again, you should be right back to the form with what you typed still there!

Advanced routing features

This is the last section of this chapter, in which we will explore routing a bit more!

Project 3 - Support Center

Dynamic routes with parameters

The last component we will add in the application is `Ticket`, which display a detailed view of one ticket by its ID. It will show the title and description inputted by the user, plus the date and the status.

1. Create a new `Ticket.vue` file and add this template with the usual loading animation and `not found` notice:

```
<template>
  <div class="ticket">
    <h2>Ticket</h2>
    <Loading v-if="remoteDataBusy"/>
    <div class="empty" v-else-if="!ticket">
      Ticket not found.
    </div>
    <template v-else>
      <!-- General info -->
      <section class="infos">
        <div class="info">
          Created on <strong>{{ ticket.date | date }}</strong>
        </div>
        <div class="info">
          Author <strong>{{ ticket.user.username }}</strong>
        </div>
        <div class="info">
          Status <span class="badge">{{ ticket.status }}</span>
        </div>
      </section>
      <!-- Content -->
      <section class="content">
        <h3>{{ ticket.title }}</h3>
        <p>{{ ticket.description }}</p>
      </section>
    </template>
  </div>
</template>
```

2. Then add an `id` prop to the component:

```
<script>
export default {
  props: {
    id: {
      type: String,
      required: true,
    },
  },
}
</script>
```

Dynamic remote data

The `id` prop will be the ID of the ticket for which we will fetch the details. The server provides a dynamic route in the form of `/ticket/<id>`, with `<id>` being the ID of the ticket.

It would be nice to be able to use our `RemoteData` mixin, but it currently lacks support for dynamic paths! What we could do is to pass a function instead of a plain string as the values of the mixin's parameter:

1. In the `RemoteData` mixin, we just need to modify the way we process the parameter in the `created` hook. If the value is a function, we will use the `$watch` method to watch its value instead of directly calling the `fetchResource` method:

```
created () {
  for (const key in resources) {
    let url = resources[key]
    // If the value is a function
    // We watch its result
    if (typeof url === 'function') {
      this.$watch(url, (val) => {
        this.fetchResource(key, val)
      }, {
        immediate: true,
      })
    } else {
      this.fetchResource(key, url)
    }
  }
},
```

Project 3 - Support Center

> **TIP:** Don't forget the `immediate: true` option for the watcher since we want to call `fetchResource` a first time before watching the value.

2. In the `Ticket` component, we can now use this mixin to load the data of the ticket depending on the `id` prop:

   ```
   import RemoteData from '../mixins/RemoteData'

   export default {
     mixins: [
       RemoteData({
         ticket () {
           return `ticket/${this.id}`
         },
       }),
     ],
     // ...
   }
   ```

   Let's try this in the `Tickets` component.

3. Add the new `Ticket` component to it with a new `id` data property:

   ```
   import Ticket from './Ticket.vue'

   export default {
     //...
     components: {
       Ticket,
     },
     data () {
       return {
         id: null,
       }
     },
   }
   ```

4. Then in the template, add a `Ticket` component:

   ```
   <Ticket v-if="id" :id="id"/>
   ```

[224]

5. In the ticket list, change the title to a link that sets the `id` data property on `click`:

   ```
   <a @click="id = ticket._id">{{ ticket.title }}</a>
   ```

If you click on the tickets in the application, you should have the details in the following list:

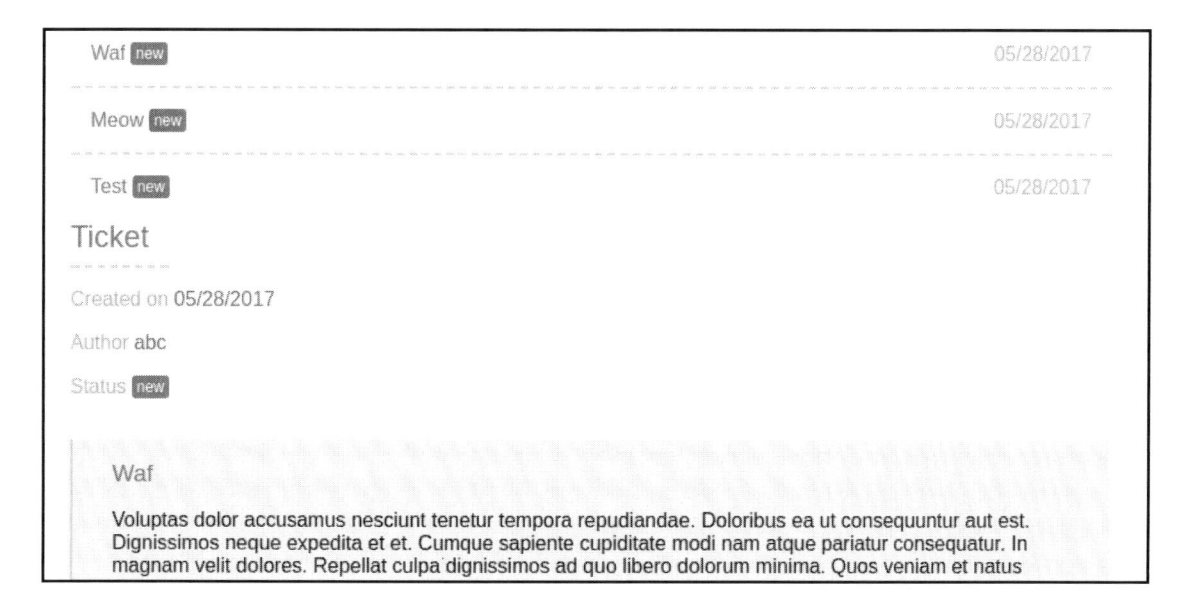

The dynamic route

Since we are going to put the ticket details in another route, you can undo what we just did in the `Tickets` component.

The route will be a child route of the tickets route, and will be of the form `/tickets/<id>` where `<id>` is the ID of the ticket being displayed. This is possible thanks to the dynamic route matching feature of vue-router!

Project 3 - Support Center

You can add dynamic segments to your route path with the semicolon. Then, each segment will be exposed in the route `params` object. Here are some examples of routes with parameters:

Pattern	Example path	`$route.params` value
`/tickets/:id`	`/tickets/abc`	`{ id: 'abc' }`
`/tickets/:id/comments/:comId`	`/tickets/abc/comments/42`	`{ id: 'abc', comId: '42' }`

1. Let's add the new route in the `router.js` file as a child route of `/tickets`:

   ```
   import Ticket from './components/Ticket.vue'

   const routes = [
     // ...
     { path: '/tickets', component: TicketsLayout,
       meta: { private: true }, children: [
       // ...
       { path: ':id', name: 'ticket', component: Ticket },
     ] },
   ]
   ```

2. In the `Tickets` component list, we need to change the title element to a link pointing to the new route:

   ```
   <router-link :to="{name: 'ticket', params: { id: ticket._id }}">
   {{ ticket.title }}</router-link>
   ```

   Now if you click on a ticket, the `$route.params` object will have the `id` property set to the of the ticket.

[226]

We could change our `Ticket` component to use this with a computed property instead of a prop:

```
computed: {
  id () {
    return $route.params.id
  },
},
```

But this is a bad idea--we are coupling the component to the route! This means we won't be able to reuse it in another way easily. The best practice is to use props to pass info to components, so let's continue to do that!

3. So we are going to keep the ID prop of the `Ticket` component and tell `vue-router` to pass all the route parameters to it as prop with the `props` attribute:

```
{ path: ':id', /* ... */, props: true },
```

This is equivalent to this more flexible syntax based on a function that gets the route object as the argument:

```
{ path: ':id', /* ... */, props: route => ({ id: route.params.id })
},
```

Another syntax based on an object exists too (useful when the props are static):

```
{ path: ':id', /* ... */, props: { id: 'abc' } },
```

We won't use this third syntax since our `id` prop should be equal to the dynamic parameter of the route.

> **TIP**: If you need to combine static and dynamic props, use the function syntax! This is also useful if the route parameters and the component props names don't match.

Now, the `id` parameter is passed as a prop to the component and you should see the ticket details page when clicking on a ticket in the list:

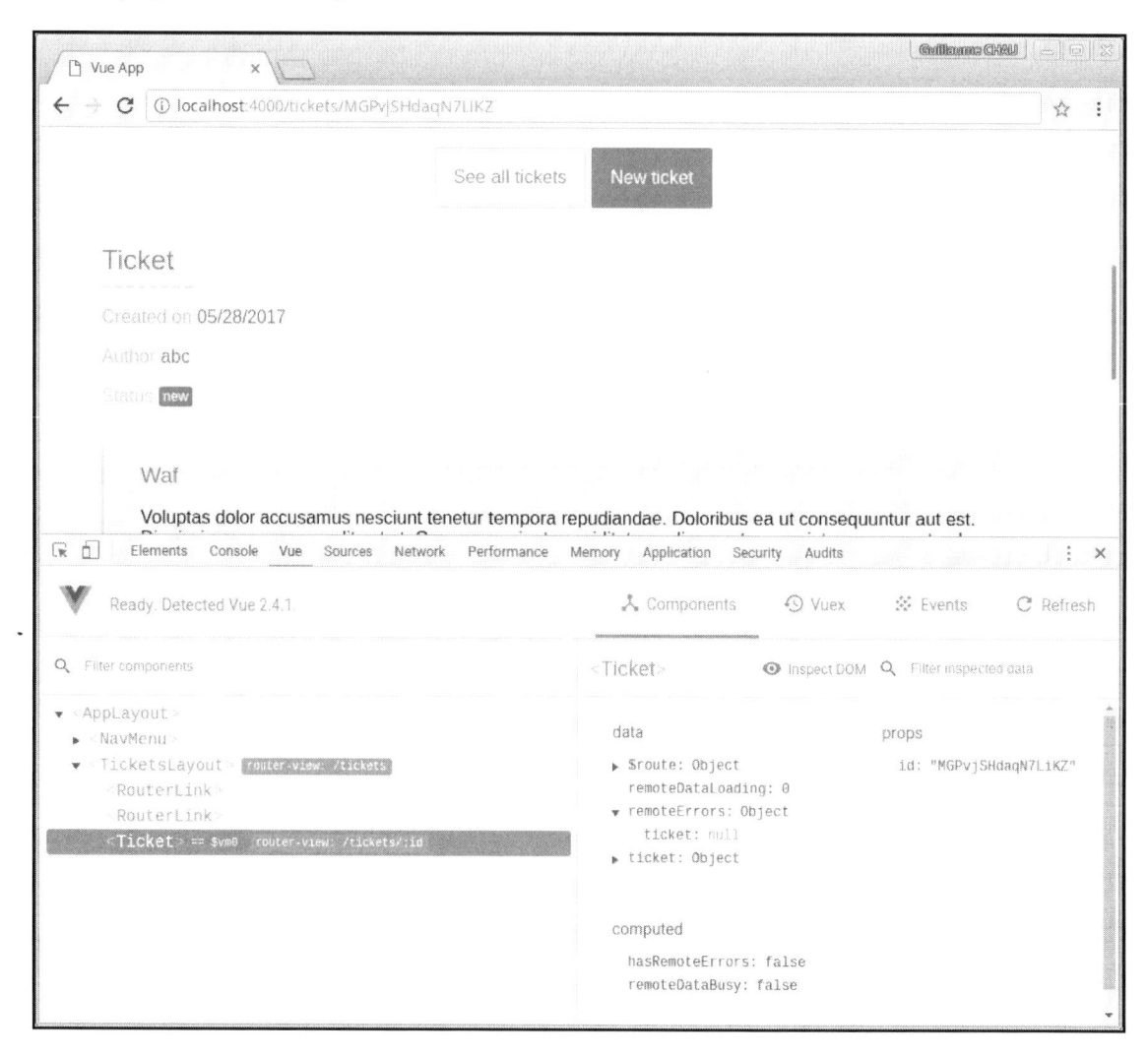

Not found page

Currently, if you enter an invalid URL into the app, you are greeted with a boring blank page. This is the default behavior of `vue-router`, but it can thankfully be changed! We will now customize the "not found" page of our app!

1. Let's create a better "not found" page with a new `NotFound.vue` component:

```
<template>
  <main class="not-found">
    <h1>This page can't be found</h1>
    <p class="more-info">
      Sorry, but we can't find the page you're looking for.<br>
      It might have been moved or deleted.<br>
      Check your spelling or click below to return to the
      homepage.
    </p>
    <div class="actions">
      <router-link tag="button" :to="{name: 'home'}">Return to
      home</router-link>
    </div>
  </main>
</template>

<style lang="stylus" scoped>
.more-info {
  text-align: center;
}
</style>
```

2. Now in the `router.js` file, we just need to add a new route matching the `'*'` path:

```
import NotFound from './components/NotFound.vue'

const routes = [
  // ...
  { path: '*', component: NotFound },
]
```

This means that for any route, we display the `NotFound` component. The very important fact is that we put this route at the end of the `routes` array--this ensures that all the legit routes will be matched before matching this last particular, catch-all route.

You can now try a URL that doesn't exist, like `/foo`, to have the page displayed:

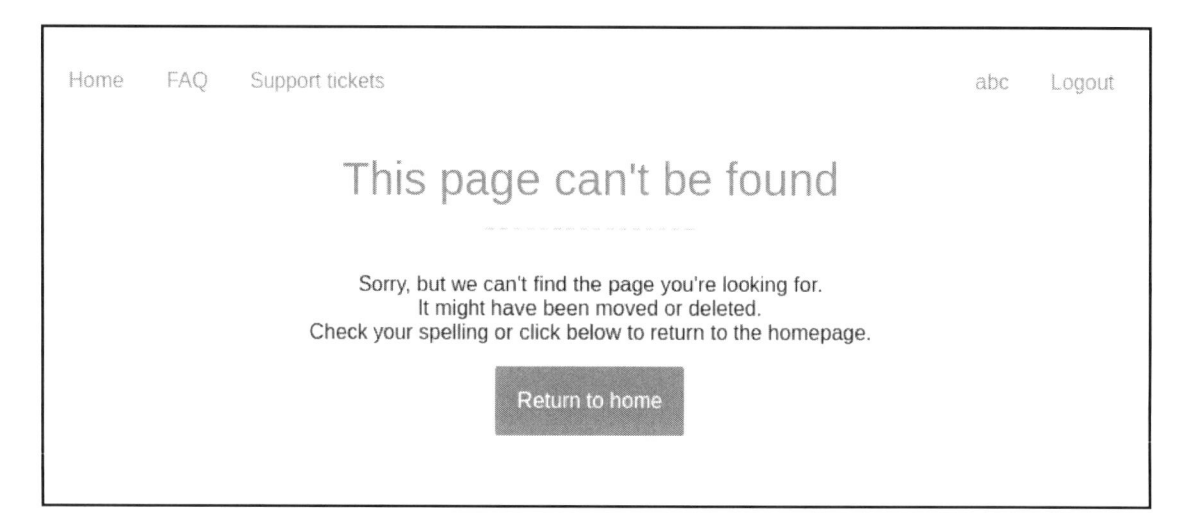

Transitions

Animating the route changes is very easy--this is done in exactly the same way we did before:

- In the `AppLayout` component, wrap the router view with this transition:

```
<transition name="fade" mode="out-in">
  <router-view />
</transition>
```

The `router-view` special component will be replaced by the different component of the routes we have, and thus trigger the transition.

Scrolling behavior

The history mode of the router allows us to manage the page scrolling when a route changes. We can reset the position to the top every time, or restore the position the user was in before changing the route (this is very useful when they go back in the browser).

When creating the router instance, we can pass a `scrollBehavior` function that will get three arguments:

- `to` is the target route object.
- `from` is the previous route object.
- `savedPosition` is the scroll position that has been automatically saved for each entry in the browser history. Each new entry will not have this until the route changes.

The `scrollBehavior` function expects an object that can take two different forms. The first is the coordinate of the scroll we want to apply; for example:

```
{ x: 100, y: 200 }
```

The second one is a selector of the HTML element we want the page to scroll to, with an optional offset:

```
{ selector: '#foo', offset: { x: 0, y: 200 } }
```

1. So to scroll to the top of the page when the route changes, we need to write this:

   ```
   const router = new VueRouter({
     routes,
     mode: 'history',
     scrollBehavior (to, from, savedPosition) {
       return { x: 0, y: 0 }
     },
   })
   ```

   To scroll to the `<h1>` element each time, we could do this:

   ```
   return { selector: 'h1' }
   ```

2. Instead, we will check if the route has a hash to mimic the browser behavior:

   ```
   if (to.hash) {
     return { selector: to.hash }
   }
   return { x: 0, y: 0 }
   ```

3. Finally, we can restore the scroll position if there is any:

```
if (savedPosition) {
  return savedPosition
}
if (to.hash) {
  return { selector: to.hash }
}
return { x: 0, y: 0 }
```

It's that simple! The app now should behave like an old multi-page website. You can then customize the way the scroll behaves with offset or route meta properties.

Summary

In this chapter, we created a fairly big application with the help of Vue and the official `vue-router` library. We created a few routes and connected them with links that turned into a real navigation menu. Then, we created a generic and reusable component to build the application forms, which helped us make the login and signup forms. We then integrated the user authentication system with the router, so our application could react in smart ways to page refreshes or session expirations. Finally, we went deeper into the features and capabilities of `vue-router` to enhance our application and user experience even further.

We are done with the app, but feel free to improve it on your own! Here are some ideas you could implement:

- Add comments to the tickets. Display the list of comments with the name of the corresponding user.
- Add close this ticket button, preventing users from adding new comments.
- Display a special icon next to a closed ticket in the tickets list!
- Add roles to users. For example, normal users could open tickets, but only admin users could close them.

In the next chapter, we will create a geolocated blogging application and we will learn how to scale our apps more with a centralized state solution and how to integrate third-party libraries to extend the features of Vue.

6
Project 4 - Geolocated Blog

In this chapter, we will build our fourth app. We will cover new topics, such as:

- Managing the state of the app in a centralized store using the official Vuex library
- Using the Google OAuth API to connect our users to the app
- Integrating Google Maps to our app with the `vue-googlemaps` third-party library
- Rendering functions and JSX
- Functional components--making lighter and faster components

The app will be a Geolocated Blog that will mainly display a big map where the user will add blog posts. Here are the main features of the app:

- A login page will ask the user to authenticate using their Google account
- The main view will be a Google map embedded in the app, with a marker for each post
- Clicking on the markers will display the content in a side panel to the right, with the description of the location, the post, a like counter, and a list of comments
- Clicking anywhere else on the map will display a form in the side panel so the user can create a new post at this location
- The top bar of the application will display the current user's avatar and name, with a button to center the map on their position and another to log out

Project 4 - Geolocated Blog

The final application will look as follows:

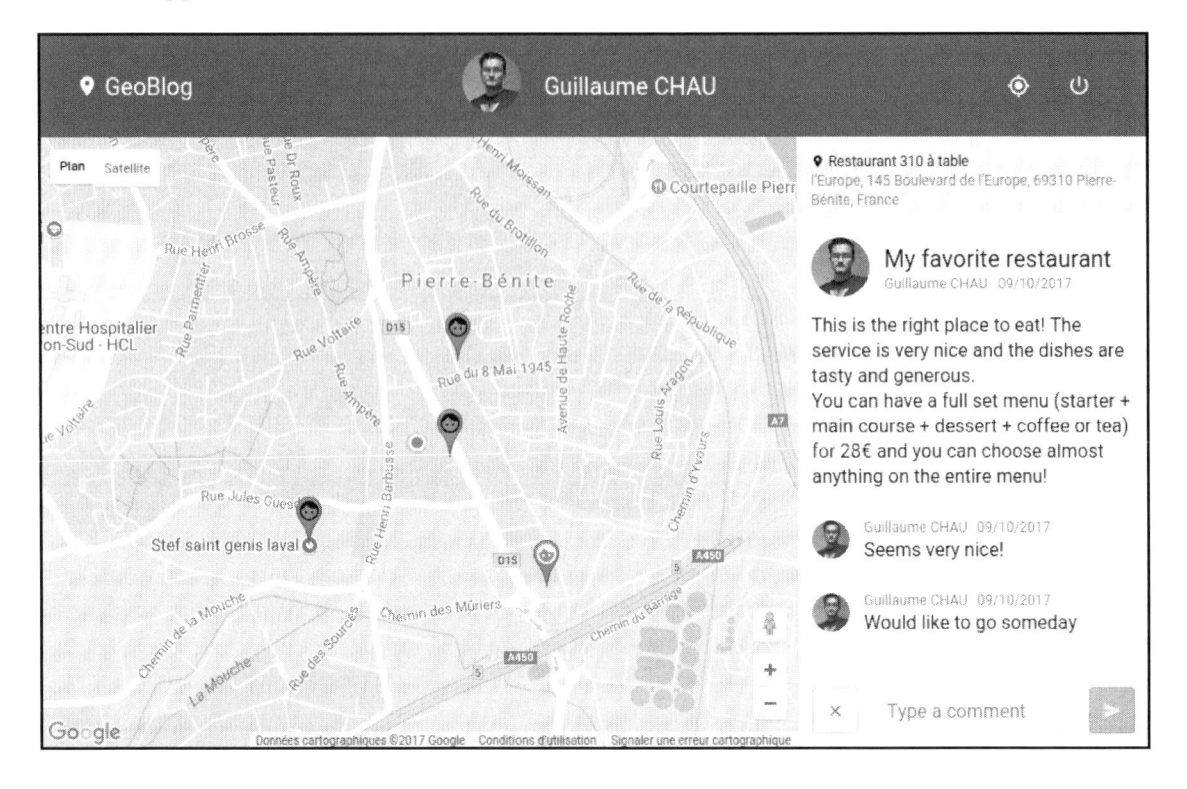

Google Auth and state management

In this first section, we will create our first Vuex store to help us manage the state of our application. We will use it to store the current user logging in through the Google OAuth API, which allows them to use their Google account to connect to our app.

Project setup

First, let's set up the basic structure of our new project. We will continue using the router and a few parts of `Chapter 5`, *Project 3 - Support Center*.

Creating the app

In this section, we will setup the base app structure for our Geolocated Blog.

1. Like we did in Chapter 5, *Project 3 - Support Center*, we will initialize a Vue project with `vue-init` and install the babel, routing, and stylus packages:

    ```
    vue init webpack-simple geoblog</strong>
    cd geoblog
    npm install
    npm install --save vue-router babel-polyfill
    npm install --save-dev stylus stylus-loader babel-preset-vue
    ```

    > **TIP**: Don't forget to add the `"vue"` preset in the `.babelrc` file.

2. Then remove the content of the `src` directory.
3. We will reuse the `$fetch` plugin we made in Chapter 5, *Project 3 - Support Center*, so copy the `src/plugins/fetch.js` file too in the new project.
4. In the `src` folder, add the `main.js` file that starts our app like we did in Chapter 5, *Project 3 - Support Center*:

    ```
    import 'babel-polyfill'
    import Vue from 'vue'
    import VueFetch, { $fetch } from './plugins/fetch'
    import App from './components/App.vue'
    import router from './router'
    import * as filters from './filters'

    // Filters
    for (const key in filters) {
      Vue.filter(key, filters[key])
    }

    Vue.use(VueFetch, {
      baseUrl: 'http://localhost:3000/',
    })

    function main () {
      new Vue({
        ...App,
        el: '#app',
    ```

```
    router,
  })
}

main()
```

5. We will still use `moment.js` to display dates, so you can install it with this command:

   npm i -S moment

   > **TIP:** This shorter notation is equivalent to `npm install --save`. For development dependencies, you can use `npm i -D` instead of `npm install --save-dev`.

6. Create the same simple date filter as before in a new `src/filters.js` file:

   ```
   import moment from 'moment'

   export function date (value) {
     return moment(value).format('L')
   }
   ```

7. In the `$fetch` plugin, you can remove the references to the `state.js` file since we won't have one this time:

   ```
   // Remove this line
   import state from '../state'
   ```

8. Also the way we log out the user if a request receives a `403` HTTP code will be different, so you can remove the relevant code too:

   ```
   } else if (response.status === 403) {
     // If the session is no longer valid
     // We logout
     // TODO
   } else {
   ```

9. Finally, download (https://github.com/Akryum/packt-vue-project-guide/tree/master/chapter6-full/client/src/styles) and put them in a `src/styles` directory.

Some routing

The app will have three pages:

- The login page with a **Sign in with Google** button
- The main Geolocated Blog page with the map
- A "not found" page

We will now create the main component and set up those pages with bare components:

1. Create a new `src/components` folder and copy the `NotFound.vue` component from Chapter 5, *Project 3 - Support Center*.
2. Then add the `App.vue` file with the `router-view` component and the main stylus file:

   ```
   <template>
     <div class="app">
       <router-view />
     </div>
   </template>

   <style lang="stylus">
   @import '../styles/main';
   </style>
   ```

3. Add the `GeoBlog.vue` file, which will be pretty bare for now:

   ```
   <template>
     <div class="geo-blog">
       <!-- More to come -->
     </div>
   </template>
   ```

4. Add the `Login.vue` file with the Sign in with Google button. The button calls an `openGoogleSignin` method:

   ```
   <template>
     <div class="welcome">
       <h1>Welcome</h1>

       <div class="actions">
         <button @click="openGoogleSignin">
           Sign in with Google
         </button>
       </div>
   ```

```
      </div>
    </template>

    <script>
    export default {
      methods: {
        openGoogleSignin () {
          // TODO
        },
      },
    }
    </script>
```

5. Create a `router.js` file similar to what we did in Chapter 5, *Project 3 - Support Center*. It will contain the three routes:

```
import Vue from 'vue'
import VueRouter from 'vue-router'

import Login from './components/Login.vue'
import GeoBlog from './components/GeoBlog.vue'
import NotFound from './components/NotFound.vue'

Vue.use(VueRouter)

const routes = [
  { path: '/', name: 'home', component: GeoBlog,
    meta: { private: true } },
  { path: '/login', name: 'login', component: Login },
  { path: '*', component: NotFound },
]

const router = new VueRouter({
  routes,
  mode: 'history',
  scrollBehavior (to, from, savedPosition) {
    if (savedPosition) {
      return savedPosition
    }
    if (to.hash) {
      return { selector: to.hash }
    }
    return { x: 0, y: 0 }
  },
})

// TODO Navigation guards
```

```
    // We will get to that soon

    export default router
```

The router should be already imported in the main file and injected in the application. We are now ready to continue!

State management with Vuex

This is the exciting section of this chapter where we will use the second very important official Vue library--Vuex!

Vuex allows us to use a centralized store to manage the global state of our app.

Why do I need this?

The big question is why we need a centralized state management solution in the first place. You may have noticed in the previous projects that we have already used a very simple `state.js` file with an object containing the global data we needed across our components. Vuex is the next step in that direction. It introduce a few new concepts to help us manage and debug the state of our application in a formal and efficient way.

When your application grows, you or your team will add many more features and components (maybe well over a hundred). Lots of them will share data. With the increasing complexity of the interconnections between your components, you will end up with a mess, with too many components whose data you need to keep in sync. At this point, the state of your app will no longer be predictable and understandable, and your app will become very difficult to evolve or maintain. For example, imagine that a button buried inside four or five components in the component tree needs to open a side panel located in the far opposite-- you may have to use a lot of events and props to pass the information up and down through many components. You effectively have two sources of truth, which means the two components share data that has to be somehow in sync or else your app breaks because you no longer know which component is right.

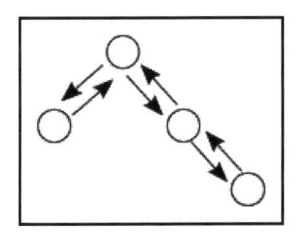

Project 4 - Geolocated Blog

The recommended solution to this problem is Vuex, from Veu. It is inspired by the Flux concept that Facebook developed, which gave birth to the Redux library (well known in the React community). Flux is a set of guiding principles that emphasize the use of a one-way flux of information through the components with a centralized store. The benefits are that your application logic and flow will be easier to reason about, so it improves maintainability by a great margin. The downside is that you may have to understand some new concepts and incidentally write a little more code. Vuex effectively implements some of these principles to help you improve the architecture of your applications.

A real example of this was the Facebook notification system--the chat system was complex enough that it was difficult to determine what message you had seen. Sometimes, you might get a notification for a new message you already read, so Facebook worked on this Flux concept to fix this issue by changing the application architecture.

For our first example, the button and the side panel component don't need to synchronize their state across the whole application. Instead, they use the centralized store to get data and dispatch actions--this implies they don't need to know each other and they don't rely on their ancestors or children components to synchronize their data. It mean there is now a single source of truth, which is the centralized store--you don't need to keep data in sync between components anymore.

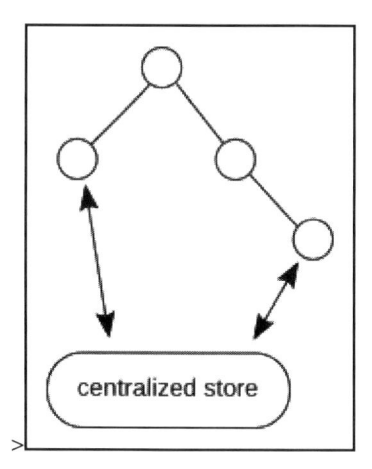

We will now architect our applications around the Vuex library and its principles.

> **TIP**: Vuex is recommended for most applications, but you don't have to use it if it's not necessary, in very small projects such as prototypes or simple widgets.

[240]

The Vuex Store

The central element of Vuex is the store. It is a special object that allows you to centralize the data of your app into a model that follows good design-patterns and helps prevent errors like we saw in the previous section. It will be the main architecture of our data and what we do with it.

The store contains the following:

- The state, which is a reactive data object that holds the state of your app
- Getters, which are the equivalent of computed properties for the store
- Mutations, which are functions used to modify the application state
- Actions, which are functions that usually call asynchronous APIs and then mutations

So a store should look like this:

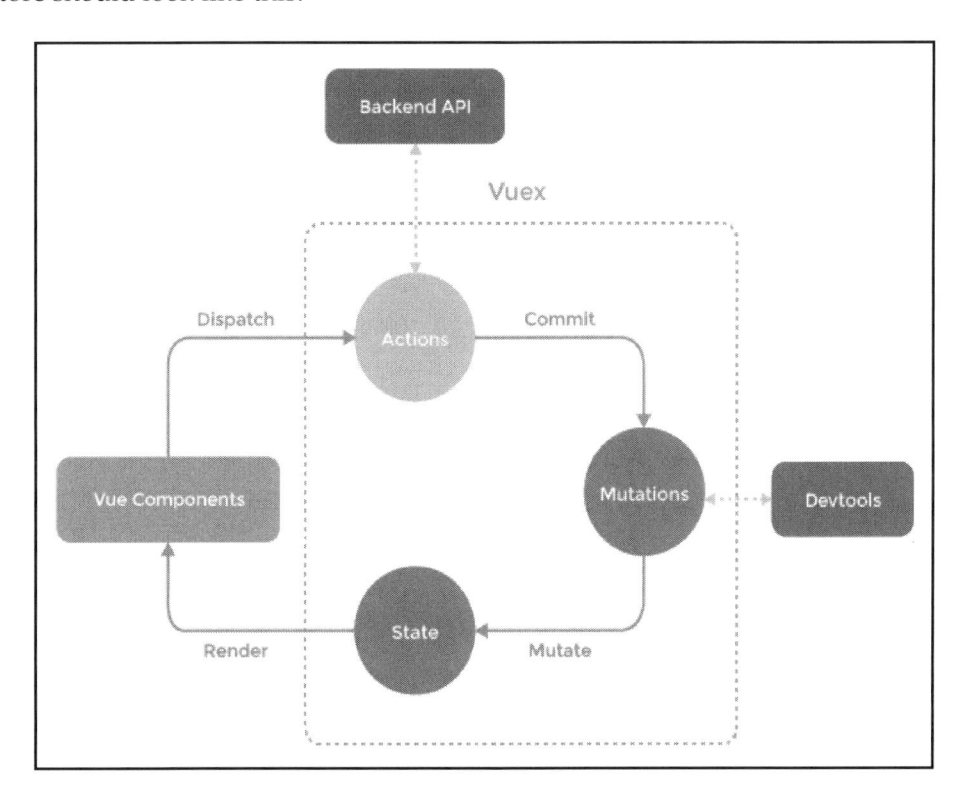

That's a lot of new vocabulary to understand, so let's create a store while walking through these new concepts. You will see that it's not as difficult as it might seem:

1. Download vuex with the 'npm i -S vuex' command. Create a new `store` folder and add a `index.js` file that installs the Vuex plugin:

```
import Vue from 'vue'
import Vuex from 'vuex'

Vue.use(Vuex)
```

2. Create the store with the `Vuex.Store` constructor:

```
const store = new Vuex.Store({
  // TODO Options
})
```

3. Export it as default like we do for the router:

```
export default store
```

4. In the main `main.js` file, import the store:

```
import store from './store'
```

> **TIP:** Webpack will detect that `store` is a folder and will automatically import the `index.js` file inside it.

5. To enable the store in our application, we need to inject it just like the router:

```
new Vue({
  ...App,
  el: '#app',
  router,
  // Injected store
  store,
})
```

6. All the components now have access to the store with the `$store` special property, similar to `vue-router` special objects such as `$router` and `$route`. For example, you could write this inside a component:

```
this.$store
```

[242]

The state is the source of truth

The main piece of the store is its state. It represents the data shared across the components of your app. The first principle is--this is the **single source of truth** for your shared data. Since components will all read data from it, and it will always be right.

For now, the state will only have a `user` property, which will contain the logged user data:

1. In the store options, add to the state a function that returns an object:

   ```
   const store = new Vuex.Store({
     state () {
       return {
         user: null,
       }
     },
   })
   ```

   Also, the next very important principle is--the state is **read-only**. You shouldn't modify the state directly, or else you lose the benefits of using Vuex (which is to make the shared state easy to reason about). If you have lots of components modifying the state as they wish anywhere in the app, it will be harder to follow the flow of the data and debug it using the dev tools. The only valid way of changing the state is through mutations, as we will see in a moment.

2. To try reading the state, let's create the `AppMenu.vue` component in the `components` folder. It will display user info, the `center-on-user` button, and the `logout` button:

   ```
   <template>
     <div class="app-menu">
       <div class="header">
         <i class="material-icons">place</i>
         GeoBlog
       </div>

       <div class="user">
         <div class="info" v-if="user">
           <span class="picture" v-if="userPicture">
             <img :src="userPicture" />
           </span>
           <span class="username">{{ user.profile.displayName }}
           </span>
         </div>
         <a @click="centerOnUser"><i class="material-
   ```

```
            icons">my_location</i>
          </a>
          <a @click="logout"><i class="material-
          icons">power_settings_new</i>
          </a>
        </div>
      </div>
    </template>

    <script>
    export default {
      computed: {
        user () {
          return this.$store.state.user
        },
        userPicture () {
          return null // TODO
        },
      },
      methods: {
        centerOnUser () {
          // TODO
        },
        logout () {
          // TODO
        },
      },
    }
    </script>
```

> The `user` object will have a profile property from Google, with the display name and the photo of the user.

3. Add this new `AppMenu` component in `GeoBlog.vue`:

```
    <template>
      <div class="geo-blog">
        <AppMenu />
        <!-- Map & content here -->
      </div>
    </template>

    <script>
    import AppMenu from './AppMenu.vue'
```

```
export default {
  components: {
    AppMenu,
  },
}
</script>
```

For now our user is not logged in, so nothing is displayed.

Mutations update the state

As we consider the state as read-only, the only way to modify it is through mutations. A mutation is a synchronous function that takes the state as the first argument and an optional payload argument, and then updates the state. It means you are not allowed to do asynchronous operations (like a request to the server) in a mutation:

1. Let's add our first mutation, of type `'user'`, which will update the user in the state:

   ```
   const store = new Vuex.Store({
     state () { /* ... */ },

     mutations: {
       user: (state, user) => {
         state.user = user
       },
     },
   })
   ```

   > **TIP**: Mutations are very similar to events--they have a type (here it's `'user'`) and a handler function.

   The word used to indicate that we are calling a mutation is **commit**. We can't directly call them--it's like events, we ask the store to trigger the mutations corresponding to a specific type.

   To invoke our mutation handler, we need to use the `commit` store method:

   store.commit(`'user'`, userData)

2. Let's try this in the `logout` function in the `AppMenu` component so we can test the mutation:

```
logout () {
  // TODO
  if (!this.user) {
    const userData = {
      profile: {
        displayName: 'Mr Cat',
      },
    }
    this.$store.commit('user', userData)
  } else {
    this.$store.commit('user', null)
  }
},
```

Now if you click on the **logout** button, you should see the user info being toggled.

Strict mode

Mutations are synchronous for debugging reasons. The way the state is handled makes it easy to track it and debug faulty behavior in the application since the dev tools can take snapshots of it. But if your mutations make asynchronous calls, then the debugger has no way to tell what the state is before and after the mutation, making it untraceable:

1. To help you avoid modifying the state outside synchronous mutations, you can enable strict mode like this:

```
const store = new Vuex.Store({
  strict: true,
  // ...
})
```

This will throw an error when the state is modified outside of a synchronous mutation preventing the debugging tools from working correctly.

> You shouldn't enable strict mode in production, since it will have an impact on performance. Use this expression to do that--`strict: process.env.NODE_ENV !== 'production'`, which will ensure the `NODE_ENV` standard environment variable tells you in which development mode you are (usually development, testing, or production).

2. Let's try changing the state directly in the `logout` test method:

```
logout () {
  if (!this.user) {
    // ...
    this.$store.state.user = userData
  } else {
    this.$store.state.user = null
  }
},
```

Then click again on the **logout** button and open the browser console--you should see that Vuex has thrown errors because you are modifying the state outside of proper mutations:

```
▶[Vue warn]: Error in callback for watcher "function () { return this._data.$$state }": "Error: [vuex] Do not mutate vuex store state outside mutation handlers."
```

Time-travel debugging

One of the benefits of using the Vuex approach is the debugging experience. In more complex apps, this is very useful to track the state of the app mutation-by-mutation.

Revert to the mutations call in the `logout` method. Click a few times on the **logout** button, then open the Vue dev tools and open the **Vuex** tab. You should see a list of mutations that were committed to the store:

[247]

On the right, you can see the state that was recorded for the selected mutation and its payload (the argument passed to it).

You can go back to any state snapshot by hovering over a mutation and clicking on the **Time Travel** icon button:

Your app will be back in the state it was originally! You can now go step-by-step and replay the evolution of the app state as the mutations are committed.

Getters compute and return data

Getters work like computed properties for the store. They are functions that take the state and the getters as arguments, and return some state data:

1. Let's create a `user` getter that returns the user held by the state:

    ```
    const store = new Vuex.Store({
      // ...
      getters: {
        user: state => state.user,
      },
    })
    ```

2. In our `AppMenu` component, we can use this getter instead of accessing the state directly:

    ```
    user () {
      return this.$store.getters.user
    },
    ```

This doesn't seem to be different from before. But accessing the state directly isn't recommended--you should always use getters since it allows you to modify the way you get the data without having to change the components using it. For example, you can change the structure of the state and adapt the corresponding getters without having an impact on the component.

3. Let's also add a `userPicture` getter that we will implement later when we have the real Google profile:

   ```
   userPicture: () => null,
   ```

4. In the `AppMenu` component, we can already use it:

   ```
   userPicture () {
     return this.$store.getters.userPicture
   },
   ```

Actions for store operations

The final element composing the store is actions. They are different from mutations, because they don't modify the state directly, but they can both **commit mutations** and make **asynchronous operations**. Similar to the mutations, actions are declared with a type and a handler. The handler can't be called directly, you need to dispatch an action type like this:

```
store.dispatch('action-type', payloadObject)
```

An action handler takes two arguments:

- `context`, which provides the `commit`, `dispatch`, `state`, and `getters` utilities linked to the store
- `payload`, which is the argument provided to the `dispatch` call

1. Let's add our first actions, of type `'login'` and `'logout'`, which don't expect a payload:

   ```
   const store = new Vuex.Store({
     // ...
     actions: {
       login ({ commit }) {
         const userData = {
           profile: {
              displayName: 'Mr Cat',
           },
   ```

```
      }
      commit('user', userData)
    },

    logout ({ commit }) {
      commit('user', null)
    },
  }
})
```

2. In the `AppMenu` component, we can test them by replacing the code of the methods corresponding to the two buttons:

```
methods: {
  centerOnUser () {
    // TODO
    // Testing login action
    this.$store.dispatch('login')
  },
  logout () {
    this.$store.dispatch('logout')
  },
},
```

Now, if you click on the buttons in the menu, you should see the user profile appear and disappear.

> **TIP**: Similarly to getters, you should always use actions instead of mutations inside your components. There is a good chance that the features of your app will evolve, so it's a good idea to be able to change the action code rather than the component code (for example, if you need to call a new additional mutation). Look at actions as abstraction for your general application logic.

Mapping helpers

Vuex provides a few helper functions to add state, getters, mutations, and actions. Since we should only use getters and actions in our components to help separate the state and related logic from the components, we will only use `mapGetters` and `mapActions`.

These functions generate appropriate computed properties and methods to the components that rely on the corresponding getters and actions from the store, so you don't have to type `this.$store.getters` and `this.$store.dispatch` each time. The argument is either:

- An array of types that are mapped with the same name as? the component
- An object, whose keys are the aliases on the component and the value are the types

For example, the following code using the array syntax:

```
mapGetters(['a', 'b'])
```

Is equivalent to this in the component:

```
{
    a () { return this.$store.getters.a },
    b () { return this.$store.getters.b },
}
```

And the following code using the object syntax:

```
mapGetters({ x: 'a', y: 'b' })
```

Is equivalent to this:

```
{
    x () { return this.$store.getters.a },
    y () { return this.$store.getters.b },
}
```

Let's refactor our `AppMenu` component to use those helpers:

1. First import those in the component:

```
import { mapGetters, mapActions } from 'vuex'
```

2. Then, we can rewrite the component like this:

```
export default {
  computed: mapGetters([
    'user',
    'userPicture',
  ]),
  methods: mapActions({
    centerOnUser: 'login',
    logout: 'logout',
  }),
}
```

Now, the component will have two computed properties that return the corresponding store getters, and two methods that dispatch the `login` and `logout` action types.

User state

In this section, we will add the user system to allow users to log in with their Google account.

Setting up Google OAuth

Before we can use the Google API, we have to configure a new project in the Google Developers Console:

1. Go to the Developer Console at `console.developers.google.com`.
2. Create a new project using the Projects drop-down at the top of the page and give it a name. When project creation is finished, select it.
3. To retrieve the user profile, we need to enable the Google+ API. Go to **APIs & services** | **Library** and click on **Google+ API** under the **Social APIs** section. On the **Google+ API** page, click on the **Enable** button. You should then see a usage dashboard with some empty graphs.
4. Next we need to create application credentials to authenticate our server to Google. Go to **APIs & services** | **Credentials** and select the **OAuth consent screen** tab. Make sure you select an email address and enter a *Product name shown to users*.

5. Select the **Credentials** tab, click on the **Create credentials** drop-down, and then select **OAuth client ID**. Select **Web application** as the application type, then enter the URL where the server will be up in the Authorized JavaScript origins field. For now, it will be `http://localhost:3000`. Press the *Enter* key to add it to the list. Then add the URL to which Google will redirect the user after the Google login screen into the **Authorized redirect URIs**-- `http://localhost:3000/auth/google/callback` and press the *Enter* key. This URL corresponds to a special route on the server. When you are done, click on the **Create client ID** button.

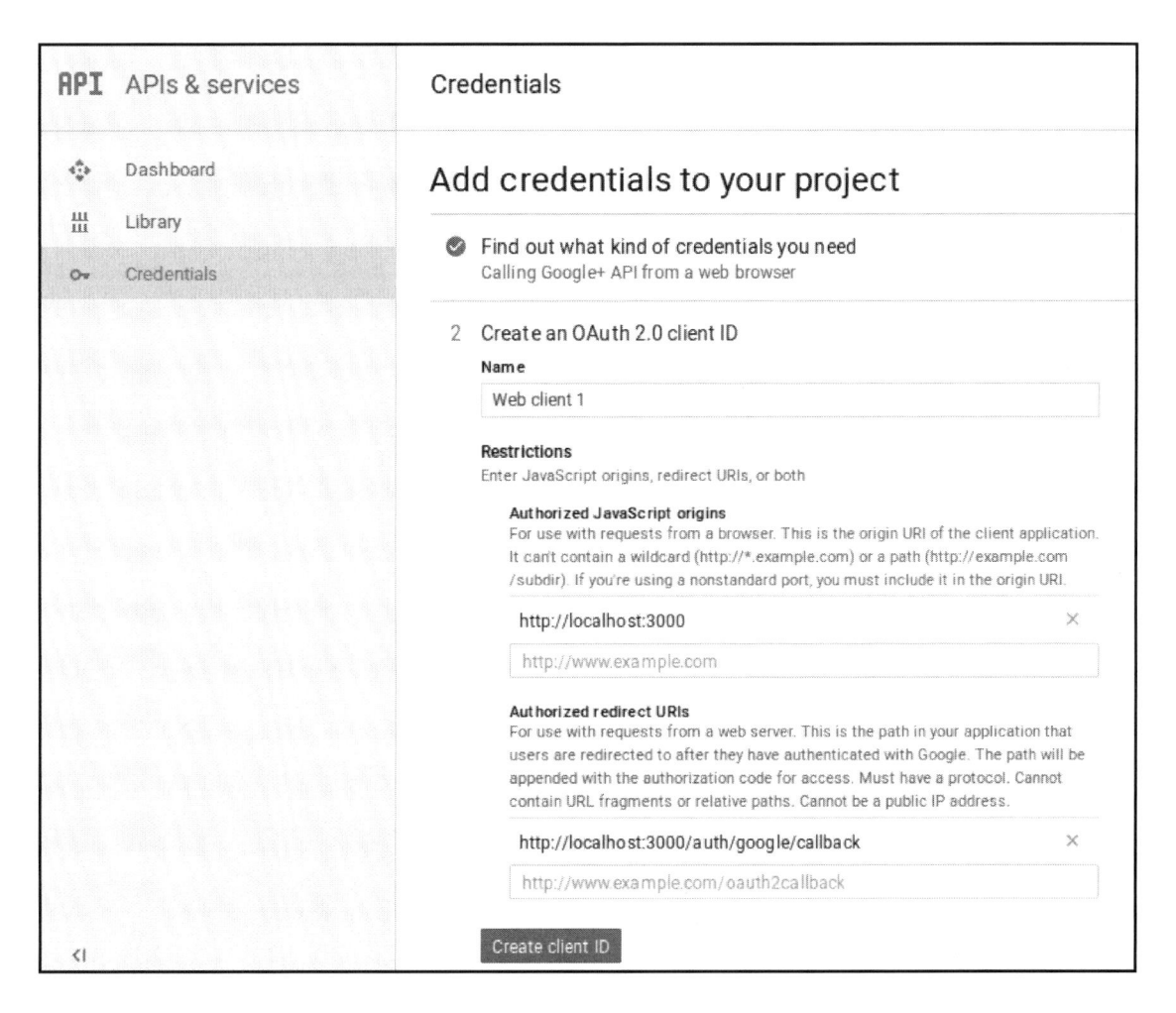

Project 4 - Geolocated Blog

6. Then copy or download the credentials containing the client ID and a secret that you shouldn't share with anybody outside of your team. These two keys will allow the Google API to authenticate your application and will display its name when the users log in through the Google login page.
7. Download the API server of the project (https://github.com/Akryum/packt-vue-project-guide/tree/master/chapter6-full/server), and extract it outside of the `Vue app` directory. Open a new Terminal inside this new folder, and install server dependencies with the usual command:

   npm install

8. Next, you need to export the two `GOOGLE_CLIENT_ID` and `GOOGLE_CLIENT_SECRET` environment variables with the corresponding values in the credentials file you downloaded from the Google Developers Console. For example, on Linux:

   ```
   export GOOGLE_CLIENT_ID=xxx
   export GOOGLE_CLIENT_SECRET=xxx
   ```

Or on Windows:

```
set GOOGLE_CLIENT_ID=xxx
set GOOGLE_CLIENT_SECRET=xxx
```

> **TIP:** You need to do that each time you want to start the server in a new Terminal session.

9. You can start the server with the `start` script:

   npm run start

Login button

The `Login` component contains the button that should open a popup displaying the Google login page. The popup will first load a route on the Node.js server, which will redirect to the Google OAuth page. When the user is logged in and has authorized our app, the popup is redirected to our nodejs server again and will send a message to the main page before closing:

1. Edit the `openGoogleSignin` method to open the popup to the `/auth/google` route on the server that will redirect the user to Google:

   ```
   openGoogleSignin () {
     const url = 'http://localhost:3000/auth/google'
     const name = 'google_login'
     const specs = 'width=500,height=500'
     window.open(url, name, specs)
   },
   ```

   After the user is successfully authenticated via Google, the callback page on the server will send a message to the Vue app window using the standard postMessage API.

   When we receive the message, we need to check that it comes from the right domain (`localhost:3000` for our server).

2. Create a new `handleMessage` method with a destructured message parameter:

   ```
   handleMessage ({data, origin}) {
     if (origin !== 'http://localhost:3000') {
       return
     }

     if (data === 'success') {
       this.login()
     }
   },
   ```

3. We will dispatch the `'login'` action type to the store, which will fetch the user data soon. Map it to the component:

   ```
   import { mapActions } from 'vuex'

   export default {
     methods: {
       ...mapActions([
         'login',
       ]),

       // ...
     },
   }
   ```

[255]

4. Then we use the `mounted` lifecycle hook (outside of the methods) to add an event listener to the window:

```
mounted () {
  window.addEventListener('message', this.handleMessage)
},
```

5. And finally, we don't forget to remove this listener when the component is being destroyed:

```
beforeDestroy () {
  window.removeEventListener('message', this.handleMessage)
},
```

User in the store

The store will have two actions related to the user--`login` and `logout`. We already have them, we now need to implement what they will do. We will also add some user-related features in this section, such as loading the user session when the app starts and displaying its profile picture in the top bar:

1. Let's implement the `login` action in the store. It will fetch user data, just like we did in Chapter 5, *Project 3 - Support Center*, and then `commit` the data to the state (don't forget to import '$fetch'):

```
async login ({ commit }) {
  try {
    const user = await $fetch('user')
    commit('user', user)

    if (user) {
      // Redirect to the wanted route if any or else to home
      router.replace(router.currentRoute.params.wantedRoute ||
        { name: 'home' })
    }
  } catch (e) {
    console.warn(e)
  }
},
```

As you can see, an action can perform asynchronous operations, for example here requesting data to the server. If the user is connected, we redirect them to the page they wanted or the home page, like we did in Chapter 5, *Project 3 - Support Center*.

2. The 'logout' action needs to send the /logout request to the server and redirect the user back to the login screen if the current route is private:

```
logout ({ commit }) {
  commit('user', null)

  $fetch('logout')

  // If the route is private
  // We go to the login screen
  if (router.currentRoute.matched.some(r => r.meta.private)) {
    router.replace({ name: 'login', params: {
      wantedRoute: router.currentRoute.fullPath,
    }})
  }
},
```

According to the information we have put in the router.js file, if the user was on the 'home' route, it will be redirected to the login page.

Adapting the router

We now have to restore the navigation guards to the router like in Chapter 5, *Project 3 - Support Center*--that way, the user won't be able to enter the private route if they are not connected:

In the router.js file, restore the beforeEach navigation guard by using the user store getter to check whether the user is connected or not. It should be quite similar to the one we have already implemented:

```
import store from './store'

router.beforeEach((to, from, next) => {
  console.log('to', to.name)
  const user = store.getters.user
  if (to.matched.some(r => r.meta.private) && !user) {
    next({
      name: 'login',
      params: {
        wantedRoute: to.fullPath,
      },
```

```
    })
    return
  }
  if (to.matched.some(r => r.meta.guest) && user) {
    next({ name: 'home' })
    return
  }
  next()
})
```

Adapting the fetch plugin

The `$fetch` plugin needs some changes as well, since we need to log the user out if their session has expired:

1. In this case, we just need to dispatch the `'logout'` action:

    ```
    } else if (response.status === 403) {
      // If the session is no longer valid
      // We logout
      store.dispatch('logout')
    } else {
    ```

2. Don't forget to import the store:

    ```
    import store from '../store'
    ```

You can now try logging in through Google to your app!

Check the user session on start

When the application starts, we want to check whether the user has an active session like we did in Chapter 5, *Project 3 - Support Center*:

1. For that, we will create a new generic `'init'` action in the store; this will dispatch the `'login'` action, but could eventually dispatch more actions:

    ```
    actions: {
      async init ({ dispatch }) {
        await dispatch('login')
      },

      // ...
    },
    ```

2. In the `main.js` file, we can now dispatch and wait for this action:

```
async function main () {
  await store.dispatch('init')

  new Vue({
    ...App,
    el: '#app',
    router,
    store,
  })
}

main()
```

Now you can log in through Google and refresh the page without being brought back to the login page.

The profile picture

Finally, we can implement the `userPicture` getter to return the first value contained in the `photos` array of the Google profile:

```
userPicture: (state, getters) => {
  const user = getters.user
  if (user) {
    const photos = user.profile.photos
    if (photos.length !== 0) {
      return photos[0].value
    }
  }
},
```

As you can see, we can reuse existing getters inside other getters with the second argument!

You should now have the complete toolbar displayed in the app when you are connected:

GeoBlog   Guillaume CHAU

Synchronizing the store and the router

We can integrate the router into the store with the official `vuex-router-sync` package. It will expose the current route in the state (`state.route`) and will commit a mutation each time the route changes:

1. Install it with the usual command:

   ```
   npm i -S vuex-router-sync
   ```

2. To use it, we need the `sync` method in the main `main.js` file:

   ```
   import { sync } from 'vuex-router-sync'

   sync(store, router)
   ```

Now, you can access the `state.route` object and time-travel debugging will apply to the router as well.

Embedding Google Maps

In this second part, we are going to add a map to the home page and control it through the Vuex store.

Installation

To integrate Google Maps, we will need an API and a third-party package called `vue-googlemaps`.

Getting the API key

To use Google Maps in our app, we need to enable the corresponding API and generate an API key:

1. In the Google Developers Console, go back to the **APIs & services** | **Library** and click on **Google Maps JavaScript API** under the **Google Maps APIs** section. On the API page, click on the **Enable** button.
2. Then go to **Credentials** and create a new API key.

Installing the library

We will now install the `vue-googlemaps` library, which will help us integrate Google Maps into our app.

1. In the app, install the `vue-googlemaps` package with the following command:

   npm i -S vue-googlemaps

2. In the main `main.js` file, you can enable it in the app with the API key from Google:

   ```
   import VueGoogleMaps from 'vue-googlemaps'

   Vue.use(VueGoogleMaps, {
     load: {
       apiKey: 'your_api_key_here',
       libraries: ['places'],
     },
   })
   ```

   > **TIP:** We also specify we want to load the Google Maps Places library, useful for showing info on a location.

   We now have access to the components of the library!

3. In the `App.vue` component, add the style of the library:

   ```
   <style lang="stylus">
   @import '~vue-googlemaps/dist/vue-googlemaps.css'
   @import '../styles/main'
   </style>
   ```

   > **TIP:** We use the ~ character because Stylus doesn't support absolute paths. Here we want to access a npm module, so we add this to tell the `stylus-loader` that this is an absolute path.

Adding a map

The map will be the main component of the app, and it will contain:

- The user position indicator
- A marker for each post
- The eventual "ghost" marker for the post being created

We will now set up a simple map that will fill the main page:

1. Create a new `BlogMap.vue` component with the `center` and `zoom` properties:

```
<template>
  <div class="blog-map">
    <googlemaps-map
      :center="center"
      :zoom="zoom"
      :options="mapOptions"
      @update:center="setCenter"
      @update:zoom="setZoom"
    />
  </div>
</template>

<script>
export default {
  data () {
    return {
      center: {
        lat: 48.8538302,
        lng: 2.2982161,
      },
      zoom: 15,
    }
  },

  computed: {
    mapOptions () {
      return {
        fullscreenControl: false,
      }
    },
  },

  methods: {
    setCenter (value) {
```

```
      this.center = value
    },
    setZoom (value) {
      this.zoom = value
    },
  },
}
</script>
```

2. Then, you need to add it to the `GeoBlog.vue` component:

```
<template>
  <div class="geo-blog">
    <AppMenu />
    <div class="panes">
      <BlogMap />
      <!-- Content here -->
    </div>
  </div>
</template>
```

Don't forget to import it and to put it in the `components` option!

Connecting the BlogMap and the store

Right now the state related to the map is local to the `BlogMap` component--let's move it to the store!

Vuex modules

In the Vuex store, we can divide our state in modules, to have better organization. A module contains a state, getters, mutations, and actions, just like the main store. The store and each module can contain any number of modules, so the store can have nested modules inside other modules--it's up to you to find the structure that works best for your project.

In this application, we will create two modules:

- `maps` related to the map
- `posts` related to the blog posts and comments

For now, we will focus on the `maps` module. It's best to at least separate each module in a different file or directory:

1. Create a new `maps.js` file in the `store` folder that exports as default a module definition and the state of the map:

```
export default {
  namespaced: true,

  state () {
    return {
      center: {
        lat: 48.8538302,
        lng: 2.2982161,
      },
      zoom: 15,
    }
  },
}
```

2. Then to add the module to the store, put it in a new `modules` option in the `store/index.js` file:

```
import maps from './maps'

const store = new Vuex.Store({
  // ...
  modules: {
    maps,
  },
})
```

By default, the state in the getters, mutations, and actions of the module will be the state of this module. Here it will be `store.state.maps`.

Namespaced module

The `namespaced` option tells Vuex to also add the `'maps/'` namespace before all the getter, mutation, and action types of the module. It will also add them to the `commit` and `dispatch` calls inside the namespaced module.

Let's add a few getters that will be used by the `BlogMap` component:

```
getters: {
  center: state => state.center,
  zoom: state => state.zoom,
},
```

The `maps/center` and the `maps/zoom` getters will be added to the store. To read them, you could do:

```
this.$store.getters['maps/center']
```

With the getter helper:

```
mapGetters({
  center: 'maps/center',
  zoom: 'maps/zoom',
})
```

You can also specify a namespace parameter:

```
...mapGetters('maps', [
  'center',
  'zoom',
]),
...mapGetters('some/nested/module', [
  // ...
]),
```

The last way to do it is to generate helpers based on a specific namespace with the `createNamespacedHelpers` method:

```
import { createNamespacedHelpers } from vuex
const { mapGetters } = createNamespacedHelpers('maps')

export default {
  computed: mapGetters([
    'center',
    'zoom',
  ]),
}
```

Accessing global elements

In the namespaced module getters, you can access the root state and root getters (which means any getter) like this:

```
someGetter: (state, getters, rootState, rootGetters) => { /* ... */ }
```

In the actions, you have access to `rootGetters` in the context and you can use the `{ root: true }` option for the `commit` and `dispatch` calls:

```
myAction ({ dispatch, commit, getters, rootGetters }) {
  getters.a // store.getters['maps/a']
  rootGetters.a // store.getters['a']
  commit('someMutation') // 'maps/someMutation'
  commit('someMutation', null, { root: true }) // 'someMutation'
  dispatch('someAction') // 'maps/someAction'
  dispatch('someAction', null, { root: true }) // 'someAction'
}
```

BlogMap module and component

In this section, we are going to wire the `BlogMap` component to the `maps` namespaced module.

Mutations

Let's add the `center` and `zoom` mutations in the `maps` module:

```
mutations: {
  center (state, value) {
    state.center = value
  },
  zoom (state, value) {
    state.zoom = value
  },
},
```

Actions

Then, we set up the actions that commit those mutations:

```
actions: {
  setCenter ({ commit }, value) {
    commit('center', value)
  },

  setZoom ({ commit }, value) {
    commit('zoom', value)
  },
},
```

Mapping in the component

Back to our `BlogMap` component; we can use the helpers to map the getters and the actions:

```
import { createNamespacedHelpers } from 'vuex'

const {
  mapGetters,
  mapActions,
} = createNamespacedHelpers('maps')

export default {
  computed: {
    ...mapGetters([
      'center',
      'zoom',
    ]),

    mapOptions () {
      // ...
    },
  },

  methods: mapActions([
    'setCenter',
    'setZoom',
  ]),
}
```

Now the state of the map is managed in the Vuex store!

User position

Now, we will add the user position indicator, which will give us the position so we can store it in the store:

1. Add the `googlemaps-user-position` component inside the map:

    ```
    <googlemaps-map
      ...
    >
      <!-- User Position -->
      <googlemaps-user-position
        @update:position="setUserPosition"
      />
    </googlemaps-map>
    ```

2. Now we need to add this `userPosition` info in the `maps` module:

    ```
    state () {
      return {
        // ...
        userPosition: null,
      }
    },
    getters: {
      // ...
      userPosition: state => state.userPosition,
    },
    mutations: {
      // ...
      userPosition (state, value) {
        state.userPosition = value
      },
    },
    actions: {
      // ...
      setUserPosition ({ commit }, value) {
        commit('userPosition', value)
      },
    }
    ```

3. And then map the `setUserPosition` action in the `BlogMap` component using the appropriate helper.

Centering on the user

This user position will be very useful to center the map on the user:

1. Let's create a new `centerOnUser` action in the `maps` module:

    ```
    async centerOnUser ({ dispatch, getters }) {
      const position = getters.userPosition
      if (position) {
        dispatch('setCenter', position)
      }
    },
    ```

    With this, we can also change the `setUserPosition` action--if it's the first time we get the user position (which means it's `null` in the state), we should center the map on the user.

2. The `setUserPosition` action should now look like this:

    ```
    setUserPosition ({ dispatch, commit, getters }, value) {
      const position = getters.userPosition
      commit('userPosition', value)
      // Initial center on user position
      if (!position) {
        dispatch('centerOnUser')
      }
    },
    ```

    You can try it now, and have the map centered on you with a little blue dot.

    > **TIP:** By default, the user indicator is disabled if the accuracy of your position is more than 1,000 meters, so it's possible that this won't work depending on your hardware. You can use a higher value with the `minmumAccuracy` prop of the `googlemaps-user-position` component.

3. We also have a `'center on user'` button in the toolbar, so we need to replace the `centerOnUser` action mapping in the `AppMenu` component:

    ```
    methods: mapActions({
      logout: 'logout',
      centerOnUser: 'maps/centerOnUser',
    }),
    ```

Blog posts and comments

In this last part, we are going to add the blog content to the app. Each blog post will have a position and an optional place ID from Google Maps (so the place can be described, for example, as "Restaurant A"). We will load the posts that fit in the visible bounds of the map and each one will appear as a marker with a custom icon. When clicking on a marker, the right side panel will display the post content and a list of comments. Clicking anywhere else on the map will create a draft post at this location in the Vuex store and display a form to write its content and save it in the right side panel.

Posts store module

Let's start by creating a new `posts` namespaced Vuex module to manage shared data related to the blog posts:

1. Create a new `store/posts.js` file with those state properties:

```
export default {
  namespaced: true,

  state () {
    return {
      // New post being created
      draft: null,
      // Bounds of the last fetching
      // To prevent refetching
      mapBounds: null,
      // Posts fetched in those map bounds
      posts: [],
      // ID of the selected post
      selectedPostId: null,
    }
  },
}
```

2. Next we need a few getters:

```
getters: {
  draft: state => state.draft,
  posts: state => state.posts,
  // The id field on posts is '_id' (MongoDB style)
  selectedPost: state => state.posts.find(p => p._id ===
state.selectedPostId),
  // The draft has more priority than the selected post
  currentPost: (state, getters) => state.draft ||
    getters.selectedPost,
},
```

3. And some mutations (note that we mutate posts and mapBounds together so they stay consistent):

```
mutations: {
  addPost (state, value) {
    state.posts.push(value)
  },

  draft (state, value) {
    state.draft = value
  },

  posts (state, { posts, mapBounds }) {
    state.posts = posts
    state.mapBounds = mapBounds
  },

  selectedPostId (state, value) {
    state.selectedPostId = value
  },

  updateDraft (state, value) {
    Object.assign(state.draft, value)
  },
},
```

4. Finally, add it to the store like we did for the `maps` module:

```
import posts from './posts'

const store = new Vuex.Store({
  // ...
  modules: {
    maps,
    posts,
  },
})
```

Rendering functions and JSX

In `Chapter` 4, *Advanced Project Setup*, I already wrote about render functions and JSX, which are different ways other than templates to write the view of the components. Before continuing, we will go into more detail about those and then we will put them into practice.

Writing the view in JavaScript with render functions

Vue compiles our templates into `render` functions. This means that all the component views are JavaScript code in the end. Those render functions will compose the Virtual DOM tree of elements to be displayed in the page real DOM.

Most of the time, templates are fine, but you may come across cases where you need the full programmatic power of JavaScript to create a component view. Instead of specifying a template, you write a `render` function to your component. For example:

```
export default {
  props: ['message'],
  render (createElement) {
    return createElement(
      // Element or Component
      'p',
      // Data Object
      { class: 'content' },
      // Children or Text content
      this.message
    )
  },
}
```

The first argument is `createElement`, the function you need to call to create elements (which can be either DOM elements or Vue components). It takes up to three arguments:

- `element` (required), which can be the name of an HTML tag, the ID of a registered component, or directly a component definition object. It can be a function returning one of these.
- `data` (optional) is the Data Object, which specifies things such as CSS classes, props, events, and so on.
- `children` (optional) is either a text string or an array of children constructed with `createElement`.

> **TIP**
> We will use `h` as an alias of `createElement`, the argument of the `render` function, since it's the common name used by everyone (and it's required by JSX as we will see in a bit). h comes from the hyperscript term describing "writing HTML using JavaScript".

The first example would be equivalent to this template:

```
<template>
  <p class="content">{{ message }}</p>
</template>
```

Dynamic templates

The main advantages of writing render functions directly are that they are closer to compiler and you have the full power of JavaScript available to manipulate the template. The obvious drawback is that it doesn't look like HTML anymore, but this can be alleviated by JSX as we will see in the *What is JSX* section.

For example, you could create a component that renders a title at any level we want:

```
Vue.component('my-title', {
  props: ['level'],
  render (h) {
    return h(
      // Tag name
      `h${this.level}`,
      // Default slot content
      this.$slots.default,
    )
  }
})
```

[273]

> **TIP**
> Here we skipped the data object argument since it is optional. We only passed the tag name and the content.

And then, for example, we would use it in our template to render an `<h2>` title element:

```
<my-title level="2">Hello</my-title>
```

The equivalent in template would be quite tedious to write:

```
<template>
  <h1 v-if="level === 1">
    <slot></slot>
  </h1>
  <h2 v-else-if="level === 2">
    <slot></slot>
  </h2>
  <h3 v-else-if="level === 3">
    <slot></slot>
  </h3>
  <h4 v-else-if="level === 4">
    <slot></slot>
  </h4>
  <h5 v-else-if="level === 5">
    <slot></slot>
  </h5>
  <h6 v-else-if="level === 6">
    <slot></slot>
  </h6>
</template>
```

Data objects

The second optional argument is the data object, which allows you to pass additional information about the element to `createElement` (or `h`). For example, you can specify CSS classes in the same way we use the `v-bind:class` directive in our classic templates, or we can add event listeners.

Chapter 6

Here is an example of a data object that covers most features:

```
{
  // Same API as `v-bind:class`
  'class': {
    foo: true,
    bar: false
  },
  // Same API as `v-bind:style`
  style: {
    color: 'red',
    fontSize: '14px'
  },
  // Normal HTML attributes
  attrs: {
    id: 'foo'
  },
  // Component props
  props: {
    myProp: 'bar'
  },
  // DOM properties
  domProps: {
    innerHTML: 'baz'
  },
  // Event handlers are nested under "on", though
  // modifiers such as in v-on:keyup.enter are not
  // supported. You'll have to manually check the
  // keyCode in the handler instead.
  on: {
    click: this.clickHandler
  },
  // For components only. Allows you to listen to
  // native events, rather than events emitted from
  // the component using vm.$emit.
  nativeOn: {
    click: this.nativeClickHandler
  },
  // Custom directives. Note that the binding's
  // oldValue cannot be set, as Vue keeps track
  // of it for you.
  directives: [
    {
      name: 'my-custom-directive',
      value: '2'
      expression: '1 + 1',
      arg: 'foo',
      modifiers: {
```

[275]

```
        bar: true
      }
    }
  ],
  // The name of the slot, if this component is the
  // child of another component
  slot: 'name-of-slot'
  // Other special top-level properties
  key: 'myKey',
  ref: 'myRef'
}
```

For example, we can apply a special CSS class if the title level is below a specific number:

```
Vue.component('my-title', {
  props: ['level'],
  render (h) {
    return h(
      // Tag name
      `h${this.level}`,
      // Data object
      {
        'class': {
          'important-title': this.level <= 3,
        },
      },
      // Default slot content
      this.$slots.default,
    )
  }
})
```

We could also put a click event listener that calls a method of the component:

```
Vue.component('my-title', {
  props: ['level'],
  render (h) {
    return h(
      // Tag name
      `h${this.level}`,
      // Data object
      {
        on: {
          click: this.clickHandler,
        },
      },
      // Default slot content
      this.$slots.default,
```

```
      )
    },
    methods: {
      clickHandler (event) {
        console.log('You clicked')
      },
    },
})
```

You can find the full description of this object in the official documentation (`https://vuejs.org/v2/guide/render-function.html#The-Data-Object-In-Depth`).

As we have seen, Vue uses render functions in pure JavaScript under-the-hood of our templates! We can even write our own render functions, using the `createElement` (or `h`) function to construct the elements to be added to the Virtual-DOM.

This way of writing our views is more flexible and powerful than templates, but is more complex and verbose. Use it when you feel comfortable with it!

Virtual DOM

The result of the `render` function is a tree of nodes created with the `createElement` (or `h`) function; these are called **VNodes** in Vue. It represent the view of the component in the Virtual DOM held by Vue. Every element in the DOM is a node--HTML elements, text, even comments are nodes:

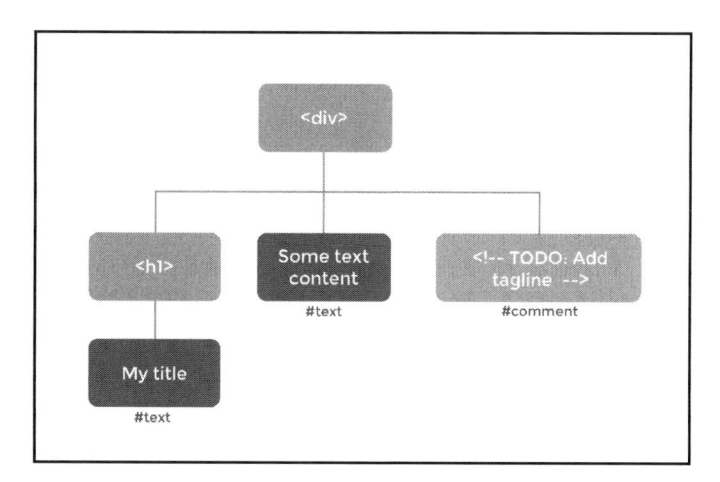

Vue doesn't directly replace the Real DOM tree with the new Virtual DOM tree, because it may engender a lot of DOM operations (add or remove nodes), which are costly. To be more performant, Vue will create a diff between the two trees, and it will only do the DOM operations necessary to update the Real DOM to match the Virtual DOM.

All of this happens automatically so that Vue keeps the Real DOM up-to-date when data changes in your application.

What is JSX?

JSX is a language created to write code that looks more like HTML inside the `render` function's JavaScript code. It is effectively an XML-like extension to JavaScript. Our first previous example looks like this in JSX:

```
export default {
  props: ['message'],
  render (h) {
    return <p class="content">
      {this.message}
    </p>
  },
}
```

This is possible thanks to Babel, the library that is in charge of compiling our ES2015 JavaScript (or more recent) code into old ES5 JavaScript, which runs in older browsers such as Internet Explorer. Babel can also be used to implement new features into the JavaScript language (such as the proposed draft features that may appear in later versions) or entirely new extensions such as JSX.

The `babel-plugin-transform-vue-jsx` included in `babel-preset-vue` takes care of transforming the JSX code into real JavaScript code that uses the `h` function. So the previous JSX example will be transformed back into:

```
export default {
  props: ['message'],
  render (h) {
    return h('p', { class: 'content' }, this.message)
  },
}
```

Chapter 6

> 💡 **TIP** That's why we need to use `h` instead of `createElement` when using JSX.

Thankfully, vue-cli already has this enabled, so we can write JSX code in our `.vue` files!

Blog content structure (in JSX!)

Let's create a new `src/components/content` folder and a new `BlogContent.vue` file inside it. This component represents the right side panel and will be responsible for displaying the right component:

- A `LocationInfo.vue` component that may display the location adress and name if selected on the map
- Below, it will display one of the following:
  - A `NoContent.vue` component if no location is selected, with a click on the map hint
  - A `CreatePost.vue` component if there is a draft post, with a form
  - A `PostContent.vue` component if a real post is selected, with the content and the comments list

1. Let's create those components as well in the `content` directory, with an empty template:

   ```
   <template></template>
   ```

   Back to our `BlogContent.vue` component! We will write this new component in JSX to practice it.

2. Start by creating the namespaced helpers:

   ```
   <script>
   import { createNamespacedHelpers } from 'vuex'

   // posts module
   const {
     mapGetters: postsGetters,
     mapActions: postsActions,
   } = createNamespacedHelpers('posts')

   </script>
   ```

[279]

> It is good practice to rename the namespaced helpers because you may add helpers for another module in the future. For example, if you don't, you may end up with two `mapGetters`, which is impossible. Here we rename `mapGetters` to `postsGetters` and `mapActions` to `postsActions`.

3. Then let's write the component definition:

```
export default {
  computed: {
    ...postsGetters([
      'draft',
      'currentPost',
    ]),

    cssClass () {
      return [
        'blog-content',
        {
          'has-content': this.currentPost,
        },
      ]
    },
  },
}
```

The `has-content` CSS class will be used on a smartphone to hide the pane when no post is selected or no draft is being edited (it will be full screen).

4. Next, we need to write the render function with JSX:

```
render (h) {
  let Content
  if (!this.currentPost) {
    Content = NoContent
  } else if (this.draft) {
    Content = CreatePost
  } else {
    Content = PostContent
  }

  return <div class={this.cssClass}>
    <LocationInfo />
    <Content />
  </div>
},
```

Chapter 6

> **TIP**: Don't forget to import the four other components as well!

In JSX, the case of the first letter of a tag is important! If it starts with a lowercase letter, it will be considered as a string parameter for the `createElement` function and will resolve either to an HTML element or a registered component (for example, `<div>`). On the other hand, if the first letter is uppercase, it will be considered as a variable! In our preceding code, `LocationInfo` is directly used from the import. For example:

```
import LocationInfo from './LocationInfo.vue'

export default {
  render (h) {
    return <LocationInfo />
  }
}
```

We also use this to dynamically choose which component will be displayed, thanks to the `Component` local variable (note the uppercase C). It wouldn't work if the first letter of the variable name was lowercase.

5. Let's rewrite our `GeoBlog.vue` component in JSX as well while adding the `BlogContent` component:

```
<script>
import AppMenu from './AppMenu.vue'
import BlogMap from './BlogMap.vue'
import BlogContent from './content/BlogContent.vue'

export default {
  render (h) {
    return <div class="geo-blog">
      <AppMenu />
      <div class="panes">
        <BlogMap />
        <BlogContent />
      </div>
    </div>
  }
}
</script>
```

[281]

> **TIP**: Don't forget to remove the `<template>` part in the file! You can't have both a render function and a template.

No content

Before continuing, let's quickly add the template of the `NoContent.vue` component, which just displays a hint when no post is selected:

```
<template>
  <div class="no-content">
    <i class="material-icons">explore</i>
    <div class="hint">Click on the map to add a post</div>
  </div>
</template>
```

Creating a post

When the user clicks on a location on the map with no marker, we create a draft post; then the form in the right side panel will edit its content. When the user clicks the **Create** button, we send the draft to the server and add the result (the new post data) to the posts list.

Draft store actions

In the `posts` namespaced store module, we will need a few new actions to create, update, and clear the draft post:

Add the `clearDraft`, `createDraft`, `setDraftLocation`, and `updateDraft` actions:

```
actions: {
  clearDraft ({ commit }) {
    commit('draft', null)
  },
  createDraft ({ commit }) {
    // Default values
    commit('draft', {
      title: '',
      content: '',
      position: null,
      placeId: null,
    })
```

```
      },

      setDraftLocation ({ dispatch, getters }, { position, placeId }) {
        if (!getters.draft) {
          dispatch('createDraft')
        }
        dispatch('updateDraft', {
          position,
          placeId,
        })
      },

      updateDraft ({ dispatch, commit, getters }, draft) {
        commit('updateDraft', draft)
      },
    },
```

The action we call when the user clicks the map is `setDraftLocation`, which will automatically create a new draft, if there isn't one, and update its location.

Blog Map changes

We need to make some changes to the `BlogMap` component to integrate our Vuex store.

1. In the `BlogMap.vue` component, we can add the Vuex helpers for the `posts` namespaced module, while renaming the ones we already have for the `maps` module:

   ```
   // Vuex mappers
   // maps module
   const {
     mapGetters: mapsGetters,
     mapActions: mapsActions,
   } = createNamespacedHelpers('maps')
   // posts module
   const {
     mapGetters: postsGetters,
     mapActions: postsActions,
   } = createNamespacedHelpers('posts')
   ```

2. Add the `draft` getter:

   ```
   computed: {
     ...mapsGetters([
       'center',
   ```

[283]

```
            'zoom',
          ]),
          ...postsGetters([
            'draft',
          ]),
          // ...
        },
```

3. Add the `setDraftLocation` action as well:

   ```
   methods: {
     ...mapsActions([
       'setCenter',
       'setUserPosition',
       'setZoom',
     ]),

     ...postsActions([
       'setDraftLocation',
     ]),
   },
   ```

Click handler

We also need to handle the clicks on the map to create a new blog post.

1. Add the `click` handler to the map:

   ```
   <googlemaps-map
     :center="center"
     :zoom="zoom"
     :options="mapOptions"
     @update:center="setCenter"
     @update:zoom="setZoom"
     @click="onMapClick"
   >
   ```

2. Add the corresponding method that dispatches the `setDraftLocation` action with the eventual `latLng` (the position) and `placeId` from Google Maps:

   ```
   onMapClick (event) {
     this.setDraftLocation({
       position: event.latLng,
       placeId: event.placeId,
     })
   },
   ```

You can now try to click on the map--two mutations (one to create the draft and one to update its location) should be recorded in the dev tools.

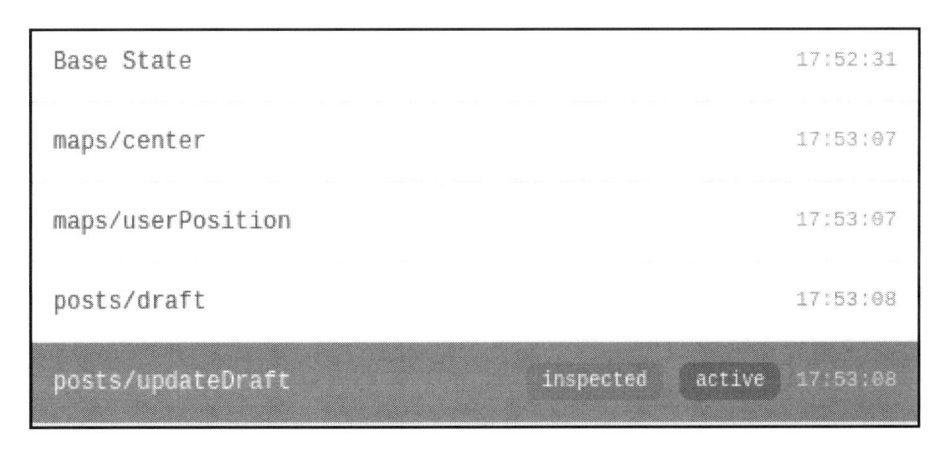

```
Base State                                      17:52:31

maps/center                                     17:53:07

maps/userPosition                               17:53:07

posts/draft                                     17:53:08

posts/updateDraft              inspected  active  17:53:08
```

Ghost marker

We would like to display a transparent marker on the position of the draft. The component to use is `googlemaps-marker`:

Add a new marker in the `googlemaps-map` component that uses the info from the `draft` getter:

```
<!-- New post marker -->
<googlemaps-marker
  v-if="draft"
  :clickable="false"
  :label="{
    color: 'white',
    fontFamily: 'Material Icons',
    text: 'add_circle',
  }"
  :opacity=".75"
  :position="draft.position"
  :z-index="6"
/>
```

> **TIP**: If you don't see the new marker, refresh the page.

Try clicking on the map to see the ghost marker in action:

Post form

Onward to the `CreatePost.vue` component! This component will display a form to enter the details of the new post like its title and content.

1. Let's first create its template with a simple form:

```
<template>
  <form
    class="create-post"
    @submit.prevent="handleSubmit">
    <input
      name="title"
      v-model="title"
      placeholder="Title"
      required />

    <textarea
      name="content"
      v-model="content"
      placeholder="Content"
      required />

    <div class="actions">
      <button
        type="button"
        class="secondary"
        @click="clearDraft">
        <i class="material-icons">delete</i>
        Discard
      </button>
      <button
        type="submit"
        :disabled="!formValid">
        <i class="material-icons">save</i>
        Post
      </button>
```

```
        </div>
    </form>
</template>
```

2. Then map the Vuex helpers from the `posts` module:

```
<script>
import { createNamespacedHelpers } from 'vuex'

// posts module
const {
  mapGetters: postsGetters,
  mapActions: postsActions,
} = createNamespacedHelpers('posts')
</script>
```

3. Add the necessary getters and methods:

```
export default {
  computed: {
    ...postsGetters([
      'draft',
    ]),
  },
  methods: {
    ...postsActions([
      'clearDraft',
      'createPost', // We will create this one very soon
      'updateDraft',
    ]),
  },
}
```

4. Then we will add a few computed properties bound to the form input elements with the `v-model` directive:

```
title: {
  get () {
    return this.draft.title
  },
  set (value) {
    this.updateDraft({
      ...this.draft,
      title: value,
    })
  },
},
```

```
content: {
  get () {
    return this.draft.content
  },
  set (value) {
    this.updateDraft({
      ...this.draft,
      content: value,
    })
  },
},

formValid () {
  return this.title && this.content
},
```

As you can see, we can use computed properties in two ways with this object notation: with a getter and with a setter! That way, we can use them to read a value, but also to easily change it:

- `get ()` is called like before when the computed property is first read or if it needs to be recomputed
- `set (value)` is called when the property is assigned a value, for example `this.a = 'new value'`

This is very useful when working with Vuex and forms, because it allow us to use a Vuex getter for the `get` part, and a Vuex action for the `set` part!

5. We also need a `handleSubmit` method that dispatches the `createPost` action that we will create very soon:

```
handleSubmit () {
  if (this.formValid) {
    this.createPost(this.draft)
  }
},
```

Making the request

We will now implement an action to send a new Geolocated Blog post to the server.

1. Let's create the new `createPost` action in the `posts` Vuex module(don't forget to import '$fetch')):

    ```
    async createPost ({ commit, dispatch }, draft) {
      const data = {
        ...draft,
        // We need to get the object form
        position: draft.position.toJSON(),
      }

      // Request
      const result = await $fetch('posts/new', {
        method: 'POST',
        body: JSON.stringify(data),
      })
      dispatch('clearDraft')

      // Update the posts list
      commit('addPost', result)
      dispatch('selectPost', result._id)
    },
    ```

    This is our most complex action yet! It prepares the data (notice how we serialize the Google Maps `position` object to a JSON-compatible plain object). Then we send a POST request to the `/posts/new` path on our server, and retrieve the result, which is the new real post object (with its `_id` field set). Finally, the draft is cleared, and the new post is added to the store and selected.

2. We also need a new `selectPost` action so the new post will be automatically selected:

    ```
    async selectPost ({ commit }, id) {
      commit('selectedPostId', id)
      // TOTO fetch the post details (comments, etc.)
    },
    ```

[289]

Project 4 - Geolocated Blog

You can now create posts by clicking on the map!

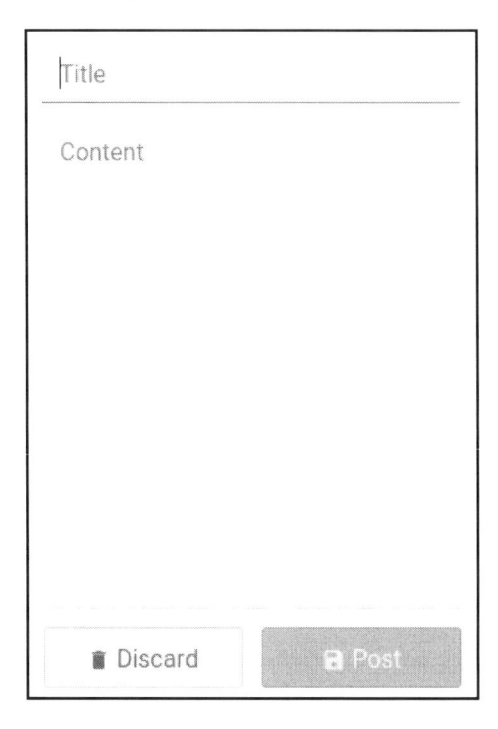

Fetching posts

In this section, we will fetch the posts from the server and display them on the map.

Store action

We will fetch the posts each time the map bounds have changed due to the user panning or zooming the map.

Fetch posts action

Let's create the posts-fetching action, but we need to tackle a problem first, though. What the following happen:

1. The user moves the map.
2. A request A is made to the server.

[290]

3. The user moves the map again.
4. A request B is sent.
5. For some reason, we receive the request B response before request A.
6. We set the list of posts from request B.
7. The response of request A is received.
8. The list of posts is replaced from a no longer up-to-date request.

That's why we need to abort the previous requests if a new one is made. To do that, we will use a unique identifier for each request:

1. Declare the unique identifier at the top of the `posts.js` file:

   ```
   let fetchPostsUid = 0
   ```

2. Now we can add the new `fetchPosts` action, which fetches the posts in the map bounds only if it's different from last time (with an additional `force` parameter in the payload):

   ```
   async fetchPosts ({ commit, state }, { mapBounds, force }) {
     let oldBounds = state.mapBounds
     if (force || !oldBounds || !oldBounds.equals(mapBounds)) {
       const requestId = ++fetchPostsUid

       // Request
       const ne = mapBounds.getNorthEast()
       const sw = mapBounds.getSouthWest()
       const query = `posts?ne=${
         encodeURIComponent(ne.toUrlValue())
       }&sw=${
         encodeURIComponent(sw.toUrlValue())
       }`
       const posts = await $fetch(query)

       // We abort if we started another query
       if (requestId === fetchPostsUid) {
         commit('posts', {
           posts,
           mapBounds,
         })
       }
     }
   },
   ```

> The `++fetchPostsUid` expression add 1 to `fetchPostsUid` and then returns the new value.

> We encode the map bounds as two points: North-East and South-West.

The way we abort the query is by comparing the unique ID we stored before making the request (`requestId`) and the current ID counter (`fetchPostsUid`). If they are different, we don't commit the result because it means another request was made (since we increment the counter each time).

Action dispatching

In the `maps` store, let's create a `setBounds` action that will be dispatched when the maps is idle after being panned or zoomed. This action will dispatch the `fetchPosts` from the `posts` module:

1. Use the `{ root: true }` option to dispatch the action in a non-namespaced way so you can reach the `posts` module one:

   ```
   setBounds ({ dispatch }, value) {
     dispatch('posts/fetchPosts', {
       mapBounds: value,
     }, {
       root: true,
     })
   },
   ```

   > We have created another action in the `maps` module because it is related to the map and it could do more in the future than just dispatching another action.

2. In the `BlogMap.vue` component, map the new `setBounds` action on the right helper and add a `'map'` ref and an `'idle'` event listener to the map:

```
<googlemaps-map
  ref="map"
  :center="center"
  :zoom="zoom"
  :options="mapOptions"
  @update:center="setCenter"
  @update:zoom="setZoom"
  @click="onMapClick"
  @idle="onIdle"
>
```

3. And add the corresponding `onIdle` method to dispatch the `setBounds` action and pass the map bounds:

```
onIdle () {
  this.setBounds(this.$refs.map.getBounds())
},
```

Refresh the app and look for the `posts` mutations in the dev tools when you pan or zoom the map.

Displaying markers

Still in the `BlogMap` component, we will use the `googlemaps-marker` again to loop through the posts and display a marker for each of them. Map the `posts` and `currentPost` getters, plus the `selectPost` action, on the right helper and add the markers loop inside the `googlemaps-map` component:

```
<googlemaps-marker
  v-for="post of posts"
  :key="post._id"
  :label="{
    color: post === currentPost ? 'white' : 'black',
    fontFamily: 'Material Icons',
    fontSize: '20px',
    text: 'face',
  }"
  :position="post.position"
  :z-index="5"
  @click="selectPost(post._id)"
/>
```

[293]

Project 4 - Geolocated Blog

You can now refresh the app and see the posts you added earlier appear on the map! If you click on a post marker, its icon should turn white too.

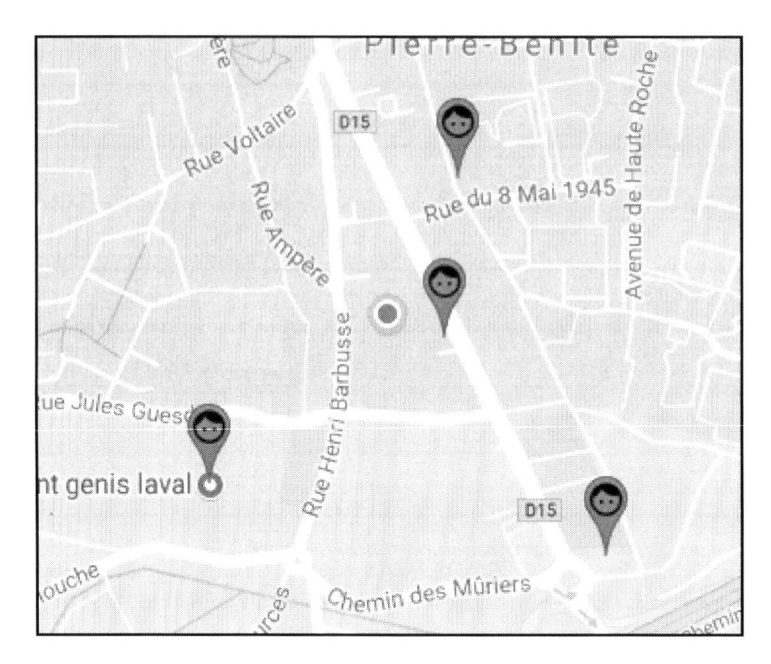

Login and logout

We are not done with the post-fetching yet--we need to react to a user logging in or out:

- When the user log out, we will clear the posts list and the last registered map bounds so the posts can be fetched again
- When the user log in, we will fetch the posts again and eventually re-select the previously selected post

Logout

First, we will implement the logout action.

1. Let's add a `logout` action in the `posts` Vuex module that clears the posts fetching data:

   ```
   logout ({ commit }) {
     commit('posts', {
       posts: [],
       mapBounds: null,
     })
   },
   ```

2. We can call this from the `logout` action in the main store (in the `store/index.js` file):

   ```
   logout ({ commit, dispatch }) {
     commit('user', null)
     $fetch('logout')
     // ...
     dispatch('posts/logout')
   },
   ```

   This is going to work, but we can improve this code--we could define the `logout` action of the `posts` namespaced submodule as a root action. That way, when we dispatch the `'logout'` action, both the `logout` and the `posts/logout` will be called!

3. Use this object notation in the `posts` module for the `logout` action:

   ```
   logout: {
     handler ({ commit }) {
       commit('posts', {
         posts: [],
         mapBounds: null,
       })
     },
     root: true,
   },
   ```

   The `handler` property is the function called on this action, and the `root` Boolean property indicates if this is a root action. Now the `logout` action is no longer namespaced regarding the action dispatching system, and will be called if a non-namespaced `'logout'` action is dispatched.

> **TIP:** The state, getters, commit, and dispatch made inside this `logout` action are still namespaced to the module. Only its invocation is no longer namespaced!

4. You can remove the `dispatch('posts/logout')` line from the `logout` action on the main store.

Login

When the user is successfully logged in, we will dispatch a non-namespaced `'logged-in'` action.

1. Back in the `posts` module, add the `logged-in` action using the new object notation:

```
'logged-in': {
  handler ({ dispatch, state }) {
    if (state.mapBounds) {
      dispatch('fetchPosts', {
        mapBounds: state.mapBounds,
        force: true,
      })
    }
    if (state.selectedPostId) {
      dispatch('selectPost', state.selectedPostId)
    }
  },
  root: true,
},
```

2. In the main store `login` action, dispatch this new `logged-in` action if the user is successfully authenticated:

```
if (user) {
  // ...
  dispatch('logged-in')
}
```

Selecting a post

This is the last section of this chapter! We will now create the post content component that will display the title, content, location info, and the comment list. A post details object is the same as a post object plus the author data, the list of the comments, and the authors for each comment.

Post details

Let's first modify our `posts` Vuex module in preparation for the posts details.

Store changes for post selection and sending

1. Add a `selectedPostDetails` data property in the state and add the corresponding getter and mutation:

   ```
   state () {
     return {
       // ...
       // Fetched details for the selected post
       selectedPostDetails: null,
     }
   },

   getters: {
     // ...
     selectedPostDetails: state => state.selectedPostDetails,
   },

   mutations: {
     // ...
     selectedPostDetails (state, value) {
       state.selectedPostDetails = value
     },
   },
   ```

2. In the `selectPost`, fetch the details with a request to the `/post/<id>` route on the server:

```
async selectPost ({ commit }, id) {
  commit('selectedPostDetails', null)
  commit('selectedPostId', id)
  const details = await $fetch(`posts/${id}`)
  commit('selectedPostDetails', details)
},
```

3. Also add a new `unselectPost` action:

```
unselectPost ({ commit }) {
  commit('selectedPostId', null)
},
```

Post Content component

We the user clicks on a blog marker on the map, we need to display its content in the side pane. We will do this in a dedicated `PostContent` component.

1. Let's implement the `content/PostContent.vue` component by starting the initial template:

```
<template>
  <div class="post-content">
    <template v-if="details">
      <div class="title">
        <img :src="details.author.profile.photos[0].value" />
        <span>
          <span>{{ details.title }}</span>
          <span class="info">
            <span class="name">
              {{ details.author.profile.displayName }}</span>
            <span class="date">{{ details.date | date }}</span>
          </span>
        </span>
      </div>
      <div class="content">{{ details.content }}</div>
      <!-- TODO Comments -->
      <div class="actions">
        <button
          type="button"
          class="icon-button secondary"
          @click="unselectPost">
          <i class="material-icons">close</i>
```

```
        </button>
        <!-- TODO Comment input -->
      </div>
    </template>
    <div class="loading-animation" v-else>
      <div></div>
    </div>
  </div>
</template>
```

The first part is the header with the author avatar, the title, author name, and creation date. Then we display the post content, followed by the comment list, and an action toolbar at the bottom. It will also display a loading animation before we receive the post details response from the server.

2. Then we need a script section with the `details` getter and the `unselectPost` action from the `posts` module:

```
<script>
import { createNamespacedHelpers } from 'vuex'

// posts module
const {
  mapGetters: postsGetters,
  mapActions: postsActions,
} = createNamespacedHelpers('posts')

export default {
  computed: {
    ...postsGetters({
      details: 'selectedPostDetails',
    }),
  },

  methods: {
    ...postsActions([
      'unselectPost',
    ]),
  },
}
</script>
```

Now you can try selecting a post marker and see its content displayed in the right side panel:

Location info and scoped slots

We are going to display information about the current post location at the top of the right sidebar, with the name and the address. The components from `vue-googlemaps` that we are going to use take advantage of a Vue feature called "scoped slots."

Scoped slots to pass data to the parent

You should already know what slots are--they allow us to put elements or components inside other components. With scoped slots, the component where the `<slot>` parts are declared can pass down data to the view that is being embedded in the slot.

For example, we could have this component with a default slot that has a list of results in the `results` property:

```
<template>
  <div class="search">
    <slot />
  </div>
</template>

<script>
export default {
```

```
    computed: {
      results () {
        return /* ... */
      },
    },
  }
</script>
```

We could pass this property to the external view that includes parts of templates through the slot like this:

```
<slot :results="results" />
```

When using this component, you can retrieve the scoped data by wrapping your code with a template with a `slot-scope` attribute. All the scoped data will be available in this attribute object:

```
<Search>
  <template slot-scope="props">
    <div>{{props.results.length}} results</div>
  </template>
</Search>
```

> **TIP:** The `<template>` tag is not necessary if it has only one child.

This is how the components of the `vue-googlemaps` library that we will use shortly will give us back the data from Google Maps.

Scoped slots are very useful too when combined with a loop:

```
<slot v-for="r of results" :result="r" />
```

When using it, the content of the slot will be repeated and will pass down the current item:

```
<Search>
  <div slot-scope="props" class="result">{{props.result.label}}</div>
</Search>
```

[301]

Project 4 - Geolocated Blog

In this example, if the `results` computed property returns three items, we will have three `<div>` displaying the result labels.

Implementing of the component

We will now use this new Scoped slot concept to display the information about the place associated with the Blog post.

1. Let's create a small component named `PlaceDetails.vue` in the `components/content` folder that displays the name and the address of a location:

```
<script>
export default {
  props: {
    name: String,
    address: String,
  },

  render (h) {
    return <div class="details">
      <div class="name"><i class="material-icons">place</i>
        {this.name}</div>
      <div class="address"> {this.address}</div>
    </div>
  },
}
</script>
```

Then we will implement the `LocationInfo.vue` component.

2. First the template, where we use either the `googlemaps-place-details` component, if we have a Google Maps `placeId` stored on the post, or else the `googlemaps-geocoder` component that will find the most relevant corresponding addresses from the position of the post, and all by retrieving the results with scoped slots:

```
<template>
  <div class="location-info" v-if="currentPost">
    <!-- Place -->
    <googlemaps-place-details
      v-if="currentPost.placeId"
      :request="{
        placeId: currentPost.placeId
      }">
```

```
        <PlaceDetails
          slot-scope="props"
          v-if="props.results"
          :name="props.results.name"
          :address="props.results.formatted_address" />
      </googlemaps-place-details>

      <!-- Position only -->
      <googlemaps-geocoder
        v-else
        :request="{
          location: currentPost.position,
        }">
        <PlaceDetails
          slot-scope="props"
          v-if="props.results"
          :name="props.results[1].placeDetails.name"
          :address="props.results[0].formatted_address" />
      </googlemaps-geocoder>
    </div>
    <div v-else></div>
  </template>
```

3. In the script part map the `currentPost` getter from the `posts` module and import the `PlaceDetails` component we just created:

```
<script>
import PlaceDetails from './PlaceDetails.vue'
import { createNamespacedHelpers } from 'vuex'

// posts module
const {
  mapGetters: postsGetters,
} = createNamespacedHelpers('posts')

export default {
  components: {
    PlaceDetails,
  },

  computed: postsGetters([
'currentPost',
  ]),
  }
</script>
```

Now, if you select or draft a post, you should see the location info display at the top of the right side panel:

> 📍 Restaurant 310 à table
> l'Europe, 145 Boulevard de l'Europe, 69310 Pierre-Bénite, France

Comments - functional components

This is the last section of the chapter, where we will implement post components and learn more about faster functional components.

Store changes for comments

Before going into functional components, we need to lay the groundwork in the Vue

1. In the `posts` Vuex module, we need a new mutation that will add a comment to a post directly:

   ```
   addComment (state, { post, comment }) {
     post.comments.push(comment)
   },
   ```

2. Add the new `sendComment` action too that sends a query to the server to the `/posts/<id>/comment` route and adds it to the selected post:

   ```
   async sendComment ({ commit, rootGetters }, { post, comment }) {
     const user = rootGetters.user
     commit('addComment', {
       post,
       comment: {
         ...comment,
         date: new Date(),
         user_id: user._id,
         author: user,
       },
     })

     await $fetch(`posts/${post._id}/comment`, {
       method: 'POST',
   ```

```
        body: JSON.stringify(comment),
      })
    },
```

> **TIP:** We use `rootGetters` from the action context to retrieve the user data, because it is not in this namespaced module.

Functional component

Each component instance in Vue has to set up a few things when it is created, such as the data reactivity system, component life cycles, and so on. There is a lighter variant of components called functional components. They don't have any state of their own (you can't use the `this` keyword) and can't be displayed in dev tools, but they have a very nice advantage in some cases--they are much faster and use less memory!

The Comments on our blog posts are good candidates for being functional because we could have to display a lot of them.

To create a function component, add the `functional: true` option to its definition object:

```
export default {
  functional: true,
  render (h, { props, children }) {
    return h(`h${props.level}`, children)
  },
}
```

Since the component doesn't have a state and we don't have access to `this`, the render function gets a new `context` parameter containing the props, event listeners, children content, slots, and other data. You can find a full list on the official documentation (https://vuejs.org/v2/guide/render-function.html#Functional-Components).

> **TIP:** When writing functional components, you don't always need to declare props. You get everything as props, but they also get passed down in `context.data`.

Not that you can also use a template with the `functional` attribute instead of the `functional: true` option:

```
<template functional>
  <div class="my-component">{{ props.message }}</div>
</template>
```

1. Now create a new `Comment.vue` component alongside the `PostContent.vue` one:

    ```
    <script>
    import { date } from '../../filters'

    export default {
      functional: true,

      render (h, { props }) {
        const { comment } = props
        return <div class="comment">
          <img class="avatar" src=
          {comment.author.profile.photos[0].value} /&gt;
          <div class="message">
            <div class="info">
            <span class="name">{comment.author.profile.displayName}
            </span>
              <span class="date">{date(comment.date)}</span>
            </div>
            <div class="content">{comment.content}</div>
          </div>
        </div>
      },
    }
    </script>
    ```

2. Back to our `PostContent` component; let's add the comment list in the center of the pane and the comment form to the bottom of the pane:

    ```
    <div class="comments">
      <Comment
        v-for="(comment, index) of details.comments"
        :key="index"
        :comment="comment" />
    </div>
    <div class="actions">
      <!-- ... -->
      <input
        v-model="commentContent"
    ```

```
            placeholder="Type a comment"
            @keyup.enter="submitComment" />
          <button
            type="button"
            class="icon-button"
            @click="submitComment"
            :disabled="!commentFormValid">
            <i class="material-icons">send</i>
          </button>
        </div>
```

3. Then add the `Comment` component, the `commentContent` data property, the `commentFormValid` computed property, the `sendComment` Vuex action, and the `submitComment` method in the script section:

```
        import Comment from './Comment.vue'

        export default {
          components: {
            Comment,
          },
          data () {
            return {
              commentContent: '',
            }
          },
          computed: {
            ...postsGetters({
              details: 'selectedPostDetails',
            }),
            commentFormValid () {
              return this.commentContent
            },
          },
          methods: {
            ...postsActions([
              'sendComment',
              'unselectPost',
            ]),
            async submitComment () {
              if (this.commentFormValid) {
                this.sendComment({
                  post: this.details,
                  comment: {
                    content: this.commentContent,
                  },
                })
```

Project 4 - Geolocated Blog

```
            this.commentContent = ''
        }
      },
    },
  }
}
```

You can now add comments to the selected post:

My favorite restaurant
Guillaume CHAU 09/10/2017

This is the right place to eat! The service is very nice and the dishes are tasty and generous.
You can have a full set menu (starter + main course + dessert + coffee or tea) for 28€ and you can choose almost anything on the entire menu!

Guillaume CHAU 09/10/2017
Seems very nice!

Guillaume CHAU 09/10/2017
Would like to go someday

× Type a comment ▶

Summary

In this chapter, we introduced the very important notion of state management through the usage of the official Vuex library. This will help you build more complex applications and improve their maintainability a lot. We used the Google OAuth API to authenticate our users, embed Google Maps, and a whole Geolocated Blog! All of this was achieved by using a Vuex store integrated into our application, making our components simpler and our code easier to evolve.

Here are some ideas if you want to improve the app further:

- Display the number of thumbs-up on the post markers
- Allow editing or deletion of comments
- Add real-time updates with web-sockets

In the next chapter, we will learn more about server-side rendering, internationalization, testing, and deployment.

7
Project 5 - Online Shop and Scaling Up

In this chapter, we will quickly set up a "Fashion Store" app in order to focus on more advanced topics, such as follows:

- Improving the compatibility of our CSS code with PostCSS and autoprefixer
- Linting our code with ESLint to improve its quality and style
- Unit testing our Vue components
- Localizing the app and taking advantage of the code-splitting feature of webpack
- Enabling server-side rendering of the app in Nodejs
- Building the app for production

The app will be a simple wearable online shop that will look like this:

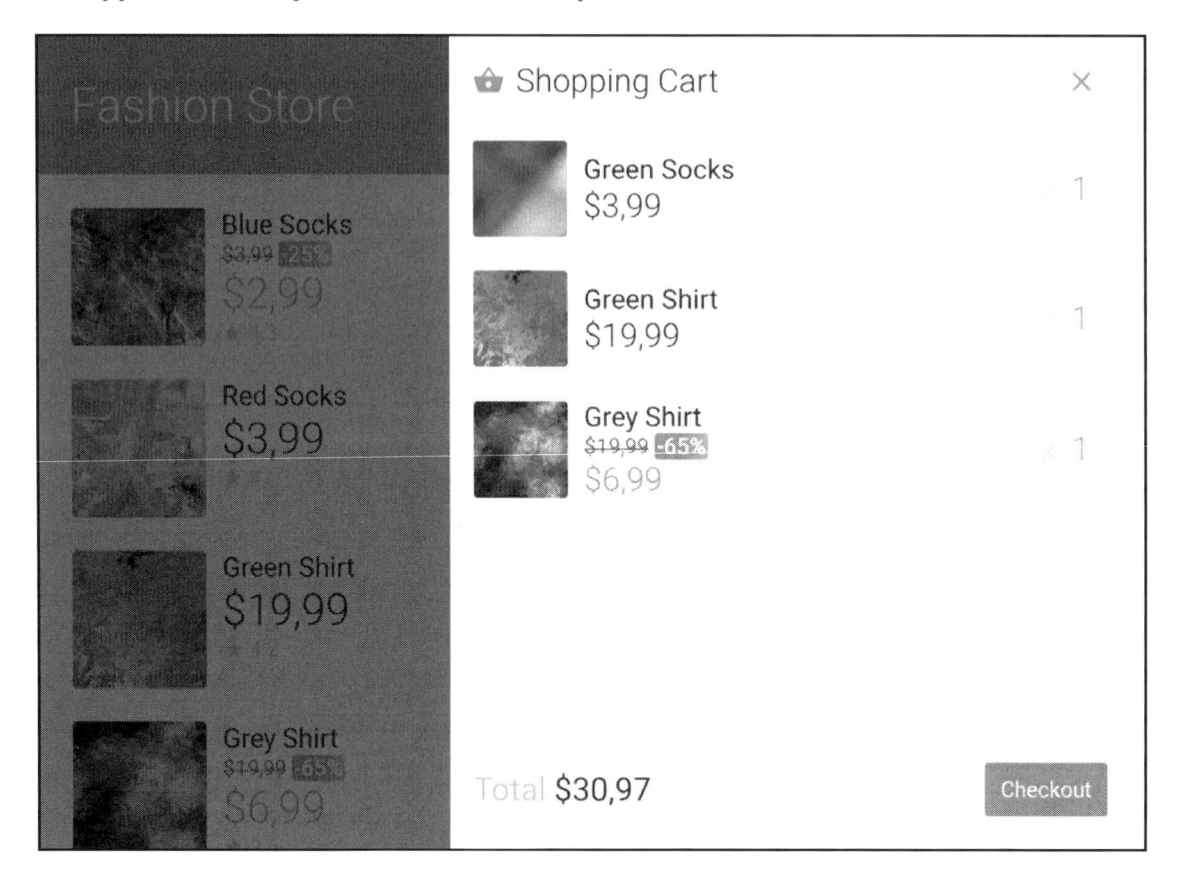

Advanced development workflow

In this first section, we will improve our development workflow with new tools and packages. However, first, we need to set up our Fashion Store project.

Setting up the project

1. Generate a new project using the `vue init` command like we did in Chapter 5, *Project 3 - Support Center*, and Chapter 6, *Project 4 - Geolocated Blog*:

   ```
   vue init webpack-simple e-shop
   cd e-shop
   npm install
   npm install -S babel-polyfill
   ```

2. We will also install stylus:

   ```
   npm i -D stylus stylus-loader
   ```

3. Remove the content of the `src` folder. Then, download the sources files (https://github.com/Akryum/packt-vue-project-guide/tree/master/chapter7-download/src) and extract them in the `src` folder. Those contains all the app source code that have been already done so that we can move forward faster.

4. We need to install a few more packages in the dependencies:

   ```
   npm i -S axios vue-router vuex vuex-router-sync
   ```

   > axios is a great library for making requests to the server and is recommended by the Vue.js team.

Generating a quick development API

Previously, we had a full node server for the backend, but this time we will not focus on the app features. So, we will use the `json-server` package to generate a very simple local API for the purpose of this chapter:

1. Install `json-server` as a dev dependency:

   ```
   npm i -D json-server
   ```

2. When we run this package, it will locally expose a simple REST API and use a `db.json` file to store the data. You can download it (https://github.com/Akryum/packt-vue-project-guide/blob/master/chapter7-download/db.json) and put it in the project root directory. If you open it, you will see a few items for sale and a comment.

3. Then, we will need to add a script to launch the json server. Add a new `db` script to the `package.json` file:

```
"db": "json-server --watch db.json"
```

The preceding command will run the `json-server` package command-line tool and watch the `db.json` file you just downloaded for changes so that you can edit it easily. To try it, use `npm run`:

```
npm run db
```

By default, it will listen to the port `3000`. You can already try it by opening the `http://localhost:3000/items` REST address in your browser:

```
localhost:3000/items

JSON    Données brutes    En-têtes
Enregistrer  Copier

0:
    id:             1
    title:          "Blue Socks"
    price:          2.99
    originalPrice:  3.99
    rating:         4.3
    img:            "http://lorempixel.com/400/400/abstract/1/"
1:
    id:             2
    title:          "Green Socks"
    price:          3.99
    rating:         3.9
    img:            "http://lorempixel.com/400/400/abstract/2/"
```

Launching the app

We are now ready to start the app. Open a new terminal and use `npm run` as usual:

```
npm run dev
```

It should open a new browser window with the right address, and you should be able to use the app:

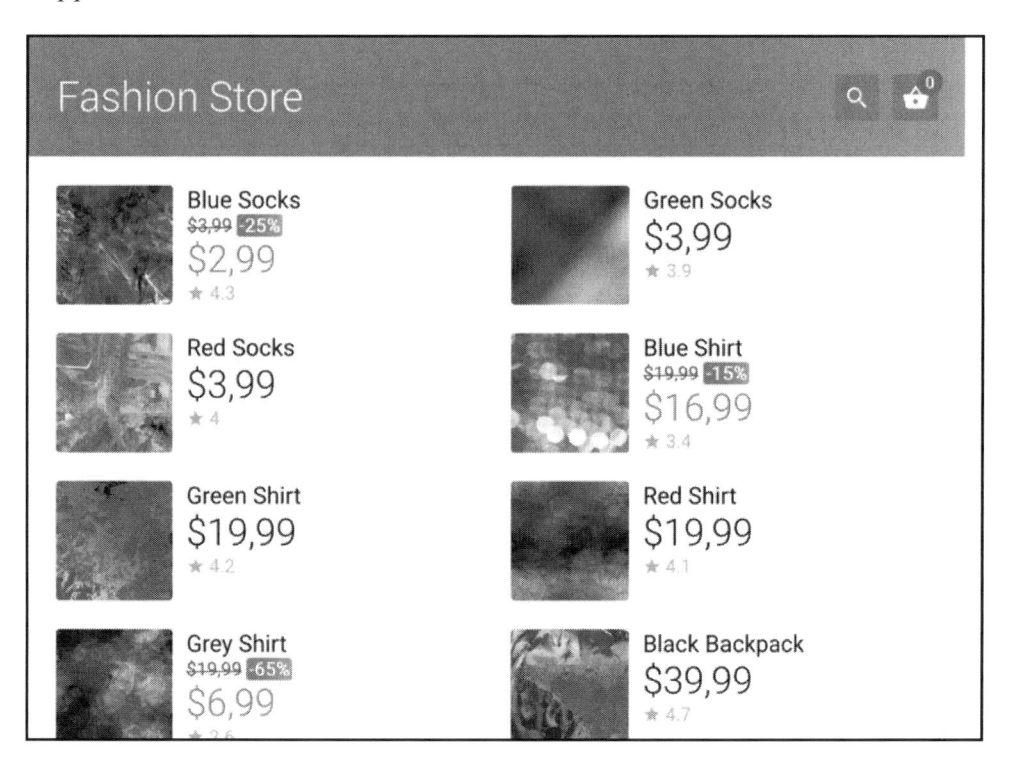

Auto-prefixing CSS with PostCSS

When writing CSS (or Stylus) code, we want it to be compatible with most browsers. Fortunately, there are tools that will do this automatically for us, for example, by adding vendor-prefixed versions of the CSS properties (such as `-webkit-user-select` and `-moz-user-select`).

PostCSS is a library specialized in CSS postprocessing. It has a very modular architecture; it works by adding plugins to it that process the CSS in various ways.

We don't have to install it. `vue-loader` already has PostCSS included. We only have to install the plugins we want. In our case, we need the `autoprefixer` package to make our CSS code compatible with more browsers.

1. Install the `autoprefixer` package:

   ```
   npm i -D autoprefixer
   ```

2. For PostCSS to be active, we will need to add a configuration file called `postcss.config.js` in the project root directory. Let's tell PostCSS we want to use `autoprefixer` in this file:

   ```
   module.exports = {
     plugins: [
       require('autoprefixer'),
     ],
   }
   ```

   That's it! Our code will now be processed by `autoprefixer`. For example, consider this Stylus code:

   ```
   .store-cart-item
     user-select none
   ```

   The final CSS will be as follows:

   ```
   .store-item[data-v-1af8c5dc] {
     -webkit-user-select: none;
     -moz-user-select: none;
     -ms-user-select: none;
     user-select: none;
   }
   ```

Targeting specific browsers with browserslist

We can change what browsers are targeted by `autoprefixer` with the `browserslist` configuration. It consists of a list of rules to determine which browsers to support. Open the `package.json` file and look for the `browserslist` field. It should already have the default values of the `webpack-simple` template, as follows:

```
"> 1%",
"last 2 versions",
"not ie <= 8"
```

The first rule takes the browsers that have more than 1% of usage share on the internet. The second one additionally selects the last two versions of every browsers. Finally, we state that we don't support Internet Explorer 8 or older.

> The data used is provided by the site (https://caniuse.com/), which is specialized in browser compatibility data.

You can now target even older browsers by customizing this field. For example, to target Firefox 20 and later versions, you would add the following rule:

```
"Firefox >= 20"
```

You can find more information about browserslist in its repository (https://github.com/ai/browserslist).

Improving code quality and style with ESLint

Enforcing good coding practices and quality is essential when working on a project with other developers. It ensures that no syntax or basic errors are made (such as forgetting to declare a variable), and it helps to keep the source code clean and consistent. This process is called **linting**.

ESLint is the recommended linting tool by the Vue.js team. It provides a set of linting rules that can be turned on and off to check the code quality. More rules can be added by plugins and some packages define a preset of enabled rules.

1. We will use the StandardJS preset and the `eslint-plugin-vue` package, which adds more rules that help follow the official Vue styleguide (https://vuejs.org/v2/style-guide/):

   ```
   npm i -D eslint eslint-config-standard eslint-plugin-vue@beta
   ```

2. The `eslint-config-standard` package has four peer dependencies that we need to install as well:

   ```
   npm i -D eslint-plugin-import eslint-plugin-node eslint-plugin-promise eslint-plugin-standard
   ```

3. In order to use babel for the JavaScript code when ESLint parses the files, we will need an additional package:

```
npm i -D babel-eslint
```

Configuring ESLint

Create a new `.eslintrc.js` file in the project root directory and write the following configuration:

```js
module.exports = {
  // Use only this configuration
  root: true,
  // File parser
  parser: 'vue-eslint-parser',
  parserOptions: {
    // Use babel-eslint for JavaScript
    'parser': 'babel-eslint',
    'ecmaVersion': 2017,
    // With import/export syntax
    'sourceType': 'module'
  },
  // Environment global objects
  env: {
    browser: true,
    es6: true,
  },
  extends: [
    // https://github.com/feross/standard/blob/master/RULES.md#javascript-standard-style
    'standard',
    // https://github.com/vuejs/eslint-plugin-vue#bulb-rules
    'plugin:vue/recommended',
  ],
}
```

First, we use `vue-eslint-parser` to read the files (including the `.vue` files). It uses `babel-eslint` when parsing the JavaScript code. We also specify the EcmaScript version of JavaScript and that we use the `import/export` syntax for the modules.

Then, we tell ESLint that we expect to be in a browser and ES6 (or ES2015) JavaScript environment, which means we should be able to access globals such as `window` or Promise without ESLint raising undefined variable errors.

We also specify which configurations (or presets) we would like to use--`standard` and `vue/recommended`.

Customizing the rules

We can change what rules are enabled and modify their options with the `rules` object. Add the following to the ESLint configuration:

```
rules: {
  // https://github.com/babel/babel-eslint/issues/517
  'no-use-before-define': 'off',
  'comma-dangle': ['error', 'always-multiline'],
},
```

The first line disables the `no-use-before-define` rule, which has a bug when using the `...` destructuration operator. The second one changes the `commad-dangle` rule to enforce putting a trailing `,` comma at the end of all the array and object lines.

> **TIP**
> The rules have a status, which can take on those three values--`'off'` (or 0), `'warn'` (or 1), and `'error'` (or 2).

Running ESLint

To run eslint on the `src` folder, we will need a new script in the `package.json`:

```
"eslint": "eslint --ext .js,.jsx,.vue src"
```

You should note some errors in the console:

```
* 3 problems (3 errors, 0 warnings)
  2 errors, 0 warnings potentially fixable with the `--fix` option.
```

Some of those issues can be fixed by ESLint by adding the `--fix` argument to the preceding `eslint` command:

```
"eslint": "eslint --ext .js,.jsx,.vue src --fix"
```

Run it again, and you should see only one error remaining:

```
/src/main.js
  20:3  error  Do not use 'new' for side effects  no-new

✘ 1 problem (1 error, 0 warnings)
```

ESLint tells us we shouldn't create new objects without keeping their reference in a variable. If we look at the corresponding code, we see that we indeed create a new instance of Vue in the `main.js` file:

```
new Vue({
  el: '#app',
  router,
  store,
  ...App,
})
```

> **TIP**: If you look at the ESLint error, you can see the code of the rule--`no-new`. You can open the `https://eslint.org/` website and type it in the search field to get the rule definition. If it's a rule added by a plugin, it should have the name of the plugin followed by a slash, for example, `vue/require-v-for-key`.

This code is written as intended, since this is the standard way of declaring a Vue app. So, we need to disable this rule for this specific line of code by adding a special comment just before:

```
// eslint-disable-next-line no-new
new Vue({
  ...
})
```

ESLint inside Webpack

For now, we have to manually run the `eslint` script to check our code. It would be even better if we were able to check our code when it is processed by Webpack, so it would be fully automatic. Fortunately, this is possible thanks to the `eslint-loader`.

1. Install it in the dev dependencies alongside the `friendly-errors-webpack-plugin` package, which will improve the console messages:

   ```
   npm i -D eslint-loader friendly-errors-webpack-plugin
   ```

   Now we have to change the webpack configuration to add a new ESLint loader rule.

2. Edit the `webpack.config.js` file and add this new rule at the top of the `module.rules` option:

   ```
   module: {
     rules: [
       {
         test: /\.(jsx?|vue)$/,
         loader: 'eslint-loader',
         enforce: 'pre',
       },
       // ...
   ```

3. Additionally, we can enable the `friendly-errors-webpack-plugin` package. Import it at the top of the file:

   ```
   const FriendlyErrors = require('friendly-errors-webpack-plugin')
   ```

   > **TIP:** We can't use the `import/export` syntax here, since it will be executed in nodejs.

4. Then, add this plugin when we are in development mode by adding an `else` condition at the end of the configuration file:

   ```
   } else {
     module.exports.plugins = (module.exports.plugins ||
     []).concat([
       new FriendlyErrors(),
     ])
   }
   ```

Restart webpack by rerunning the `dev` script and remove a comma somewhere in the code. You should see the ESLint error displayed in the webpack output:

```
ERROR  Failed to compile with 1 errors

error  in ./src/main.js

/Users/guillaumechau/Documents/Projets/packt-vue-project-guide/chapter7-full/src/main.js
  25:11  error  Missing trailing comma  comma-dangle

✖ 1 problem (1 error, 0 warnings)
  1 error, 0 warnings potentially fixable with the `--fix` option.
```

In the browser, you should now see the error overlay:

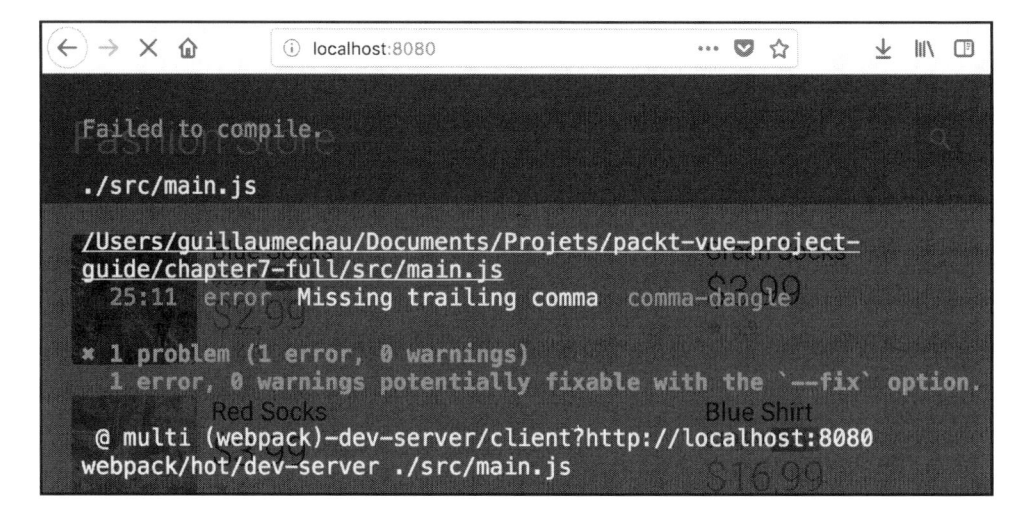

```
Failed to compile.

./src/main.js

/Users/guillaumechau/Documents/Projets/packt-vue-project-
guide/chapter7-full/src/main.js
  25:11  error  Missing trailing comma  comma-dangle

✖ 1 problem (1 error, 0 warnings)
  1 error, 0 warnings potentially fixable with the `--fix` option.

@ multi (webpack)-dev-server/client?http://localhost:8080
webpack/hot/dev-server ./src/main.js
```

If you fix the error by putting the comma back again, the overlay will close and the console will display a friendly message:

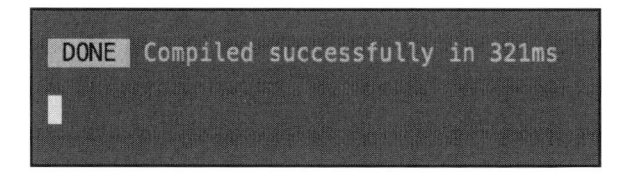

```
DONE  Compiled successfully in 321ms
```

Unit testing with Jest

Important code and components should be unit tested to ensure that they are working as intended and to prevent most regressions when the code evolves. The recommended test runner for Vue components is Jest from Facebook. It is quite fast with a cache system and has an handy snapshot feature to help detect regressions even more.

1. First, install Jest and the official Vue unit testing tools:

   npm i -D jest vue-test-utils

2. We also need a few utilities related to Vue to compile the .vue files with jest-vue and to take snapshots of the components:

   npm i -D vue-jest jest-serializer-vue vue-server-renderer

   > **TIP**: The recommended way to get the HTML render of a component in node is using the `vue-server-renderer` package used to do server-side rendering as we will see later in the chapter.

3. Finally, we will need some babel packages to support babel compilation and webpack dynamic imports inside Jest:

   npm i -D babel-jest babel-plugin-dynamic-import-node

Configuring Jest

To configure Jest, let's create a new `jest.config.js` file in the project root directory:

```
module.exports = {
  transform: {
    '.+\\.jsx?$': '<rootDir>/node_modules/babel-jest',
    '.+\\.vue$': '<rootDir>/node_modules/vue-jest',
  },
  snapshotSerializers: [
    '<rootDir>/node_modules/jest-serializer-vue',
  ],
  mapCoverage: true,
}
```

The `transform` option defines processors for the JavaScript and Vue files. Then, we tell Jest to use `jest-serializer-vue` to serialize the snapshots of the components. We will also enable the source maps with the `mapCoverage` option.

You can find more configuration options at the Jest website (https://facebook.github.io/jest/).

Babel configuration for Jest

To support JavaScript `import/export` modules and dynamic imports inside Jest, we will need to change our babel configuration when the tests are run.

> When using Jest, we are not using webpack and the loaders we use to build the real application.

We need to add two babel plugins to the configuration, when the `NODE_ENV` environment variable is set to `"test"`:

```
{
  "presets": [
    ["env", { "modules": false }],
    "stage-3"
  ],
  "env": {
    "test": {
      "plugins": [
        "transform-es2015-modules-commonjs",
        "dynamic-import-node"
      ]
    }
  }
}
```

The `transform-es2015-modules-commonjs` plugin adds support for `import/export` syntax to Jest, and the `dynamic-import-node` adds support for dynamic imports.

> When run, Jest will automatically set the `NODE_ENV` environment variable to `'test'`.

Our first unit test

To be recognized by Jest anywhere by default, we need to call our test files `.test.js` or `.spec.js`. We will test the `BaseButton.vue` component; go ahead and create a new `BaseButton.spec.js` file next to it in the `src/components` folder.

1. First, we will import the component and the `shallow` method from `vue-test-utils`:

   ```
   import BaseButton from './BaseButton.vue'
   import { shallow } from 'vue-test-utils'
   ```

2. Then, we will create a tests suite with the `describe` function:

   ```
   describe('BaseButton', () => {
     // Tests here
   })
   ```

3. Inside the tests suite, we can add our first unit test with the `test` function:

   ```
   describe('BaseButton', () => {
     test('click event', () => {
       // Test code
     })
   })
   ```

4. We will test whether the `click` event is emitted when we click on the component. We need to create a wrapper object around the component that will provide useful functions to test the component:

   ```
   const wrapper = shallow(BaseButton)
   ```

5. Then, we will simulate a click on the component:

   ```
   wrapper.trigger('click')
   ```

6. Finally, we will check whether the `click` event was emitted using the Jest `expect` method:

   ```
   expect(wrapper.emitted().click).toBeTruthy()
   ```

7. Now, let's add a script in the `package.json` file to run Jest:

   ```
   "jest": "jest"
   ```

8. Then, use the usual `npm run` command:

   npm run jest

   The tests are launched and should pass as follows:

   ```
   PASS  src/components/BaseButton.spec.js
     BaseButton
       ✓ click event (13ms)

   Test Suites: 1 passed, 1 total
   Tests:       1 passed, 1 total
   Snapshots:   0 total
   Time:        1.809s
   Ran all test suites.
   ```

   To learn more about unit testing Vue components, you can visit the official guide at https://vue-test-utils.vuejs.org/

ESLint and Jest globals

If we run ESLint now, we will get errors related to the Jest keywords such as `describe`, `test`, and `expect`:

```
4:1  error  'describe' is not defined    no-undef
5:3  error  'test' is not defined        no-undef
```

We need to make a tiny change to our ESLint configuration--we have to specify the `jest` environment; edit the `.eslintrc.js` file:

```
// Environment global objects
env: {
  browser: true,
  es6: true,
  jest: true,
},
```

Now, ESLint will know about the Jest keywords and will stop complaining.

Jest snapshots

Snapshots are strings that are saved and compared each time tests are run to detect potential regression. They are mostly used to save the HTML render of component, but can be used for any value as long as it make sense to store it between tests and compare it.

For our Vue component, we will snapshot the HTML render of it using the server-side Rendering tool called `vue-server-renderer`. We will need the `createRenderer` method from this package:

```
import { createRenderer } from 'vue-server-renderer'
```

At the start of the test, we instanciate a renderer instance, then we wrap the component with `shallow` and start rendering the component to a String. Finally, we compare the result with the previous one. Here is an example of snapshot test for the `BaseButton` component, passing some props values and the default slot content:

```
test('snapshot', () => {
  const renderer = createRenderer()
  const wrapper = shallow(BaseButton, {
    // Props values
    propsData: {
      icon: 'add',
      disabled: true,
      badge: '3',
    },
    // Slots content
    slots: {
      default: '<span>Add Item</span>',
    },
  })
  renderer.renderToString(wrapper.vm, (err, str) => {
    if (err) throw new Error(err)
    expect(str).toMatchSnapshot()
  })
})
```

> **TIP**
>
> If the snapshot test is run for the first time, it will create and save the snapshot to a __snapshots__ folder next to it. If you are using a versioning system such as git, you need to add these snapshot files to it.

Updating the snapshots

If you modify a component, there is a chances that its HTML render will change too. This means its snapshots will no longer be valid and the Jest tests will fail. Fortunately, the `jest` command has a `--updateSnapshots` argument. When used, all the failing snapshots will be resaved and will pass.

1. Let's add a new script in our `package.json` file:

   `"jest:update": "jest --updateSnapshot"`

2. Modify the `BaseButton` component by changing a CSS class, for example. If your run the Jest tests again, you should get an error that says, the snapshots don't match anymore.

   ```
   FAIL  src/components/BaseButton.spec.js
   BaseButton
     ✓ click event (21ms)
     ✓ icon prop (14ms)
     ✗ snapshot (20ms)

   ● BaseButton › snapshot

     expect(value).toMatchSnapshot()

     Received value does not match stored snapshot 1.
   ```

3. Now, update the snapshot with the new script:

   `npm run jest:update`

   All the tests should pass now, and the `BaseButton` snapshot should be updated:

   ```
   PASS  src/components/BaseButton.spec.js
   BaseButton
     ✓ click event (14ms)
     ✓ icon prop (10ms)
     ✓ snapshot (13ms)

   › 1 snapshot updated.
   Snapshot Summary
   › 1 snapshot updated in 1 test suite.
   ```

> **TIP:** You should run this command only when you are sure there are no regressions elsewhere. A good idea is to run the tests normally just before, to make sure only the modified component snapshot fails, as expected. After you have updated the snapshots, use the normal test command.

Complementary topics

In this section, we will cover a few more topics that can be useful for bigger apps.

Internationalization and code-splitting

If the app is to be used by people in different countries, it should be translated to be more user-friendly and appealing. To localize the texts of the app, you can use the recommended `vue-i18n` package:

```
npm i -S vue-i18n
```

Using `vue-i18n`, we will add a link in the `AppFooter` component to a new page where the user can select the language. Only the link and this page will be translated, but you can translate more parts of the app if you wish. `vue-i18n` works by creating a `i18n` object from it with the translated messages and injecting it into the Vue app.

1. In the `src/plugins.js` file, install the new plugin into Vue:

   ```
   import VueI18n from 'vue-i18n'

   // ...

   Vue.use(VueI18n)
   ```

2. Let's create a new folder called `i18n` in the project directory. Download the `locales` folder (https://github.com/Akryum/packt-vue-project-guide/tree/master/chapter7-download/locales) containing the translation files and put it inside. You should have, for example, the `en` translations in the `i18n/locales/en.js` file.

3. Create a new `index.js` file that exports the list of available languages:

   ```
   export default [
     'en',
     'fr',
     'es',
     'de',
   ]
   ```

   We will need two new utility functions:

   - `createI18n`: To create the `i18n` object, with a `locale` parameter.
   - `getAutoLang`: That returns the two-letter language code set by the user in the browser, for example, `en` or `fr`. Most of the time, this will be the OS language setting.

4. In the `src/utils` folder, create a new `i18n.js` file and import both `VueI18n` and the list of available locales we defined earlier:

   ```
   import VueI18n from 'vue-i18n'
   import langs from '../../i18n'
   ```

5. At the time of writing, we need the `babel-preset-stage-2` (or less) to allow Babel to parse the dynamic imports. In the `package.json` file, change the `babel-preset-stage-3` package:

   ```
   "babel-preset-stage-2": "^6.24.1",
   ```

6. Run `npm install` to update your packages.
7. Edit the `.babelrc` file in the root folder and change `stage-3` to `stage-2`.
8. In order to switch to stage-2, do the following installation:

   npm install --save-dev babel-preset-stage-2

Code-splitting with dynamic imports

When we create the `i18n` object, we want to load only the translations of the selected locale via the `locale` argument. To do that, we will make a dynamic import of the file with the `import` function. It takes the path as the argument and returns a Promise, which will eventually resolve to the corresponding JavaScript module once it is loaded from the server.

In webpack, this dynamic import feature is sometimes referred as 'code splitting', because webpack will move the asynchronous module to another compiled JavaScript file called a chunk.

Here is an example of an asynchronous module loaded with a dynamic import:

```
async function loadAsyncModule () {
  await module = await import('./path/to/module')
  console.log('default export', module.default)
  console.log('named export', module.myExportedFunction)
}
```

You can use variables in the imported path, as long as it has some information about where webpack can find the files. For example, this code will not work:

```
import(myModulePath)
```

However, the following one will work fine as long as the variable path is simple (without ../):

```
import(`./data/${myFileName}.json`)
```

> **TIP**
> In this example, all the files with the json extension in the data folder will be added to the build into asynchronous chunks, because webpack can't guess which ones you will really use at runtime.

Asynchronously loading big JavaScript modules with dynamic imports can reduce the size of the initial JavaScript code sent to the browser when opening the page. In our app, it allows us to load only the relevant translations file instead of including them all in the initial JavaScript file.

> **TIP**
> If a module is already imported with a normal import in the main code (the initial chunk), it will already be loaded and will not be split into another chunk. In that case, you won't have the benefits of the code-splitting feature and the initial file size won't be reduced. Note that you can synchronously use other modules with the normal import keyword inside the dynamically loaded module: they will be put together in the chunk (if they aren't already included in the initial chunk).

The i18n object is created with the VueI18n constructor from the vue-i18n package. We will pass the locale argument.

Here is what the `createI18n` function should look like:

```
export async function createI18n (locale) {
  const { default: localeMessages } = await
import(`../../i18n/locales/${locale}`)
  const messages = {
    [locale]: localeMessages,
  }

  const i18n = new VueI18n({
    locale,
    messages,
  })

  return i18n
}
```

> **TIP**
> As you can see, we need to take the `default` value of the module, because we exported the messages using `export default`.

The code using `async/await` above can be written using Promises:

```
export function createI18n (locale) {
  return import(`../../i18n/locales/${locale}`)
    .then(module => {
      const localeMessages = module.default
      // ...
    })
}
```

Automatically loading the user locale

Next, we can use `navigator.language` (or `userLanguage` for Internet Explorer compatibility) to retrieve the locale code. Then, we will check whether it is available in the `langs` list or if we have to use the default `en` locale.

1. The `getAutoLang` function should look like this:

```
export function getAutoLang () {
  let result = window.navigator.userLanguage ||
  window.navigator.language
  if (result) {
    result = result.substr(0, 2)
```

Chapter 7

```
  }
  if (langs.indexOf(result) === -1) {
    return 'en'
  } else {
    return result
  }
}
```

> **TIP**: Some browsers may return the code in the en-US format, but we only need the first two characters.

2. In the `src/main.js` file, import the two new utility functions:

   ```
   import { createI18n, getAutoLang } from './utils/i18n'
   ```

3. Then, modify the `main` function:
   1. Retrieve the preferred locale using `getAutoLang`.
   2. Create and wait for the `i18n` object with the `createI18n` function.
   3. Inject the `i18n` object into the root Vue instance.

It should now look like this:

```
async function main () {
  const locale = getAutoLang()
  const i18n = await createI18n(locale)
  await store.dispatch('init')

  // eslint-disable-next-line no-new
  new Vue({
    el: '#app',
    router,
    store,
    i18n, // Inject i18n into the app
    ...App,
  })
}
```

> **TIP**: Don't forget the `await` keyword in front of `createI18n`, or else you will get the Promise instead.

[333]

You can now open the network pane in the browser devtools and refresh the page. The translations module corresponding to the selected locale will be loaded by webpack in a separate request. In this example screenshot, this is the `2.build.js` file that is asynchronously loaded:

Changing Language page

For now, nothing really changed in the app, so let's add the page that will allow us to select the language.

1. In the `src/router.js` file, import the `PageLocale` component:

   ```
   import PageLocale from './components/PageLocale.vue'
   ```

2. Then, add the `locale` route in the `routes` array, just before the last one (with the `*` path):

   ```
   { path: '/locale', name: 'locale', component: PageLocale },
   ```

3. In the `AppFooter.vue` component, add this router link to the template:

   ```
   <div v-if="$route.name !== 'locale'">
     <router-link :to="{ name: 'locale' }">{{ $t('change-lang') }}
     </router-link>
   </div>
   ```

   As you can see in the preceding code, we use the `$t` provided by `vue-i18n` to display a translated text. The argument correspond to the key in the locale file. You should now see the link in the app footer:

[334]

The links takes us to the language selection page, which is already fully translated using `vue-i18n`:

Changer de langue

English | Français | Español | Deutsch

Retour

You can look at its source code in the `components/PageLocale.vue` file.

When you click on a locale button, the corresponding translations are loaded if they aren't already. In the network pane of the browser devtools, you should see a request made to other chunks each time:

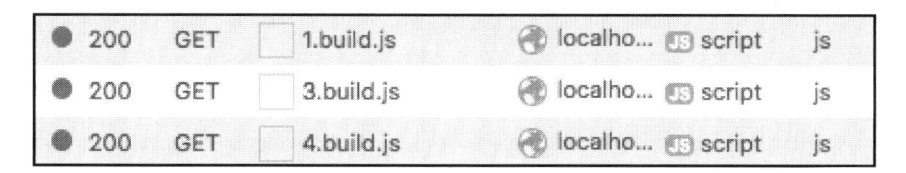

200	GET	1.build.js	localho...	script	js
200	GET	3.build.js	localho...	script	js
200	GET	4.build.js	localho...	script	js

Server-side rendering

Server-side Rendering (**SSR**) consists of running and rendering the app on the server, before sending the HTML back to the browser. This has two main advantages:

- Better **Search Engine Optimization** (**SEO**), since the initial content of the application will be rendered in the page HTML. This is important since no search engine is indexing an asynchronous JavaScript app (for example, when you have a spinner).
- Slower networks or devices will display contents faster--the rendered HTML doesn't need the JavaScript to be shown to the user.

Project 5 - Online Shop and Scaling Up

However, using SSR also brings some trade-offs:

- The code need to be able to run on the server (unless it is in client-side only hooks such as `mounted`). Also, some libraries may not play well on the browser and may require special treatments.
- The load will increase on the server, since it is doing more work.
- The development setup is a bit more complex.

So using SSR isn't always a good idea, especially if the time the first content is shown isn't critical (for example, an admin dashboard).

Universal App Structure

Writing a Universal App that runs both on the client and the server requires changing the architecture of the source code.

When running on the client, we are in a fresh context each time the page is loaded. That's why we used singletons instance of the root instance, the router, and the store until now. However, now we need to have a fresh context on the server as well--the problem is, Node.js is stateful. The solution is creating a fresh new root instance, router, and store for each request handled by the server.

1. Let's start with the router. In the `src/router.js` file, wrap the router creation into a new exported `createRouter` function:

```
export function createRouter () {
  const router = new VueRouter({
    routes,
    mode: 'history',
    scrollBehavior (to, from, savedPosition) {
      // ...
    },
  })

  return router
}
```

2. We will do the same with the Vuex store. In the `src/store/index.js` file, wrap the code into a new exported `createStore` function:

```
export function createStore () {
  const store = new Vuex.Store({
    strict: process.env.NODE_ENV !== 'production',

    // ...

    modules: {
      cart,
      item,
      items,
      ui,
    },
  })

  return store
}
```

3. Let's also rename the `src/main.js` file to `src/app.js`. This will be our universal file that creates the router, the store, and the Vue root instance. Change the `main` function into an exported `createApp` function, which takes a `context` argument and returns the app, the router, and the store:

```
export async function createApp (context) {
  const router = createRouter()
  const store = createStore()

  sync(store, router)

  const i18n = await createI18n(context.locale)
  await store.dispatch('init')

  const app = new Vue({
    router,
    store,
    i18n,
    ...App,
  })

  return {
    app,
    router,
    store,
  }
}
```

> Don't forget to change the imports for `createRouter` and `createStore`.

On the server, we won't select the initial locale the same way as in the client since we won't have access to `window.navigator`. That's why we are passing the locale in the `context` argument:

```
const i18n = await createI18n(context.locale)
```

We also removed the `el` option from the root instance definition since it doesn't make sense on the server.

Client entry

On the browser, the code will be started in the client entry file that we will write now.

1. Create a new `src/entry-client.js` file that will be the entry point for the client bundle. It will get the user language, call the `createApp` function, and then mount the app into the page:

   ```
   import { createApp } from './app'
   import { getAutoLang } from './utils/i18n'

   const locale = getAutoLang()
   createApp({
     locale,
   }).then(({ app }) => {
     app.$mount('#app')
   })
   ```

2. You can now change the entry path in the `webpack.config.js` file:

   ```
   entry: './src/entry-client.js',
   ```

   You can restart the `dev` script and check whether the app still works in the browser.

Server entry

Create a new `src/entry-server.js` file that will be the entry point for the server bundle. It will export a function that gets a `context` object from the HTTP server we will build later. It should return a Promise that resolves with the Vue app when it's ready.

We will pass an `url` attribute to the context so that we can set the current route like this:

```
router.push(context.url)
```

Similarly to the client entry, we also use the `createApp` function to create the root app instance, the router, and the store. `entry-server.js` should look like this:

```
import { createApp } from './app'

export default context => {
  return new Promise(async (resolve, reject) => {
    const { app, router, store } = await createApp(context)
    // Set the current route
    router.push(context.url)
    // TODO get matched components to preload data
    // TODO resolve(app)
  })
}
```

> We return a Promise because we will send the application `app` when we will have finished all the operations.

The `app` root instance will be send back to what we call the renderer (kind of like when we did Jest snapshots) using `resolve(app)`. First, we need to take care of preloading the Vuex store.

State management

When processing a request, we need to fetch the data on the relevant components before rendering the app. That way, the data will already be displayed when the HTML is loaded by the browser. For example, `PageHome.vue` fetches the store items and `PageStoreItem.vue` retrieves the item details and comments.

We will add a new `asyncData` custom option to those, so we can call it on the server when doing SSR.

1. Edit the `PageHome.vue` component by adding this function that dispatches the `fetchItems` action of the `items` store module:

   ```
   asyncData ({ store }) {
     return store.dispatch('items/fetchItems')
   },
   ```

2. In the `PageStoreItem.vue` component, we need to call the `fetchStoreItemDetails` action of the `item` store module, with the `id` parameter of the route passed by the server:

   ```
   asyncData ({ store, route }) {
     return store.dispatch('item/fetchStoreItemDetails', {
       id: route.params.id,
     })
   },
   ```

3. Now that our components are ready, we will go back to `entry-server.js`. We can use the `router.getMatchedComponents()` method to get the list of components that matched with the current route:

   ```
   export default context => {
     return new Promise(async (resolve, reject) => {
       const { app, router, store } = await createApp(context)
       router.push(context.url)
       // Wait for the component resolution
       router.onReady(() => {
         const matchedComponents = router.getMatchedComponents()
         // TODO pre-load data
         // TODO resolve(app)
       }, reject)
     })
   }
   ```

4. We can then call all the `asyncData` options of these components and wait for them to finish. We pass both the store and the current route to them, and when they have all completed, we send the Vuex store state back to the renderer with `context.state = store.state`. Use `Promise.all(array)` to wait for all the `asyncData` calls:

```
router.onReady(() => {
  const matchedComponents = router.getMatchedComponents()

  Promise.all(matchedComponents.map(Component => {
    if (Component.asyncData) {
      return Component.asyncData({
        store,
        route: router.currentRoute,
      })
    }
  })).then(() => {
    // Send back the store state
    context.state = store.state

    // Send the app to the renderer
    resolve(app)
  }).catch(reject)
}, reject)
```

If an error occurs, it will reject the Promise we returned to the renderer.

Restoring the Vuex state on the client

The store state is serialized by the server on a `__INITIAL_STATE__` variable in the HTML page. We can use this to set the state even before the app is mounted, so the components will have access to it.

Edit the `entry-client.js` file and use the `store.replaceState` method before mounting the app:

```
createApp({
  locale,
}).then(({ app, store }) => {
  if (window.__INITIAL_STATE__) {
    store.replaceState(window.__INITIAL_STATE__)
  }

  app.$mount('#app')
})
```

[341]

Now, the store will have the data sent by the server.

Webpack configuration

Our app code is now ready. Before continuing, we need to refactor our webpack configuration.

We will need a slightly different webpack configuration for the client and the server. It is a good idea to have a common configuration file, which is then extended for the client and the server. We can do this easily with the `webpack-merge` package that merges multiples webpack configuration objects into one.

For the server configuration, we also need the `webpack-node-externals` package to prevent webpack from bundling the packages in `node_modules`--this is not necessary since we will run inside nodejs and not in the browser. All the corresponding imports will be left as `require` statements so that node will load them itself.

1. Install the packages in the dev dependencies:

   ```
   npm i -D webpack-merge webpack-node-externals
   ```

2. Create a new `webpack` folder in the project root directory, then move and rename the `webpack.config.js` file to `webpack/common.js`. Some changes are needed.

3. Remove the `entry` option from the configuration. This will be specified in the specific extended configurations.

4. Update the `output` option to target the correct folder and to generate better chunk names:

   ```
   output: {
     path: path.resolve(__dirname, '../dist'),
     publicPath: '/dist/',
     filename: '[name].[chunkhash].js',
   },
   ```

Client configuration

Next to `webpack/common.js`, create a new `client.js` file that extends the base configuration:

```
const webpack = require('webpack')
const merge = require('webpack-merge')
const common = require('./common')
const VueSSRClientPlugin = require('vue-server-renderer/client-plugin')

module.exports = merge(common, {
  entry: './src/entry-client',
  plugins: [
    new webpack.optimize.CommonsChunkPlugin({
      name: 'manifest',
      minChunks: Infinity,
    }),
    // Generates the client manifest file
    new VueSSRClientPlugin(),
  ],
})
```

The `VueSSRClientPlugin` will generate a `vue-ssr-client-manifest.json` file that we will give to the renderer. This way, it will know more about the client. Also, it will automatically inject the script tags and the critical CSS to the HTML.

> The Critical CSS is the style of the components rendered by the server. Those styles will be directly injected to the page HTML so that the browser doesn't have to wait for the CSS to be loaded; it can display those components sooner.

The `CommonsChunkPlugin` will put the webpack runtime code into a leading chunk so that asynchronous chunks can be injected right after it. It also improves caching of the app and vendor code.

Server configuration

Next to `webpack/common.js`, create a new `server.js` file that extends the base configuration:

```
const merge = require('webpack-merge')
const common = require('./common')
const nodeExternals = require('webpack-node-externals')
const VueSSRServerPlugin = require('vue-server-renderer/server-plugin')

module.exports = merge(common, {
```

```
    entry: './src/entry-server',
    target: 'node',
    devtool: 'source-map',
    output: {
      libraryTarget: 'commonjs2',
    },
    // Skip webpack processing on node_modules
    externals: nodeExternals({
      // Force css files imported from no_modules
      // to be processed by webpack
      whitelist: /\.css$/,
    }),
    plugins: [
      // Generates the server bundle file
      new VueSSRServerPlugin(),
    ],
})
```

Here, we change multiple options, such as the `target` and `output.libraryTarget` ones, to adapt to the node.js environment.

Using the `webpack-node-externals` package, we tell webpack to ignore the modules located in the `node_modules` folder (which means the dependencies). Since we are in nodejs and not in a browser, we don't have to bundle all the dependencies into the bundle, so this will improve the build times.

Finally, we use `VueSSRServerPlugin` to generate the server bundle file that will be used by the renderer. It contains the compiled server-side code and a lot of other informations so that the renderer can support source maps (with the `source-map` value of `devtool`), hot-reloading, critical CSS injection, and other injections in conjunction with the client manifest data.

Server-side setup

In development, we can't use `webpack-dev-server` directly anymore with SSR. Instead, we will set up the express server with webpack. Download the `server.dev.js` file (https://github.com/Akryum/packt-vue-project-guide/blob/master/chapter7-download/server.dev.js) and put it in the project root directory. This file exports a `setupDevServer` function that we will use to run webpack and update the server.

We will also need some packages for the development setup:

```
npm i -D memory-fs chokidar webpack-dev-middleware webpack-hot-middleware
```

We can create virtual file systems with `memory-fs`, watch files with `chokidar`, and enable webpack Hot Module Replacement in an express server with the last two middleware.

Page template

Create a new `index.template.html` file alongside `index.html` and copy its contents. Then, replace the body content with the special `<!--vue-ssr-outlet-->` comment:

```html
<!DOCTYPE html>
<html lang="en">
  <head>
    <meta charset="utf-8">
    <title>Fashion Store</title>
  </head>
  <body>
    <!--vue-ssr-outlet-->
  </body>
</html&gt;
```

This special comment will be replaced by the rendered markup on the server.

Express server

On the nodejs side, we will use `express` package to create our HTTP server. We will also need the `reify` package so that we can require files that uses the `import`/`export` syntax inside nodejs (which doesn't support it natively).

1. Install the new packages:

```
npm i -S express reify
```

2. Download this incomplete `server.js` file (https://github.com/Akryum/packt-vue-project-guide/blob/master/chapter7-download/server.dev.js) and put it in the project root directory. It already creates an express server and configures the necessary express routes.

For now, we will focus on the development part.

Creating and updating the renderer

To render our app, we will need a renderer created with the `createBundleRenderer` function from the `vue-server-renderer` package.

> A bundle renderer is quite different from a normal renderer. It uses a server bundle file (that will be generated, thanks to our new webpack configuration) with an optional client manifest that allows the renderer to have more information about the code. This enables more features such as source maps and hot-reloading.

In the `server.js` file, replace the `// TODO development` comment with this code:

```
const setupDevServer = require('./server.dev')
readyPromise = setupDevServer({
  server,
  templatePath,
  onUpdate: (bundle, options) => {
    // Re-create the bundle renderer
    renderer = createBundleRenderer(bundle, {
      runInNewContext: false,
      ...options,
    })
  },
})
```

Thanks to the `server.dev.js` file, we can add support of webpack hot-reloading to our express server. We also specify the path to the HTML page template, so we can reload it too when changed.

When the setup triggers an update, we create or recreate the bundle renderer.

[346]

Rendering the Vue app

Next, we will need to implement the code that renders the app and send the HTML result back to the client.

Replace the `// TODO render` comment with this:

```
const context = {
  url: req.url,
  // Languages sent by the browser
  locale: req.acceptsLanguages(langs) || 'en',
}
renderer.renderToString(context, (err, html) => {
  if (err) {
    // Render Error Page or Redirect
    res.status(500).send('500 | Internal Server Error')
    console.error(`error during render : ${req.url}`)
    console.error(err.stack)
  }
  res.send(html)
})
```

Thanks to the `req.acceptsLanguages` method from express, we can easily select the preferred language of the user.

> When performing the request, the web browser will send a list of "accepted languages" by the user. This is generally the language set for either their browser or OS.

We then use the `renderToString` method that will call the function we exported in the `entry-server.js` file, wait for the returned Promise to complete and then render the app into an HTML string. Finally, we send the result to the client (unless there is an error during the render).

Running our SSR app

Now is the time to run the app. Change the `dev` script to run our express server instead of `webpack-dev-server`:

```
"dev": "node server",
```

Restart the script and refresh the app. To be sure that the SSR is working correctly, view the source of the page:

```
1  <!DOCTYPE html>
2  <html lang="en">
3    <head>
4      <meta charset="utf-8">
5      <title>Fashion Store</title>
6      <link rel="preload" href="/dist/manifest.c69ddec6ab4cedcb56a9.js" as="script"><link rel="preload" href="/dist/vendor.a6e8017e514f497280bd.js" as="script"><link rel="preload" href="/dist/main.de91e0e9b3d5804143cd.js" as="script"><link rel="prefetch" href="/dist/0.21bf7785b82022f8af70.js"><link rel="prefetch" href="/dist/2.508433d502229d905384.js"><link rel="prefetch" href="/dist/3.395a70fc7d3563e990b9.js"><link rel="prefetch" href="/dist/1.470b338ce90ba04e6319.js"><link rel="stylesheet" href="/dist/common.de91e0e9b3d5804143cd.css"></head>
7    <body>
8      <div id="app" data-server-rendered="true"><header class="app-header" data-v-40a9da8b><div class="content" data-v-40a9da8b><div class="state" data-v-40a9da8b data-v-40a9da8b><h1 class="app-name" data-v-40a9da8b><a href="/" class="link router-link-exact-active router-link-active" data-v-40a9da8b>Fashion Store</a></h1><button class="base-button icon-button" data-v-76e42c36 data-v-40a9da8b><i class="material-icons icon" data-v-76e42c36>search</i><span class="content" data-v-76e42c36></span><!---->
```

The app is already rendered in HTML by the server.

Unnecessary fetch

Unfortunately, something is wrong with our app. The server sends the Vuex store data alongside the HTML of the page, which means the app already has all the data it needs when running for the first time, except that the requests to retrieve the stored items of the item details and comments are still being made. You can see this because of the loading animation that appears when you first load or when you refresh one of the corresponding pages.

The solution to this is to prevent the components from fetching data if it is not necessary:

1. In the `PageHome.vue` component, we need to fetch the items only if we don't have them already:

   ```
   mounted () {
     if (!this.items.length) {
       this.fetchItems()
     }
   },
   ```

2. In the `PageStoreItem.vue` component, the details and comments should be fetched only if we don't have the data:

```
fetchData () {
  if (!this.details || this.details.id !== this.id) {
    this.fetchStoreItemDetails({
      id: this.id,
    })
  }
},
```

We no longer have the issue now.

To continue learn more about SSR, you can visit the official documentation at `https://ssr.vuejs.org/` or use an easy-to-use framework called nuxtjs (`https://nuxtjs.org/`), which abstracts a lot of boilerplate away from you.

Production build

Our app is working great in development. Let's say we have finished it and we want to deploy it to a real server.

Additional configuration

We need to add some configuration for the production build of the app to ensure that it is optimized.

Extracting the style into CSS files

Until now, the style was added to the page via the JavaScript code. This is great in development because it allows hot-reloading with webpack. However, in production, it is recommended to extract it into separate CSS files.

1. Install the `extract-text-webpack-plugin` package in the dev dependencies:

   ```
   npm i -D extract-text-webpack-plugin
   ```

2. In the `webpack/common.js` configuration file, add a new `isProd` variable:

   ```
   const isProd = process.env.NODE_ENV === 'production'
   ```

3. Modify the `vue-loader` rule to enable the CSS extraction if we are in production and to ignore the whitespaces between HTML tags:

```
{
  test: /\.vue$/,
  loader: 'vue-loader',
  options: {
    extractCSS: isProd,
    preserveWhitespace: false,
  },
},
```

4. Add the `ExtractTextPlugin` and the `ModuleConcatenationPlugin` to the production-only plugins list at the bottom of the file:

```
if (isProd) {
  module.exports.devtool = '#source-map'
  module.exports.plugins = (module.exports.plugins ||
  []).concat([
    // ...
    new webpack.optimize.ModuleConcatenationPlugin(),
    new ExtractTextPlugin({
      filename: 'common.[chunkhash].css',
    }),
  ])
} else {
  // ...
}
```

`ExtractTextPlugin` will put the style into CSS files and the `ModuleConcatenationPlugin` will optimize the compiled JavaScript code to be faster.

Production express server

The last changes we need to make to our code is the bundle renderer creation in the express server.

In the `server.js` file, replace the `// TODO production` comment with this:

```
const template = fs.readFileSync(templatePath, 'utf-8')
const bundle = require('./dist/vue-ssr-server-bundle.json')
const clientManifest = require('./dist/vue-ssr-client-manifest.json')
renderer = createBundleRenderer(bundle, {
  runInNewContext: false,
  template,
  clientManifest,
})
```

We will read the HTML page template, the server bundle, and the client manifest. Then, we create a new bundle renderer since we won't have hot-reloading in production.

New npm scripts

The compiled code will be output to a `dist` directory in the project root. Between each build, we need to remove it so we are in a clean state. To do that in a cross-platform manner, we will use the `rimraf` package that can recursively delete files and folders.

1. Install the `rimraf` package to the dev dependencies:

   npm i -D rimraf

2. Add a `build` script for both the client and server bundles:

   ```
   "build:client": "cross-env NODE_ENV=production webpack --progress
     --hide-modules --config webpack/client.js",
   "build:server": "cross-env NODE_ENV=production webpack --progress
     --hide-modules --config webpack/server.js",
   ```

   We set the `NODE_ENV` environment variable to `'production'` and run the `webpack` command with the corresponding webpack configuration file.

3. Create a new `build` script that clears the `dist` folder and runs the two other `build:client` and `build:server` scripts:

   ```
   "build": "rimraf dist && npm run build:client && npm run
     build:server",
   ```

[351]

4. Add a last script called `start` that runs the express server in production mode:

   ```
   "start": "cross-env NODE_ENV=production node server",
   ```

5. You can now run the build; use the usual `npm run` command:

   npm run build

   The `dist` folder should now contain all the chunks generated by webpack, plus the server bundle and client manifest json files:

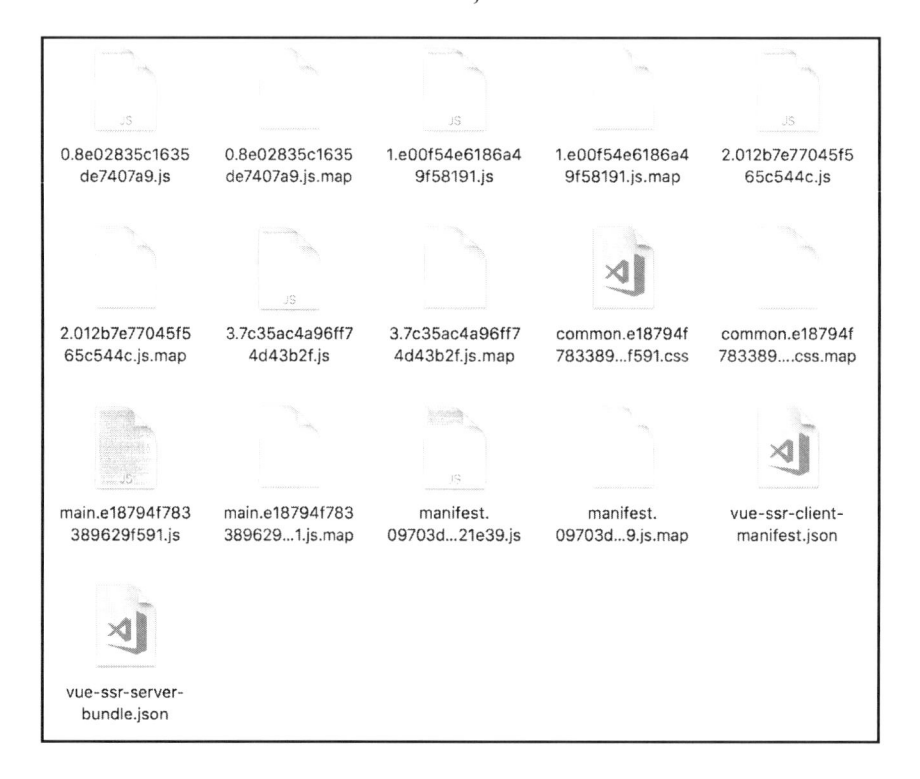

   - 0.8e02835c1635de7407a9.js
   - 0.8e02835c1635de7407a9.js.map
   - 1.e00f54e6186a49f58191.js
   - 1.e00f54e6186a49f58191.js.map
   - 2.012b7e77045f565c544c.js
   - 2.012b7e77045f565c544c.js.map
   - 3.7c35ac4a96ff74d43b2f.js
   - 3.7c35ac4a96ff74d43b2f.js.map
   - common.e18794f783389...f591.css
   - common.e18794f783389....css.map
   - main.e18794f783389629f591.js
   - main.e18794f783389629...1.js.map
   - manifest.09703d...21e39.js
   - manifest.09703d...9.js.map
   - vue-ssr-client-manifest.json
   - vue-ssr-server-bundle.json

   > **TIP**: These are the files that need to be uploaded to your real nodejs server.

6. We can now start the express server:

   npm start

[352]

Chapter 7

> **TIP**: You should also upload the `server.js`, `package.json`, and `package-lock.json` files to the real server. Don't forget to install the dependencies with `npm install`.

Summary

In this chapter, we improved our development workflow by learning how to autoprefix our CSS with PostCSS, lint our code for quality with ESLint, and unit test our components with Jest. We went even further by adding localization with the `vue-i18n` package and dynamic imports, and by refactoring the project to enable server-side rendering while still taking advantage of the awesome webpack features such as hot-reloading, code-splitting, and optimizations.

In the last chapter, we will create a simple real-time app with the Meteor fullstack framework and Vue.

8
Project 6 - Real-time Dashboard with Meteor

In this final chapter, we will use Vue with an entirely different stack--Meteor!

We will discover this full-stack JavaScript framework and build a real-time dashboard monitoring the production of some products. We will cover the following topics:

- Installing Meteor and setting up a project
- Storing data into a Meteor collection with a Meteor method
- Subscribing to the collection and using the data in our Vue components

Project 6 - Real-time Dashboard with Meteor

The app will have a main page with some indicators, such as:

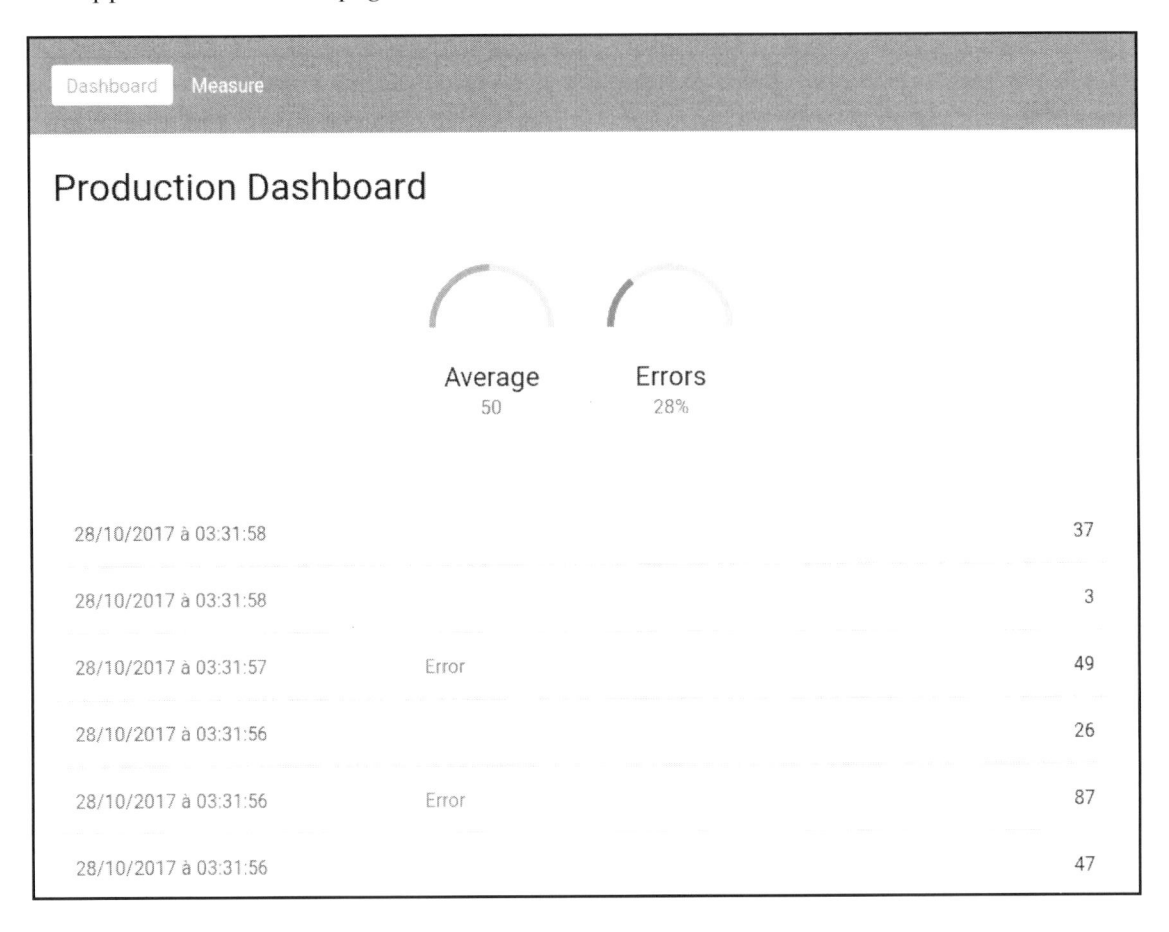

It will also have another page with buttons to generate fake measures since we won't have real sensors available.

Setting up the project

In this first part, we will cover Meteor and get a simple app up and running on this platform.

What is Meteor?

Meteor is a full-stack JavaScript framework for building web applications.

The mains elements of the Meteor stacks are as follows:

- Web client (can use any frontend library, such as React or Vue); it has a client-side database called Minimongo
- Server based on nodejs; it supports the modern ES2015+ features, including the `import/export` syntax
- Real-time database on the server using MongoDB
- Communication between clients and the server is abstracted; the client-side and server-side databases can be easily synchronized in real-time
- Optional hybrid mobile app (Android and iOS), built in one command
- Integrated developer tools, such as a powerful command-line utility and an easy-to-use build tool
- Meteor-specific packages (but you can also use npm packages)

As you can see, JavaScript is used everywhere. Meteor also encourages you to share code between the client and the server.

Since Meteor manages the entire stack, it offers very powerful systems that are easy to use. For example, the entire stack is fully reactive and real-time--if a client sends an update to the server, all the other clients will receive the new data and their UI will automatically be up to date.

> Meteor has its own build system called "IsoBuild" and doesn't use Webpack. It focuses on ease of use (no configuration), but is, as a result, also less flexible.

Installing Meteor

If you don't have Meteor on your system, you need to open the Installation Guide on the official Meteor website at `https://www.meteor.com/install`. Follow the instructions there for your OS to install Meteor.

When you are done, you can check whether Meteor was correctly installed with the following command:

```
meteor --version
```

The current version of Meteor should be displayed.

Creating the project

Now that Meteor is installed, let's set up a new project:

1. Let's create our first Meteor project with the `meteor create` command:

   ```
   meteor create --bare <folder>
   cd <folder>
   ```

   The `--bare` argument tells Meteor we want an empty project. By default, Meteor will generate some boilerplate files we don't need, so this keeps us from having to delete them.

2. Then, we need two Meteor-specific packages--one for compiling the Vue components, and one for compiling Stylus inside those components. Install them with the `meteor add` command:

   ```
   meteor add akryum:vue-component akryum:vue-stylus
   ```

3. We will also install the `vue` and `vue-router` package from npm:

   ```
   meteor npm i -S vue vue-router
   ```

   > **TIP**: Note that we use the `meteor npm` command instead of just `npm`. This is to have the same environment as Meteor (nodejs and npm versions).

4. To start our Meteor app in development mode, just run the `meteor` command:

   ```
   meteor
   ```

Chapter 8

Meteor should start an HTTP proxy, a MongoDB, and the nodejs server:

```
=> Started proxy.
   [HMR] Dev server listening on port 3003
=> Started MongoDB.
=> Started your app.

=> App running at: http://localhost:3000/
```

It also shows the URL where the app is available; however, if you open it right now, it will be blank.

Our first Vue Meteor app

In this section, we will display a simple Vue component in our app:

1. Create a new `index.html` file inside the project directory and tell Meteor we want `div` in the page body with the `app` id:

   ```
   <head>
     <title>Production Dashboard</title>
   </head>
   <body>
     <div id="app"></div>
   </body>
   ```

   > **TIP**: This is not a real HTML file. It is a special format where we can inject additional elements to the `head` or `body` section of the final HTML page. Here, Meteor will add a `title` into the `head` section and the `<div>` into the `body` section.

2. Create a new `client` folder, new `components` subfolder, and a new `App.vue` component with a simple template:

   ```
   <!-- client/components/App.vue -->
   <template>
     <div id="#app">
       <h1>Meteor</h1>
     </div>
   </template>
   ```

[359]

3. Download (https://github.com/Akryum/packt-vue-project-guide/tree/master/chapter8-full/client) this stylus file in the `client` folder and add it to the main `App.vue` component:

   ```
   <style lang="stylus" src="../style.styl" />
   ```

4. Create a `main.js` file in the `client` folder that starts the Vue application inside the `Meteor.startup` hook:

   ```
   import { Meteor } from 'meteor/meteor'
   import Vue from 'vue'
   import App from './components/App.vue'

   Meteor.startup(() => {
     new Vue({
       el: '#app',
       ...App,
     })
   })
   ```

   > **TIP**: In a Meteor app, it is recommended that you create the Vue app inside the `Meteor.startup` hook to ensure that all the Meteor systems are ready before starting the frontend.

   > This code will only be run on the client because it is located in a `client` folder.

You should now have a simple app displayed in your browser. You can also open the Vue devtools and check whether you have the `App` component present on the page.

Routing

Let's add some routing to the app; we will have two pages--the dashboard with indicators and a page with buttons to generate fake data:

1. In the `client/components` folder, create two new components--`ProductionGenerator.vue` and `ProductionDashboard.vue`.
2. Next to the `main.js` file, create the router in a `router.js` file:

```
import Vue from 'vue'
import VueRouter from 'vue-router'

import ProductionDashboard from
'./components/ProductionDashboard.vue'
import ProductionGenerator from
'./components/ProductionGenerator.vue'

Vue.use(VueRouter)

const routes = [
  { path: '/', name: 'dashboard', component: ProductionDashboard
  },
  { path: '/generate', name: 'generate',
    component: ProductionGenerator },
]

const router = new VueRouter({
  mode: 'history',
  routes,
})

export default router
```

3. Then, import the router in the `main.js` file and inject it into the app, like we did in Chapter 5, *Project 3 - Support Center*.
4. In the `App.vue` main component, add the navigation menu and the router view:

```
<nav>
  <router-link :to="{ name: 'dashboard' }" exact>Dashboard
    </router-link>
  <router-link :to="{ name: 'generate' }">Measure</router-link>
</nav>
<router-view />
```

The basic structure of our app is now done:

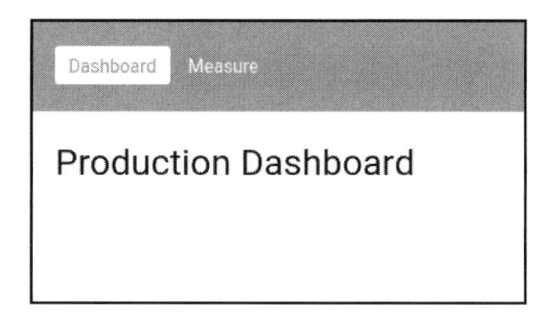

Production measures

The first page we will make is the Measures page, where we will have two buttons:

- The first one will generate a fake production measure with current `date` and random `value`
- The second one will also generate a measure, but with the `error` property set to `true`

All these measures will be stored in a collection called "Measures".

Meteor collections integration

A Meteor collection is a reactive list of objects, similar to a MongoDB collection (in fact, it uses MongoDB under the hood).

We need to use a Vue plugin to integrate the Meteor collections into our Vue app in order to update it automatically:

1. Add the `vue-meteor-tracker` npm package:

   `meteor npm i -S vue-meteor-tracker`

2. Then, install the library into Vue:

   ```
   import VueMeteorTracker from 'vue-meteor-tracker'
   ```
   `Vue.use``(VueMeteorTracker)`

3. Restart Meteor with the `meteor` command.

   The app is now aware of the Meteor collection and we can use them in our components, as we will do in a moment.

Setting up data

The next step is setting up the Meteor collection where we will store our measures data.

Adding a collection

We will store our measures into a `Measures` Meteor collection. Create a new `lib` folder in the project directory. All the code in this folder will be executed first, both on the client and the server. Create a `collections.js` file, where we will declare our `Measures` collection:

```
import { Mongo } from 'meteor/mongo'

export const Measures = new Mongo.Collection('measures')
```

Adding a Meteor method

A `Meteor` method is a special function that will be called both on the client and the server. This is very useful for updating collection data and will improve the perceived speed of the app--the client will execute on minimongo without waiting for the server to receive and process it.

> This technique is called "Optimistic Update" and is very effective when the network quality is poor.

1. Next to the `collections.js` file in the `lib` folder, create a new `methods.js` file. Then, add a `measure.add` method that inserts a new measure into the `Measures` collection:

   ```
   import { Meteor } from 'meteor/meteor'
   import { Measures } from './collections'
   
   Meteor.methods({
     'measure.add' (measure) {
       Measures.insert({
         ...measure,
         date: new Date(),
       })
     },
   })
   ```

   We can now call this method with the `Meteor.call` function:

   ```
   Meteor.call('measure.add', someMeasure)
   ```

The method will be run on both the client (using the client-side database called minimongo) and on the server. That way, the update will be instant for the client.

Simulating measures

Without further delay, let's build the simple component that will call this `measure.add` Meteor method:

1. Add two buttons in the template of `ProductionGenerator.vue`:

   ```
   <template>
     <div class="production-generator">
       <h1>Measure production</h1>

       <section class="actions">
         <button @click="generateMeasure(false)">Generate
         Measure</button>
         <button @click="generateMeasure(true)">Generate
         Error</button>
       </section>
     </div>
   </template>
   ```

2. Then, in the component script, create the `generateMeasure` method that generates some dummy data and then call the `measure.add` Meteor method:

   ```
   <script>
   import { Meteor } from 'meteor/meteor'

   export default {
     methods: {
       generateMeasure (error) {
         const value = Math.round(Math.random() * 100)
         const measure = {
           value,
           error,
         }
         Meteor.call('measure.add', measure)
       },
     },
   }
   </script>
   ```

The component should look like this:

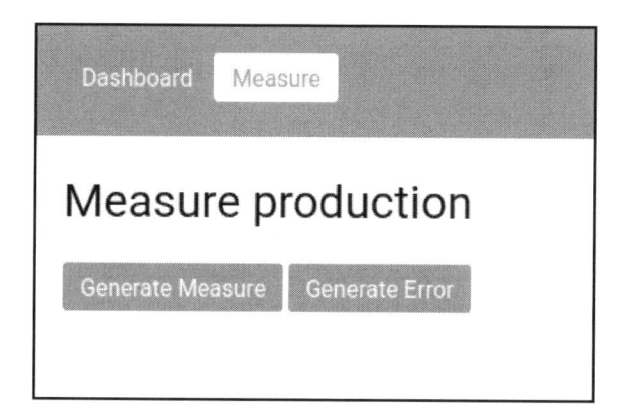

If you click on the buttons, nothing visible should happen.

Inspecting the data

There is an easy way to check whether our code works and to verify that you can add items in the `Measures` collection. We can connect to the `MongoDB` database in a single command.

In another terminal, run the following command to connect to the app's database:

```
meteor mongo
```

Then, enter this MongoDB query to fetch the documents of the `measures` collection (the argument used when creating the `Measures` Meteor collection):

```
db.measures.find({})
```

If you clicked on the buttons, a list of measure documents should be displayed:

This means that our Meteor method worked and objects were inserted in our MongoDB database.

Dashboard and reporting

Now that our first page is done, we can continue with the real-time dashboard.

Progress bars library

To display some pretty indicators, let's install another Vue library that allows drawing progress bars along SVG paths; that way, we can have semi-circular bars:

1. Add the `vue-progress-path` npm package to the project:

   ```
   meteor npm i -S vue-progress-path
   ```

   We need to tell the Vue compiler for Meteor not to process the files in `node_modules` where the package is installed.

2. Create a new `.vueignore` file in the project root directory. This file works like a `.gitignore`: each line is a rule to ignore some paths. If it ends with a slash /, it will ignore only corresponding folders. So, the content of `.vueignore` should be as follows:

   ```
   node_modules/
   ```

3. Finally, install the `vue-progress-path` plugin in the `client/main.js` file:

   ```
   import 'vue-progress-path/dist/vue-progress-path.css'
   import VueProgress from 'vue-progress-path'

   Vue.use(VueProgress, {
     defaultShape: 'semicircle',
   })
   ```

Meteor publication

To synchronize data, the client must subscribe to a publication declared on the server. A Meteor publication is a function that returns a Meteor collection query. It can take arguments to filter the data that will be synchronized.

For our app, we will only need a simple `measures` publication that sends all the documents of the `Measures` collection:

1. This code should only be run on the server. So, create a new `server` in the `project` folder and a new `publications.js` file inside that folder:

   ```
   import { Meteor } from 'meteor/meteor'
   import { Measures } from '../lib/collections'

   Meteor.publish('measures', function () {
     return Measures.find({})
   })
   ```

   > This code will only run on the server because it is located in a folder called `server`.

Creating the Dashboard component

We are ready to build our `ProductionDashboard` component. Thanks to the `vue-meteor-tracker` we installed earlier, we have a new component definition option-- `meteor`. This is an object that describes the publications that need to be subscribed to and the collection data that needs to be retrieved for that component.

1. Add the following script section with the `meteor` definition option:

   ```
   <script>
   export default {
     meteor: {
       // Subscriptions and Collections queries here
     },
   }
   </script>
   ```

2. Inside the `meteor` option, subscribe to the `measures` publication with the `$subscribe` object:

   ```
   meteor: {
     $subscribe: {
       'measures': [],
     },
   },
   ```

[367]

Project 6 - Real-time Dashboard with Meteor

> **TIP:** The empty array means we pass no parameter to the publication.

3. Retrieve the measures with a query on the `Measures` Meteor collection inside the `meteor` option:

   ```
   meteor: {
     // ...

     measures () {
       return Measures.find({}, {
         sort: { date: -1 },
       })
     },
   },
   ```

> **TIP:** The second parameter of the `find` method is an options object very similar to the MongoDB JavaScript API. Here, we are sorting the documents by their date in descending order, thanks to the `sort` property of the options object.

4. Finally, create the `measures` data property and initialize it to an empty array.

   The script of the component should now look like this:

   ```
   <script>
   import { Measures } from '../../lib/collections'

   export default {
     data () {
       return {
         measures: [],
       }
     },

     meteor: {
       $subscribe: {
         'measures': [],
       },

       measures () {
         return Measures.find({}, {
           sort: { date: -1 },
         })
   ```

[368]

```
      },
    },
  }
</script>
```

In the browser devtools, you can now check whether the component has retrieved the items from the collection.

Indicators

We will create a separate component for the dashboard indicators, as follows:

1. In the `components` folder, create a new `ProductionIndicator.vue` component.
2. Declare a template that displays a progress bar, a title, and additional info text:

   ```
   <template>
     <div class="production-indicator">
       <loading-progress :progress="value" />
       <div class="title">{{ title }}</div>
       <div class="info">{{ info }}</div>
     </div>
   </template>
   ```

3. Add the `value`, `title`, and `info` props:

   ```
   <script>
   export default {
     props: {
       value: {
         type: Number,
         required: true,
       },
       title: String,
       info: [String, Number],
     },
   }
   </script>
   ```

4. Back in our `ProductionDashboard` component, let's compute the average of the values and the rate of errors:

   ```
   computed: {
     length () {
       return this.measures.length
   ```

Project 6 - Real-time Dashboard with Meteor

```
    },

    average () {
      if (!this.length) return 0
      let total = this.measures.reduce(
        (total, measure) => total += measure.value,
        0
      )
      return total / this.length
    },

    errorRate () {
      if (!this.length) return 0
      let total = this.measures.reduce(
        (total, measure) => total += measure.error ? 1 : 0,
        0
      )
      return total / this.length
    },
  },
```

> **TIP**: In the preceding code snippet, we cached the length of the `measures` array in a `length` computed property.

5. Add two indicators in the templates - one for the average value and one for the error rate:

```
<template>
  <div class="production-dashboard">
    <h1>Production Dashboard</h1>

    <section class="indicators">
      <ProductionIndicator
        :value="average / 100"
        title="Average"
        :info="Math.round(average)"
      />
      <ProductionIndicator
        class="danger"
        :value="errorRate"
        title="Errors"
        :info="`${Math.round(errorRate * 100)}%`"
      />
```

```
    </section>
  </div>
</template>
```

> **TIP:** Don't forget to import `ProductionIndicator` into the component!

The indicators should look like this:

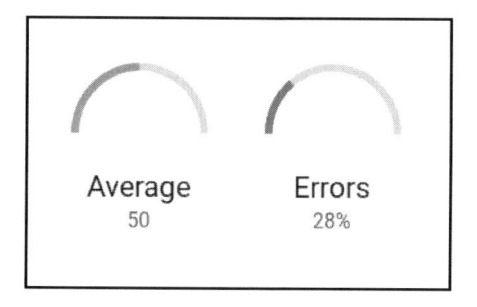

[Average 50 | Errors 28%]

Listing the measures

Finally, we will display a list of the measures below the indicators:

1. Add a simple list of `<div>` elements for each measure, displaying the date if it has an error and the value:

```
<section class="list">
  <div
    v-for="item of measures"
    :key="item._id"
  >
    <div class="date">{{ item.date.toLocaleString() }}</div>
    <div class="error">{{ item.error ? 'Error' : '' }}</div>
    <div class="value">{{ item.value }}</div>
  </div>
</section>
```

Project 6 - Real-time Dashboard with Meteor

The app should now look as follows, with a navigation toolbar, two indicators, and the measures list:

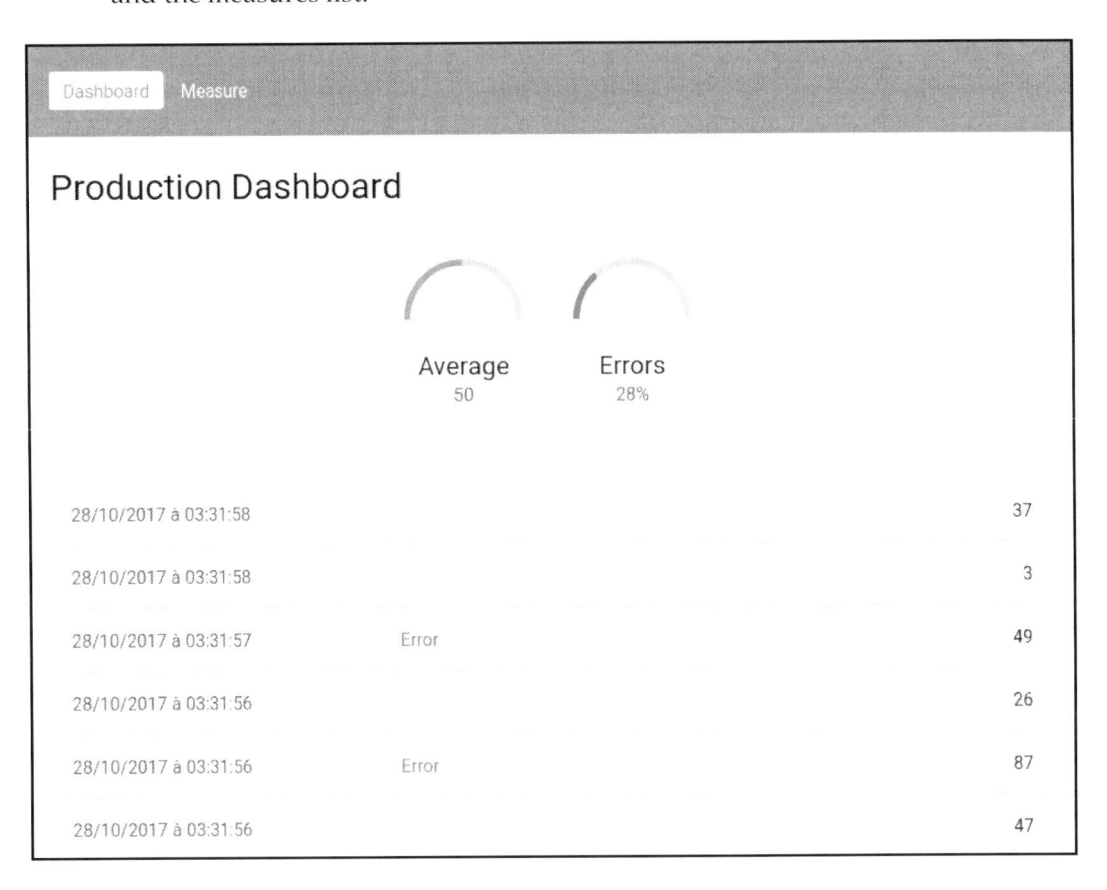

Dashboard Measure		
Production Dashboard		
	Average Errors	
	50 28%	
28/10/2017 à 03:31:58		37
28/10/2017 à 03:31:58		3
28/10/2017 à 03:31:57	Error	49
28/10/2017 à 03:31:56		26
28/10/2017 à 03:31:56	Error	87
28/10/2017 à 03:31:56		47

If you open the app in another window and put your windows side by side, you can see the full-stack reactivity of Meteor in action. Open the dashboard in one window and the generator page in the other window. Then, add fake measures and watch the data update on the other window in real time.

If you want to learn more about Meteor, check out the official website (https://www.meteor.com/developers) and the Vue integration repository (https://github.com/meteor-vue/vue-meteor).

Summary

In this final chapter, we created a project using a new full-stack framework called Meteor. We integrated Vue into the app and set up a Meteor reactive collection. Using a Meteor method, we inserted documents into the collection and displayed in real-time the data in a dashboard component.

This book may be over, but your journey using Vue is only beginning. We started with very basic concepts around templates and reactive data, writing simple applications without any build tools. Even with not much baggage, we were able to make a Mardown Notebook and even a browser Card Game with animations. Then, we started using the full set of tools at our disposal to make larger apps. The official command-line tool--vue-cli--was a great help in scaffolding our projects. The Single-File-Components (`.vue` files) make the components easy to maintain and evolve. We can even use preprocessing languages, such as stylus, very easily. The vue-router official library is mandatory for managing multiple pages, like we did in `Chapter 5`, *Project 3 - Support Center*, with a nice user system and private routes. Next, we went to a whole other level with advanced features, such as Google OAuth and Google Maps, while architecturing our Geolocated Blog in a scalable and safe way using the official Vuex library. Then, we improved the quality of our Online Shop code with ESLint and wrote unit tests for our component. We even added localization and server-side rendering to the app, so now it has a very professional feeling.

You can now practice on the projects we built by improving them, and you can even start your own. Using Vue will improve your skills, but you can also attend events, chat online with the community, get involved (`https://github.com/vuejs/vue`), or help others in learning Vue. Sharing your knowledge will only increase your own, and you will become better at what you do.

Index

A

app
  creating 10
  Vue devtools 11
  Vue.js devtools 13
asynchronous operations 249
awesome-vue
  URL 151

B

blog posts, Geolocated Blog app
  creating 270
BlogMap component changes
  about 283
  click handler 284, 285
  ghost marker 285, 286
BlogMap component
  mapping 267
BlogMap module
  actions 267
  mutations 266
BlogMap, connecting to store
  about 263
  BlogMap module and component 266
  user position 268
  Vuex modules 263, 264

C

card
  child-to-parent communication, with custom events 77, 79
  displaying 73, 75
  native events, listening on components 77
  playing 88
Castle Duel Browser Game, scenery components
  animated clouds 111, 113
  animation 113, 115
  banner bars 108, 109
  castle banners 104
  castles 103
  food and health bubbles 106, 107
  value, animating 109, 111
Castle Duel Browser Game
  card effect, applying 121
  card transition, ending 120
  card, playing 117
  card, removing from hand 119
  cards, drawing 116, 117
  cheating, avoiding 118
  endGame function 125
  gameplay 115
  nextTurn function 122
  overlay close actions 124
  project, setting up 63
  rules 59, 62
  scenery components 102
  skipTurn 122
code-splitting
  about 329
  with dynamic imports 330
commit 245
commit mutations 249
computed property 21

D

dashboard
  about 366
  component, creating 367
  indicators 369
  measures, listing 371
  Meteor publication 366

progress bars library 366
data-binding 14
development environment
  code editors 128
  command-line tool 128
  setting up 127
  vue-cli, installing 128
development workflow
  about 312
  app, launching 314
  browsers, targeting with browserslist 316
  code quality, enhancing with ESLint 317
  CSS, auto-prefixing with PostCSS 315
  development API, generating 313
  project, setting up 313
  style, enhancing with ESLint 317
  unit testing, with Jest 323
directives
  used, for adding basic interactivity 14
DOM
  basic interactivity, adding with directives 14, 15
  templates, using 13
  text, displaying 13

E

ESLint
  code quality, enhancing 317
  configuring 318
  executing 319
  inside Webpack 320
  keywords 326
  rules, customizing 319
  style, enhancing 317

F

FAQ page
  animation, loading 167
  API, consuming 162
  code, resusing with mixins 172
  error management 177
  fetch API, using 163, 167
  fetch method 171
  fetch, reusing with mixins 174
  management, loading 176

plugin options 170
plugin, creating 169
remote data, fetching 174
server, setting up 162
Vue, extending with plugin 169
filters 55
Front-end JavaScript frameworks
  URL 8
functional components
  about 304, 305
  creating 305, 306, 307, 308
  store changes, for comments 304

G

Geolocated Blog app
  about 233
  basic structure, setting up 234
  blog posts, adding 270
  comments, adding 270
  creating 235, 236
  Google Auth and state management 234
  Google Maps, embedding 260
  routing 237, 239
  state management, with Vuex 239
  user system, adding 252
Google Maps
  API key, obtaining 260
  BlogMap, connecting to store 263
  embedding 260
  installing 260
  library, installing 261
  map, adding 262, 263

I

internationalization
  about 329
  Language page, modifying 334
  user locale, loading automatically 332

J

Jest
  Babel, configuration 324
  configuring 323
  keywords 326

snapshots 327
snapshots, updating 328
unit testing 323, 325
JSX
  about 272, 278
  blog content structure 279, 281
  no content 282

L

linting 317

M

markdown note app
  about 18
  attributes, binding with v-bind 35
  button, used for calling method 34
  click events, used for calling methods 34
  conditional templates, with v-if 42, 44
  current note 40
  data, initializing 31
  dynamic CSS classes 41
  lifecycle hooks 30
  list, displaying with v-for 37
  method, used for creating note 33
  method, using 28
  multiple notes 32
  note list 32
  note toolbar 47
  note, saving 24
  note, selecting 39
  notes, saving with deep option 44
  preview pane 21
  project, setting up 19
  saved note, loading 29
  selection, saving 46
  status bar 53
  text editor, adding 20
  Vue instance, accessing 28
  watchers 25
Marked
  URL 21
Meteor
  about 357
  installing 357
  project, creating 358
  routing 360
  URL 357, 372
  Vue Meteor app 359
methods
  using 28
mutation
  about 245
  strict mode 246, 247

N

namespaced module 264
note toolbar, markdown note app
  favorite notes 50, 52
  note, deleting 49
  note, renaming 47
npm
  URL 135

P

post details
  about 297
  PostContent component 298, 300
  store changes, for post selection and sending 297, 298
post, creating
  about 282
  BlogMap changes 283
  draft store actions 282
  post form 286, 287
  request, creating 289, 290
post, selecting
  about 297
  functional components 304
  location info 300
  post details 297
  scoped slots 300
posts store module 270, 271
posts, fetching
  about 290
  login action, implementing 296
  logout action, implementing 295
  markers, displaying 293, 294
  store action 290

[377]

user logging in or out 294
posts-fetching action
  creating 290, 292
  dispatching 292, 293
preview pane
  about 21
  computed property 21
  HTML, displaying 23
  text interpolation, escaping 22
production measures
  about 362
  collection, adding 363
  data, inspecting 365
  data, setting up 362
  Meteor collections integration 362
  Meteor method, adding 363
  simulating 364
progressive framework 7
project structure
  about 149
  active class 161
  layouts, with router-view 152
  navigation menu, creating 158
  pages 151
  router links 159
  router modes 157
  router object 156
  routes, creating 154
  routing 151, 152
  setting up 150
  Vue plugins 151
props
  parent-to-child communication 71
  using, in template 72

R

read-only 243
render functions
  about 272
  data objects 274, 276
  dynamic templates 273, 274
  used, for writing view in JavaScript 272, 273
  Virtual DOM 277, 278

S

scoped slots
  for passing data to parent 300, 302
  implementing 302, 304
Search Engine Optimization (SEO) 335
Server-side Rendering (SSR)
  about 335
  app, executing 347
  client entry file 338
  Client, configuration 343
  express server 345
  npm scripts 351, 352
  page template 345
  production build 349
  Production build, configuration adding 349
  production express server 350
  renderer, creating 346
  renderer, updating 346
  server entry 339
  Server, configuration 343
  server-side setup 344
  state management 339
  style, extracting into CSS files 349
  Universal App Structure 336
  unnecessary fetch, avoiding 348
  Vue app, rendering 347
  Vuex state, restoring on client 341
  Webpack, configuration 342
Single-File Component (SFC)
  about 136
  component, using inside component 145, 147
  JSX 140, 141
  less 144
  preprocessors, adding 143
  pug, using 139
  sass 144
  scoped styles 142
  script 139
  style 141
  stylus 145
  template 138
state management, Geolocated Blog app
  actions, for store operations 249
  getters, for computing and returning data 248,

249
  helpers, mapping 250, 251, 252
  mutations update 245
  single source of truth 243
  time-travel debugging 247, 248
  Vuex Store 241, 242
  with Vuex 239, 240
status bar, markdown note app
  date filter, using 54, 56
  text stats 56
support tickets, login forms
  fetch plugin, improving 196
  form input component 184, 188
  login component 189, 193
  login operation 198
  scoped elements, styling 194
  sign up operation 197
  smart form 181
  v-model, customizing 189
support tickets
  about 179
  adding 206
  attributes, binding 216
  displaying 206
  dynamic remote data 223
  dynamic route 225, 228
  dynamic routes, with parameters 222
  form textarea 215
  form, sending 214
  guest routes 205
  login forms 181
  logout method 199
  meta properties, routing 201
  navigation guard, fixing 213
  nested routes 210
  not found page 229
  plugin 180
  private routes with navigation guards 200
  route, redirecting 204
  router navigation guards 202, 203
  routing features 221
  scrollBehavior function 230
  session expiration 208
  tickets list 206
  transitions 230

user actions 217
user authentication 179
user authentication, initializing 205
user input, backing up 218, 221
user menu 199
user, storing in centralized state 180

T

text interpolation 13

U

user interface
  animation, enhancing 86, 87
  building 67
  card list, animating 89
  card, displaying 73, 75
  card, playing 88
  components, defining 69
  components, using 69
  content distribution, with slots 94, 96
  CSS transitions 92
  dynamic component 98, 100
  game over overlay 97
  gameplay data, adding to state 68
  hand 79, 82
  hand, animating with transitions 82, 85
  key attribute 101
  key special attribute 90
  last play overlay 97
  overlay animation 101
  overlay background 102
  overlays 93
  parent-to-child communication, with Props 71
  player turn overlay 96
  props, using in template 72
  top bar 68
user position, Google Maps
  about 268
  centering, on user 269
user system, Geolocated Blog app
  Google OAuth, setting up 252, 253, 254
  login button 254, 256
  store, synchronizing with router 260
  user, in store 256, 257

[379]

user, store
  about 256
  fetch plugin, adapting 258
  profile picture, implementing 259
  router, adapting 257
  user session, checking on start 258, 259

V

VNodes 277
Vue application
  about 128
  babel Vue preset 133
  babel, configuring 133
  building, for production 136
  creating 130
  dependencies, updating 134
  executing 131
  polyfills 134
  project, scaffolding 129
  render functions 132
  updating automatically 135
  updating manually 135
  vue package, updating 136
Vue instances 10
Vue integration repository
  URL 372
Vue, features
  almighty components 67
  app state 65
  template option 64
Vue.js devtools
  references 11
Vue
  about 7
  compatibility requisites 9
  project 8
  setting up 9
  URL 7, 8
Vuex modules
  about 263, 264
  global elements, accessing 266
  namespaced module 264, 265

Printed in Great Britain
by Amazon